The Quest
of the Historical Muhammad
and
Other Studies on Formative Islam

The Quest
of the Historical Muhammad
and
Other Studies on Formative Islam

STEPHEN J. SHOEMAKER

CASCADE *Books* · Eugene, Oregon

THE QUEST OF THE HISTORICAL MUHAMMAD AND OTHER STUDIES IN FORMATIVE ISLAM

Copyright © 2024 Stephen J. Shoemaker. All rights reserved. Except for brief quotations in critical publications or reviews, no part of this book may be reproduced in any manner without prior written permission from the publisher. Write: Permissions, Wipf and Stock Publishers, 199 W. 8th Ave., Suite 3, Eugene, OR 97401.

Cascade Books
An Imprint of Wipf and Stock Publishers
199 W. 8th Ave., Suite 3
Eugene, OR 97401
www.wipfandstock.com

PAPERBACK ISBN: 979-8-3852-2038-0
HARDCOVER ISBN: 979-8-3852-2039-7
EBOOK ISBN: 979-8-3852-2040-3

Cataloguing-in-Publication data:

Names: Shoemaker, Stephen J., 1968– author.

Title: The quest of the historical Muhammad and other studies in formative Islam / Stephen J. Shoemaker.

Description: Eugene, OR: Cascade Books, 2024. | Includes bibliographical references and index.

Identifiers: ISBN 979-8-3852-2038-0 (print). | ISBN 979-8-3852-2039-7 (print). | ISBN 979-8-3852-2040-3 (epub).

Subjects: Muhammad, Prophet, -622—Biography. | Islam—Origin. | Islam—History—To 1500. | Qur'an.

Classification: BP55 S47 2024 (print). | BP55 (epub).

"A New Arabic Apocryphon from Late Antiquity: The Qur'an" is used with permission of Walter de Gruyter and Company, from *The Study of Islamic Origins: New Perspectives and Contexts*, edited by Mette Bjerregaard Mortensen et al., copyright © 2021.

"Qur'anic Eschatology in its Biblical and Late Ancient Matrix" is used with permission of Walter de Gruyter and Company, from *Dreams, Visions, Imaginations: Jewish, Christian, and Gnostic Views of the World to Come*, edited by Jens Schröter et al., copyright © 2021.

"The Jerusalem Temple and the Qur'anic Holy House" is used with permission of Schiler & Mücke, from *Abschied von der Heilsgeschichte*, edited by Robert M. Kerr and Marcus Groß, copyright © 2023.

"The Eschatological Reign of God in the Qur'an: The Amr Allā[set macron over a]h" is used with permission of Schiler & Mücke, from *Die Entstehung einer Weltreligion VI: Vom umayyadischen Christentum zum abbasidiscchen Islam*, edited by Robert M. Kerr and Marcus Groß, copyright © 2020.

For Matthew Shoemaker, brother, father, and chef extraordinaire

Contents

Acknowledgments | ix
1 The Quest of the Historical Muhammad | 1
2 A New Arabic Apocryphon from Late Antiquity: The Qur'an | 68
3 The Qur'an's Holy House: Mecca or Jerusalem? | 81
4 The Eschatological Reign of God in the Qur'an: The Amr Allāh | 96
5 Qur'anic Eschatology in Its Biblical and Late Ancient Matrix | 108

Bibliography | 133
Index | 151

Acknowledgments

THE PRESENT VOLUME IS a collection of studies that either have already appeared elsewhere or will soon be published in another collection (and in fact, language), and have gratefully been republished here (with some very minor changes) thanks to the generous permission of the initial (and future) publishers. The book's initial chapter, "The Quest of the Historical Muhammad," appears here for the first time and comprises roughly half of the entire text. This extended study was commissioned in July 2022 to serve as the introductory study for an important French collection of studies on the figure of Muhammad in history: *Le Mahomet des historiens*, edited by Mohammad Ali Amir-Moezzi and John Tolan, where it will appear, translated into French, as "Mahomet dans l'histoire" in 2025. I was thrilled to receive this invitation, since it offered the perfect venue for a study of the historical Muhammad that I had been hoping to write, particularly since I do not think that there is actually enough to say about the *historical* Muhammad to fill a whole book. I am enormously grateful to Profs. Amir-Moezzi and Tolan for allowing me to publish the text in English in advance of its appearance in French. I should also note that there are plans for the entire multivolume collection *Le Mahomet des historiens* to be published also in English, including this introductory essay on the historical Muhammad.

The other four chapters in this book were initially delivered at conferences in Europe and were eventually published in the edited volumes that came out of those conferences. It is an unfortunate reality that many such volumes, often published by Continental academic publishers, do not always find their way into North American libraries and into the hands of many Anglophone readers. For these reasons, it seemed desirable that these articles should be published together in a volume, along with this substantial study on the historical Muhammad soon to be published in French, that could make them all available together to a North American audience in particular. These reprinted articles are reproduced faithfully according to their original publication, with only minor corrections of typos, occasional slight improvements in style, and a few additions to the notes. The second chapter in this book originated as a presentation at the 3rd Early Islamic Studies Seminar / 11th Nangeroni Meeting, Gazzada, Italy, June 16–20, 2019, and was subsequently published in the proceedings of that seminar in *The Study of Islamic Origins: New Perspectives and Contexts*, edited by Mette Bjerregaard Mortensen, Guillaume Dye, Isaac Oliver and Tommaso Tesei, 29–42 (Berlin: de Gruyter, 2021). I am grateful to Walter de Gruyter for allowing permission for it to be republished in the present volume.

The third and fourth chapters were originally given as papers at successive meetings of the Inârah Institute, in Trier, May 4–7, 2022, and Mainz, May 1–4, 2019, respectively. They were published in the volumes produced on the basis of those conferences, again, respectively, *Abschied von der Heilsgeschichte*, edited by Robert M. Kerr and Marcus Groß, 179–200 (Berlin: Schiler-Mücke, 2023); and *Die Entstehung einer Weltreligion VI: Vom umayyadischen Christentum zum abbasidiscchen Islam*, edited by Robert Kerr and Markus Groß, 720–33 (Berlin: Schiler-Mücke, 2020). I am grateful to Schiler-Mücke for allowing the reprint of both of these articles. Finally, chapter 5 was prepared for a conference on "Dreams, Visions, Imaginations: Jewish, Christian and Gnostic Views of the World to Come," held in Barcelona, May 9–11, 2019. The published version then appeared in that conference volume, *Dreams, Visions, Imaginations: Jewish, Christian and Gnostic Views of the World to Come*, edited by Jens Schröter, Tobias Nicklas, and Armand Puig i Tàrrech, 461–86 (Berlin: de Gruyter, 2021). Once again, I express my gratitude to Walter de Gruyter for allowing the republication of this article in the present volume. I would also note that this final chapter and chapters 2 and 4 derive from a longer study that was presented in part at a conference on Biblical Traditions in the Qur'an at the British Academy, October 11–12, 2018, and was initially intended for publication in the forthcoming volume *Biblical Traditions in the Qur'an* under the title "Biblical Eschatology and the Qur'an" (and hence readers will notice some overlap). Nevertheless, by mutual agreement it was withdrawn from this important and long anticipated collection of studies, which will hopefully appear with Princeton University Press in the very near future.

I am especially grateful to my friends and colleagues Guillaume Dye, Robert Kerr, and Tobias Nicklas (along with the other conference organizers) for the invitations to participate in these four conferences and also to contribute to their respective edited volumes. My gratitude also extends to James Stock, Jon Stock, and Jim Tedrick at Wipf and Stock, with whom I have become good friends over the years living together in the Springfield–Eugene, Oregon, metroplex. It is wonderful to find now the opportunity to publish a book together with them, particularly in light of Wipf and Stock's enormous contribution to publishing scholarly works in religious studies, among other fields. My thanks also to the many others at the press who helped shepherd this book through the publication process, including K. C. Hanson, the editor in chief, and also Matt Wimer, Emily Callihan, and George Calihan. Finally, I dedicate this book to my brother Matt Shoemaker. I'm truly glad my parents decided to have him; he's been a great friend and brother.

1

The Quest of the Historical Muhammad[1]

IT IS AT ONCE incredibly trite and yet seemingly inevitable to begin any inquiry into the historical figure of Muhammad with the infamous words of Ernest Renan, who maintained that, in stark contrast to other religious traditions, Islam uniquely "was born in the full light of history." For Renan, this finding applied no less to Islam's founder Muhammad, of whom he said that it was possible to know "year by year the fluctuations of his thoughts, his contradictions, his weaknesses."[2] Renan himself was of course a renowned biblical scholar and the author of a famous (some would say infamous) *Life of Jesus*, a work of enormous popularity in its day. Uneven as this work was, it nonetheless marked an important milestone in the progress of research on the historical figure of Jesus, among other things as the first major Francophone and Catholic contribution to this endeavor.[3]

---

1. This study was originally commissioned for inclusion in a multi-volume collection of studies in French on the figure of Muhammad in history, where it will appear—in translation—as Shoemaker, "Mahomet dans l'histoire." I would like to express my gratitude to Ali Amir-Moezzi and John Tolan for agreeing to allow the publication of this study in English in parallel to the publication of the French translation. I should also note that this study will eventually also appear in English in the anticipated future English translation of *Le Mahomet des historiens*.

2. Renan, "Mahomet et les origines de l'Islamisme," 1065; Renan, "Muhammad and the Origins of Islam," 129.

3. Renan, *Vie de Jésus*; cf. Baird, *History of New Testament Research*, 1:375–84.

Although Renan's biography of Jesus was marred by its sentimentality and anti-Judaism (according to Renan Jesus overcame his Judaism to become a spiritual Aryan), it nonetheless was grounded in the basic principles fundamental to the quest for the historical Jesus: that the life of Jesus could be investigated just like that of any other historical figure, and the biblical texts should be subject to scrutiny just like any other historical sources.[4]

Accordingly, when Renan contrasts the perfect clarity of Islam's early history with other religious traditions whose origins are shrouded in mystery and "lost in dreams" so that "the effort of the sharpest criticism is hardly enough to distinguish the real from under the misleading appearance of myths and legends," there is little mistaking just which tradition he has foremost in mind.[5] Although he fails to specify, these remarks undoubtedly were directed at Christianity, whose early history, including the life of its founder, had progressed into greater and greater uncertainty through critical research over the preceding century. Inasmuch as Renan himself was a principal actor in this research, deeply engaged in this scholarly endeavor, one might think that his judgment regarding the beginnings of Islam would be particularly weighty. Nevertheless, as it turns out Renan could not have been more wrong, and in fact the origins of Islam are even more poorly known to the modern historian than the beginnings of Christianity. As little as we can determine about the historical Jesus with any measure of probability, we know far less about the historical Muhammad, who turns out to be almost a complete cipher.

In large part Renan's serious misjudgment reflects the immediate context in which he was writing. These comments appear in a review of several recent works on early Islam that had been published in the preceding decade, the most important of which (for our purposes) is Gustav Weil's *Mohammed der Prophet, sein Leben und seine Lehre* (1843), a work to which we will soon turn in the following section. Weil's work was highly trusting of the traditional Islamic sources at his disposal, even as he attempted to introduce a modicum of criticism by excising what he considered obviously legendary or supernatural elements. And so Renan, reviewing works outside of his field of expertise, merely reflects Weil's confident reproduction of the richly detailed traditional accounts of Muhammad's life found in the

---

4. Schweitzer, *Von Reimarus zu Wrede*; Schweitzer, *Quest of the Historical Jesus*, ch. 13; Heschel, *Aryan Jesus*, 33–38.

5. Renan, "Mahomet et les origines de l'Islamisme," 1025; Renan, "Muhammad and the Origins of Islam," 129.

earliest sources, in this case, in the recently obtained *Life of the Prophet*, or "*Sira*," by the ninth-century Islamic scholar Ibn Hishām. Renan's opinion, then, is not so much that of a biblical scholar who is approaching the search for the historical Muhammad on the same terms as the contemporary quest of the historical Jesus. He merely reflects the convictions of the experts whose work he has reviewed.[6]

Nevertheless, by the turn of the twentieth century, this naïve confidence in the early Islamic tradition from the mid-nineteenth century had been thoroughly debunked.[7] From this point onward scholars increasingly laid bare the highly tendentious and artificial nature of Muhammad's traditional biographies, leaving the historical Muhammad and the beginning of Islam cloaked within a deep darkness that Renan could hardly have imagined. Ignác Goldziher's work on the early Islamic tradition at the end of the nineteenth century exposed its profound artificiality and highly tendentious nature, eviscerating its credibility for modern historical study. Prior to Goldziher's work, scholars of early Islam generally believed that there was a core of historical truth at the basis of what the Islamic tradition remembered about its founding prophet, so that with proper, careful sifting it was possible to separate this wheat from the chaff. Goldziher, however, demonstrated that these traditions had come into being only long after Muhammad's death, and as a result, even the very earliest traditions from the oldest collections were more legendary than historical in character. These memories of Muhammad did not preserve some bedrock core of what really happened; instead, they presented Muhammad and the beginnings of Islam in a manner that suited the beliefs, practices, and concerns of the Islamic community in the middle of the eighth century.[8]

With this recognition, which was soon confirmed by other scholars, the historical figure of Muhammad quickly all but vanished.[9] Goldziher's studies were shortly followed by the important work of Henri Lammens and Leoni Caetani on the biographical and historical traditions respectively, which dimmed considerably the "full light" imagined by Renan and found

---

6. Weil, *Mohammed der Prophet*; Weil, *Historisch-kritische Einleitung*; Weil, *Geschichte der Chalifen*; Caussin de Perceval, *Essai sur l'histoire*; Irving, *Lives of Mahomet*.

7. Nevertheless, Renan's judgment is still strangely cited as "fact" in Aslan, *No God but God*, xix.

8. Goldziher, *Muhammedanische Studien*; Goldziher, *Muslim Studies*, vol. 2.

9. E.g., Nöldeke, "Zur tendenziözen Gestaltung,"; Nöldeke, "Review of Leone Caetani."

the origins of Islam instead hidden beneath a shroud of pious memories.[10] By consequence, it is now widely recognized in Western scholarship on Islamic origins that almost nothing conveyed by the early Islamic sources can be taken at face value, and indeed most of what these narratives relate concerning Muhammad and his earliest followers must be regarded with deep suspicion.[11] As no less of an authority than Marshall Hodgson concludes, "On the face of it, the documentation transmitted among Muslims about his life is rich and detailed; but we have learned to mistrust most of it; indeed, the most respected early Muslim scholars themselves pointed out its untrustworthiness."[12] Nevertheless, despite a strong consensus for over a century now regarding the profound historical unreliability of Muhammad's traditional Islamic biographies, it remains peculiar that, as we will see, many scholars of early Islam have continued to write about Muhammad's life as if nothing at all has changed. One still meets routinely invocations of a reliable "historical kernel" or a "solid core of fact" lying at the basis of these sources that allows for their relatively unproblematic use in writing a biography of the historical Muhammad.[13] Yet no matter how many times certain experts will invoke this "authentic core," their postulation is no more than a *petitio principi* that has resolved to ignore the profound problems with our source materials for the life of Muhammad.[14] Far from being a figure bathed in the "full light of history," the historical Muhammad has instead become an elusive phantom who haunts the beginnings of Islam.

The Origins of the Quest for the Historical Muhammad

From the very moment that Muhammad's new religious movement appeared on the world stage, with the Near Eastern conquests commencing in 634, non-Muslims began to write about him.[15] Indeed, the bits of infor-

---

10. Lammens, "Qoran et tradition"; Lammens, "L'Âge de Mahomet"; Lammens, *Fatima*; Lammens, "Koran and Tradition"; Lammens, "Fatima"; Lammens, "Age of Muhammad"; Caetani, *Annali dell'Islām*.

11. See, e.g., Shoemaker, "Les vies de Muhammad," 188–96; and Raven, "Sīra."

12. Hodgson, *Venture of Islam*, 160.

13. Watt, "Materials Used by Ibn Ishaq"; Watt, "Reliability of Ibn Ishaq's Sources"; cf. Andræ, *Mohammed: The Man*, 31.

14. E.g., both Donner, *Narratives of Islamic Origins*, 7–9, and Hoyland, "Writing the Biography," 597n6 note the persistence of this problem in the study of formative Islam.

15. E.g., Hoyland, "Earliest Christian Writings"; Shoemaker, *Death of a Prophet*; Shoemaker, *Prophet Has Appeared*.

mation that we can glean about Muhammad from these sources amount to his earliest biography, produced well in advance of his traditional Islamic biographies, the earliest of which dates the mid-eighth century. While their accounts are not always free from polemic, these earliest biographers of Muhammad often show genuine interest in learning more about the founder of this new religious community that invaded and subjugated their homelands: indeed, it is this first-hand experience that makes their accounts particularly valuable. It would not take long, however, before this external perspective on Muhammad turned to pure polemic, with the composition and circulation of a Christian counter-biography of Muhammad known as the *Legend of Sergius Baḥīrā*, which seems to have appeared sometime during the later eighth century, around the same time as Muhammad's first Islamic biographies.[16] This tradition of calumny would continue and even escalate during the middle ages and into the early modern period, as western intellectuals regularly sought to diminish Muhammad by portraying him as either a charlatan or a bewildered epileptic.[17] The first to break with this trend was an English scholar named Henry Stubbe, who in the later seventeenth century composed *Originall & Progress of Mahometanism*, which presented Muhammad "as a great reformer who fought the superstition and illegitimate power of Christian clergy and sought to return to a pure, unsullied monotheism."[18] Yet Stubbe's work was never published during his lifetime, and the manuscript circulated privately among friends: only in 1911 would it finally see the light of day.[19] Accordingly, it was not until the early decades of the nineteenth century that this pattern began to change significantly, when several German scholars deliberately turned away from this collective derision and sought to recover Muhammad as a historical figure, without deliberate disparagement and on the basis of the earliest Islamic sources that were then available.

Most scholars continue to regard Weil's 1843 biography, mentioned above, as the first serious attempt to write a critical biography of Muhammad, that is, as the first effort to recover the historical figure of Muhammad as opposed to the Muhammad of either Christian polemic or Muslim piety. Nonetheless, Weil himself continued to perpetuate the diagnosis of Muhammad as an epileptic, which has a long history, even as

16. Roggema, *Legend of Sergius Baḥīrā*.
17. Tolan, *Saracens*; Tolan, *Faces of Muhammad*.
18. Tolan, *Faces of Muhammad*, 12.
19. Stubbe and Matar, *Henry Stubbe*; Stubbe and Shīrānī, *Account*.

he simultaneously argued that Muhammad himself sincerely understood his ailment as a source of prophetic revelation.[20] Indeed, Weil's turn to regard Muhammad as sincere in his self-understanding as a prophet, rather than a manipulative charlatan, is one of the hallmarks of a new shift toward writing about Muhammad as a historical figure, instead of as anti-Islamic caricature. Weil's biography marks a considerable advance on previous European writings about Muhammad not only for its more sympathetic approach but also because he was the first to have at his disposal the earliest Islamic biography of Muhammad, in the form of Ibn Hishām's mid-ninth century revision of Ibn Isḥāq's mid-eighth century *Sira* (that is, his "*Life*"). To this day, Ibn Isḥāq's *Sira*, as known in primarily through the transmissions of Ibn Hishām and the early tenth century *History* of al-Ṭabarī, remains the oldest extant biography of Muhammad, problematic though it may be. For the first time, then, Weil's biography presented Muhammad as he was remembered in the earliest surviving Islamic sources, instead of relying on the more fanciful and embellished accounts of later authors, whose writings had previously been the only Islamic sources available to European scholars.

Not long before Weil began to work on his biography of Muhammad, Heinrich Ewald announced to the scholarly world the newly discovered significance of Ibn Hishām's *Sira* in an article published in the inaugural issue of the *Zeitschrift für die Kunde des Morgenlandes* (which he founded). In it Ewald laments that despite the recent publication of many noteworthy contributions to the history of Arabic and Arabia, "the main part of this history, the one without which one can least make do, that is, the history of Muhammad himself, has been left as good as completely untouched."[21] The article is, in effect, a call for someone to undertake the task of writing a truly historical, rather than polemical, account of Muhammad's life, with Ibn Hishām's biography as its basis. With this important early source newly available, the task should be a relatively easy one, he suggests. Owing to "a unique quality of the Islamic tradition," he avers, which is grounded in the Arabs' "innate resistance to the mythical" and the rapid fixation of Muhammad's biography in both memory and writing (in the ninth century?!), this account of Muhammad's life "possessed from the beginning such a transparent historicity" that its many legendary elements can be easily overlooked. On its basis "a reliable presentation of the history of

---

20. Weil, "Sur un fait."
21. Ewald, "Aus Muhammeds Leben," 89.

Muhammad" can be made, filling an important gap in our knowledge of early Islamic history.²² Indeed, so confident is Ewald in the reliability of Ibn Hishām's biography that he anticipates Renan's misplaced enthusiasm by over a decade with the promise that its study will bring beginnings of Islam "into the full light," with "the special advantage of seeing the origins of one of the most significant religions with such proximity and certainty, which for other ancient religions is extremely difficult, or even impossible, to achieve."²³

In the preface to his *Mohammed der Prophet*, Weil locates Ewald and his influence very much at the center of this project. Indeed, Ewald had acquired, seemingly not long after his 1837 article, a complete manuscript of Ibn Hishām's *Sira*, which he then lent to Weil to serve as the basis for his new biography of Muhammad.²⁴ Working as he was under Ewald's effective patronage, it is therefore not at all surprising that Weil's work thoroughly reflects Ewald's views on both the transparency of early Islamic history in general and Ibn Hishām's particularly reliable witness thereto. Although Weil promises his readers that he has subjected the information in his sources to "rigorous criticism,"²⁵ in fact his studies on Muhammad lack a true critical approach to the sources, whose content he regularly replicates as if their reports were entirely accurate and unproblematic. He has no problem in excising, as Ewald suggested, the clearly legendary and miraculous elements of his sources, but when it comes to their accounts of Muhammad's life and deeds, he treats their contents, as Ewald had characterized them, as "a reliable representation of the history of Muhammad." Weil therefore generally neglects to question what he assumed were the basic "facts" of his sources, reproducing them largely as they are found. He fails to subject either individual traditions or the sources more generally to the sort of critical scrutiny one is accustomed to expect already in this age from study of the biblical traditions, the historical Jesus, or early Judaism and Christianity more broadly. At the same time, however, Weil did succeed in finally presenting Muhammad for the first time to a European audience more or less as the Islamic world saw him.

Nevertheless, Weil's biography of Muhammad represents a failure to meet the critical spirit of the age, despite its unquestionable achievements

---

22. Ewald, "Aus Muhammeds Leben," 91.
23. Ewald, "Aus Muhammeds Leben," 90.
24. Weil, *Mohammed der Prophet*, viii–ix.
25. Weil, *Mohammed der Prophet*, x.

relative to what had come before it. As John Tolan rightly notes, "there is little trace here of the healthy skepticism toward his sources that we find in the biblical scholarship of the Tübingen school or in Geiger's deconstruction of postbiblical Jewish sources."[26] This deficiency is no wonder, given that Weil was working at the time at least in part under the tutelage of Ewald. Ewald was legendary in his day for sharply rejecting any scholarly approaches "that separated academic learning from religious and political edification." Nowhere was this tendency more evident than in his determination to protect the early history of Christianity and the historical integrity of the biblical writings from critical scrutiny, lest by conceding that the Bible is full of mysteries and uncertainty, such studies would play into the hand of "the Roman Church."[27] Ewald's infamous vitriol was particularly evident in his notorious and relentless hostility to the tradition of historical criticism represented by his pioneering peers at Tübingen, including particularly F. C. Baur, the founding father of early Christian studies for whom he held a special animus. Indeed, it was largely at Ewald's influence, so it would seem, that the study of early Islam and the Qur'an in Germany developed during the nineteenth century in relative isolation from the more critical approaches that were taking hold of and transforming the study of early Christianity at this time.[28] For example, one finds already in his 1837 article on Ibn Hishām the following remarks, directed at developments within the field of early Christian studies at this time: "The disputes about early Christianity that are now surging above all in Germany among unhistorical scholars make a most deplorable impression on those who have come to know the Orient better. . . .They have hardly the slightest idea of the facts of the questions about which they are contending."[29]

Although Ewald avoids naming any names here, one strongly suspects that his ire in this instance is directed especially at the work of David Friedrich Strauss, whose enormously controversial—and profoundly seminal—*Das Leben Jesu* appeared just two years before Ewald's article. This critical study of the life of Jesus in many ways marks the true beginning of the quest for the historical Jesus, such that Albert Schweitzer would divide research on this topic as falling "immediately into two periods, that before Strauss

26. Tolan, *Faces of Muhammad*, 218–19.
27. Engberts and Paul, "Scholarly Vices," 84.
28. Shoemaker, *Death of a Prophet*, 125–26.
29. Ewald, "Aus Muhammeds Leben," 91–92.

and that after Strauss."[30] The ensuing scholarly transition was convulsive, not least for Strauss himself. "Scarcely ever has a book let loose such a storm of controversy," Schweitzer observes.[31] Immediately after its publication, Strauss was removed from his teaching position at Tübingen and his academic career was destroyed. He never held another academic post. Yet at the same time, Strauss must be credited with almost single-handedly ushering in a new era in the critical study of religious culture.[32] Study of the historical Jesus, the New Testament, and early Christianity would never be the same going forward. And it was this new direction in critical research that Ewald so ardently despised and sought to undermine, seeing in it a pernicious "overturning and destruction of all intellectual and moral life."[33]

Accordingly, Renan's praise of "the finesse and penetration of Weil" as making him a worthy compatriot of Strauss can hardly be taken seriously.[34] For all Weil's unquestionable advances in the historical study of Muhammad, not the least of which are his avoidance of polemic and the use of an important early source, his biography is in no way deserving of comparison with the breakthrough occasioned in Strauss's scholarly masterpiece. Strauss's painstaking and skeptical interrogation of the gospel traditions bears no relation to the credulity that Weil showed his sources. A more comparable figure from this period would instead be Abraham Geiger, whose path-breaking 1833 work *Was hat Mohammed aus dem Judenthume aufgenommen* stands more in the mold of Strauss's biography and other contemporary scholars of early Christian studies.[35] Rather than relying primarily on Muhammad's medieval biographies, as Weil had done, Geiger instead turned directly to the Qur'an in an effort to reconstruct the formative history of Muhammad's new religious movement. In contrast to the Islamic tradition's pious memories of Muhammad from the ninth and tenth centuries, the Qur'an is indisputably a writing from the first century of

---

30. Schweitzer, *Von Reimarus zu Wrede*, 9; Schweitzer, *Quest of the Historical Jesus*, 10.

31. Schweitzer, *Von Reimarus zu Wrede*, 95; Schweitzer, *Quest of the Historical Jesus*, 97.

32. Fittingly, much of Schweitzer's momentous study is devoted to Strauss and his work: Schweitzer, *Von Reimarus zu Wrede*, 67–119; Schweitzer, *Quest of the Historical Jesus*, 68–120.

33. Harris, *Tübingen School*, 45.

34. Renan, "Mahomet et les origines de l'Islamisme," 1065; Renan, "Muhammad and the Origins of Islam," 129.

35. Geiger, *Was hat Mohammed*; Geiger, *Judaism and Islam*.

Islam, and indeed, is the only Islamic religious text that we may confidently assign to this period. Accordingly, as scholars have increasingly come to recognize, if we wish to know anything about Islam's earliest history, the Qur'an is our single best source by a very wide measure. By focusing on the Qur'an, then, Geiger's work unintentionally anticipates the approach that most critical historians would endorse today for recovering Islam's earliest history: a focus squarely on the content of the Qur'an.

Nevertheless, the approach to Muhammad via the Qur'an is fraught with seemingly intractable difficulties. In the first place, the Qur'an is not about Muhammad or his early community. It is about Abraham, and Moses, and Jesus, and other prophets and messengers of Allah from centuries past. It is not at all comparable, therefore, to the Christian Gospels and other New Testament writings with their focus on the ministry of Jesus and the earliest communities of his followers. Almost nothing ties the Qur'an directly to Muhammad or his historical context other than a few stray references, whose significance for understanding the text is generally not entirely clear. The failure of the Qur'an to inform us directly about Muhammad's ministry, its context, and his earliest followers is one of the primary reasons that we are in fact able to know considerably less about the beginnings of Islam than we can determine with a reasonable degree of probability about earliest Christianity. Renan, it turns out, actually had things entirely backwards. Yet although the Qur'an tells us almost nothing about the historical Muhammad and his earliest followers, it is a treasure trove of information for discerning what his early followers believed and what they remembered Muhammad as having taught. When approached in this manner, the Qur'an reveals a great deal about the faith and practice of Muhammad's earliest followers, although not necessarily what the historical Muhammad himself actually preached or believed.

Indeed, one of the primary weaknesses of Geiger's approach, at least with respect to the search for the historical Muhammad, is his assumption that the Qur'an represents in effect a transparent record of Muhammad's teaching to his followers in Mecca and Medina. Of course, this simplistic understanding of the Qur'an and its origins was not unique to Geiger. Rather, it was a scholarly limitation of the age in which he was working, a misconception that, despite the subsequent emergence of more sophisticated understandings of the development and transmission of sacred literature, remains surprisingly persistent even today.[36] While we might forgive Gei-

---

36. Shoemaker, *Creating the Qur'an*, 167–68.

ger and others of his era for their naïve assumptions in this regard, now that we have learned a great deal about the nature of oral transmission and the capacities of human memory, it is preposterous to maintain that somehow the words of the Qur'an are the very words that Muhammad spoke to his followers. Even in the unlikely event that the Qur'an as we now have it was established already under the caliph Uthman, which seems doubtful, just the two decades that elapsed between Muhammad's death and this time ensure that what we have in the Qur'an is not the actual words of Muhammad. Only a transcript made in the moment(s) when he was speaking could possibly achieve this, and even then, one cannot be certain that the result would be Muhammad's actual words. To be sure, it is not at all impossible that there are ideas and perhaps even individual phrases in the Qur'an that go back to Muhammad. Yet this must be painstakingly argued in each individual instance, as has long been the case with the sayings attributed to Jesus. Otherwise, we must assume that the words and ideas found in the Qur'an are as much as if not more a product of their transmission by Muhammad's followers, as they are likely to come from Muhammad himself.[37]

With recognition of these inescapable limitations in place, the Qur'an nonetheless offers the best path forward into the earliest history of Muhammad's new religious movement, providing us, without question, Muhammad's message as his early followers remembered it and recomposed it from memory over the course of subsequent decades. It is a testament to Geiger's work that many of his observations remain relevant and insightful to this day. Geiger approached the Qur'an with deep learning in the early Jewish tradition and sought to identify elements of the Qur'an that reflect the faith and practices of late ancient Judaism and, presumably, find their origins therein. No less than Weil, Geiger saw Muhammad as sincere in following a call to prophetic ministry, a call that drew deep inspiration from the Judaism of his age. Geiger's aim was not to somehow expose Muhammad as a fraud by identifying the Qur'an's connections with ancient Judaism. If anything, his aim was rather to elevate the stature of Judaism in his own historical context through these comparisons. The net effect, however, was a major advance in the historical study of religion, "inspired in part by the work of German Protestant biblical scholars who had submitted the Bible to critical study, seeing it not as the product of divine revelation but of human composition. Careful textual critique could place scripture in its historical context and reveal the formation and development of religious

37. Shoemaker, *Creating the Qur'an*, 117–229.

communities."³⁸ Such an approach places Geiger squarely among the company of Strauss, Baur, and others in the Tübingen school, who were major methodological influences on Geiger. Geiger himself praised Strauss's *Leben Jesu* as an "epoch-making" work that "'perfected' the first step in historical work, exposing the sources' claims as untenable."³⁹ In Geiger's *Was hat Mohammed*, then, we have a work truly worthy (in contrast to Weil's biography) of comparison with contemporary developments in study of early Christianity and the historical Jesus. It is therefore not surprising that Ewald and his students would eventually extend their derision of historical-critical approaches to Geiger's work as well.⁴⁰

Although Ewald failed spectacularly in his effort to destroy the emerging historical-critical trends within the study of early Christianity, in regard to early Islam his legacy was more successful. As an esteemed professor of Orientalistik he was able to exert considerable influence on the direction of this field, not only through his own imperious personality but also through his influence over colleagues such as Weil and the scholarly trajectory of his students, most notably Nöldeke (his favorite student), whose mid-nineteenth-century work on the Qur'an strangely continues to define the field.⁴¹ Consequently, the methodological developments that transformed the study of early Christianity during the early nineteenth century had very limited impact on study of the historical Muhammad, the Qur'an, and early Islam more generally. The study of Islamic origins has instead remained primarily philological, rather than historical, in approach, and substantial faith continues to be placed in the traditional accounts of Islam's formative history, including the canonical narrative of Qur'an's production and the medieval biographies of its founding prophet. Accordingly, the generally uncritical approach to the sources exemplified in Weil's biography of Muhammad more or less set the standard for many other studies of the historical Muhammad moving forward. And instead of Geiger's pioneering historical approach to the Qur'an, inspired by contemporary developments within early Christian studies, we find a trajectory that sought to understand text through philological analysis based in historical perspectives drawn from the later Islamic tradition. Such fetishization of philology, I would suggest, has remained a persistent hinderance to the progress of historical analysis

38. Tolan, *Faces of Muhammad*, 212–13.
39. Heschel, *Abraham Geiger*, 64–65, 108.
40. Heschel, *Abraham Geiger*, 45.
41. Shoemaker, *Death of a Prophet*, 125–26.

within the study of early Islam, no less so in its latest guise, with the elevation of historical linguistics as newest skeleton key promising to unlock the complex history of formative Islam. To be sure, philological expertise and knowledge of the history of the Arabic language are enormously significant for the historian of early Islam, particularly when done with care, but at the same time, one can only wonder at the elevated authority with which some recent scholars have invested such approaches. These disciplines provide merely one piece of the puzzle in understanding the beginnings of Islam, one that must be fully contextualized in light of all of the available evidence.

The History of the Historical Muhammad

By the second half of the nineteenth century, access to the earliest Muslim traditions about Muhammad became more widespread, with Ferdinand Wüstenfeld's edition of Ibn Hishām's biography (1857), followed soon thereafter by a German translation by Weil (1864).[42] Yet even before these publications, by the early 1850s scholars of early Islam increasingly had access to this important Islamic biography of Muhammad. In his 1851 English biography of Muhammad, Aloys Sprenger notes the availability of this work to European scholars, while also making the first effort to catalogue other important early Islamic sources for Muhammad's life. Chief among these was the *Maghāzī* (*Expeditions*) of Muhammad by al-Wāqidī, which Sprenger seems to be the first westerner to discover. He also notes the potential importance of al-Ṭabarī's *History* as a source for Muhammad's life, although in 1851 the original Arabic for this section of his chronicle still had not been found.[43] By 1858, Sprenger had apparently discovered this missing source as well, as reported by William Muir, who in the introduction to the first volume of his four-volume study provides an overview of the available sources that is both comprehensive and critical for its era.[44]

In some regards, Muir's survey of the sources holds up as useful reading even today. Among other things, he highlights the importance of focusing especially on the three earliest collections for knowledge about Muhammad and the beginnings of Islam: Ibn Hishām and al-Ṭabarī, both of whom bear witness to Ibn Isḥāq's biography of Muhammad from the middle of the eighth century, and also al-Wāqidī, who also transmits early

42. Wüstenfeld, *Leben Muhammed's*; Weil, *Leben Mohammed's*.
43. Sprenger, *Life of Mohammad*, 69–72.
44. Muir, *Life of Mahomet*, 1:ci–cii.

traditions from another early authority, Maʿmar ibn Rāshid, who was a contemporary of Ibn Isḥāq. (Maʿmar's traditions are now witnessed also via another important source, the *Muṣannaf* of ʿAbd al-Razzāq).[45] Later biographies of Muhammad, abundant in information though they may appear to be, are to be rejected by the critical historian, since their surplus is primarily a result of legendary and hagiographic accretions.[46] Yet Muir is also aware that embellishments of this sort abound equally in the earliest biographical collections too. As he notes, the basis of their traditions in at least one hundred years of purely oral transmission does not inspire much confidence. Accordingly, with this in mind Muir elaborates a lengthy set of critical principles that he believes will enable the historian to correct for these qualities in the traditional sources. While Muir's methodological precepts certainly mark a considerable advance in the study of the historical Muhammad, at the same time they are still too trusting of the sources. Muir assumes the reliability of certain qualities in these reports, on the basis of which he proposes to establish the trustworthiness of individual traditions.[47]

The result was a four-volume biography of Muhammad totaling more than 1,000 pages. Clearly Muir decided that many of the traditions from these early collections were worthy of confidence. Although Muir criticized Sprenger for being too credulous of the early sources in his 1851 biography of Muhammad, it is nonetheless hard to see how Muir himself is much more discerning. Muir's work is certainly to be commended for recognizing the highly problematic nature of Muhammad's traditional biographies and developing a set of critical principles aimed at meeting their deficiencies. Yet it turns out that Muir was far more astute at identifying the considerable shortcomings of these repositories as historical sources than he was at finding ways to address them. Indeed, with Muir we are still a very long way from the sort of methodological skepticism and rigor that characterized study of the historical Jesus in this age, continuing to entrench the separation of these two endeavors. In the end, Muir's principles yielded a biography that effectively reproduces the basic narrative of the Islamic sources, which it reads alongside of (and to illuminate) various passages from Qurʾan. Muir persistently upholds the unique value of the Qurʾan as offering "sure and steady light" into Muhammad's prophetic career, as if

---

45. Anthony, *Maʿmar*.
46. Muir, *Life of Mahomet*, 1:lxxxvii–ciii.
47. Muir, *Life of Mahomet*, 1:xxvi–lxxxvii.

its reliable witness to Muhammad's preaching could provide the necessary antidote to the failings of his traditional biographies.[48] Yet there is a vicious circle here since, without the tradition, it is almost impossible to connect the Qur'an's contents to the historical Muhammad and the formation of his new religious community.[49] In Muir's biography, then, the Qur'an is constantly presented in light of the tradition's understanding of Muhammad's life and mission, so that in actuality it serves not so much as an independent witness as instead a device for smuggling in a lot of traditional material.

In 1926 Arthur Jeffery published a survey that sought to take stock of the quest for the historical Muhammad as it had progressed so far, inspired largely by Schweitzer's virtuoso study on the investigation of the historical Jesus. The article remains useful today, not only as a survey of developments up to this point, but also for its effort to classify different approaches to writing the life of Muhammad according to various types.[50] In many respects these same categories remain useful today, as many lives continue to reflect one or another sort of type: "Pathological Lives," "Political and Economic Lives," "Eschatological Lives," and "Apologetic Lives." The first category, however, "Pathological Lives," admittedly might seem a little outdated. As noted above, following in a long tradition that originated in medieval Christian polemic, many lives of Muhammad from the nineteenth century, even those that sought deliberately to turn away from polemic, concerned themselves greatly with Muhammad's mental health and whether or not he had epilepsy. Weil, as we noted, seems to have been the first to bring this diagnosis into the realm of critical scholarship. But soon thereafter it was embraced by Nöldeke and perhaps more famously by Sprenger, whose medical credentials lent a measure of weight to the diagnosis.[51] According to Sprenger, Muhammad was, as a result of his illness, "for some time a complete maniac; and that the fit, after which he assumed his office, was a paroxysm of cataleptic insanity. This disease is sometimes accompanied by such interesting psychical phœnomena, that even in modern times it has given rise to many superstitious opinions. After this paroxysm the fits became habitual, though the moral excitement cooled down, and they assumed more and more an epileptic character."[52]

48. Muir, *Life of Mahomet*, 1:xxvii, lxxxvii.
49. Muir, *Life of Mahomet*, 1:xxviii.
50. Jeffery, "Quest."
51. Nöldeke, *Geschichte des Qorâns*, 18, 70.
52. Sprenger, *Das Leben und die Lehre*, 1:208.

Some early twentieth-century biographers sustained this assessment of Muhammad's psychological state, including most notably Frants Buhl and David Margoliouth.[53] Others, however, were more critical of these attempts to determine Muhammad's mental health, such as Hartwig Hirschfeld and Snouck Hurgronje.[54] One must admit, it is a bit presumptuous to assume the ability to pathologize an individual at a distance of centuries, and on the basis of sources known to be highly problematic and deeply unreliable. Accordingly, it would seem that this particular interpretation of Muhammad's mental state and prophecy has vanished from more recent scholarship, and good riddance. Among other factors, the projection of modern cultural assumptions about disease back into late ancient Arabia offers a poor prism for understanding Muhammad and the beliefs held by his earliest followers. Indeed, no doubt for Muhammad and the earliest Muslims, any such "convulsions" were clear signs of prophecy, not illness, whatever their cause may have been. It is therefore more than a little surprising to find this view of Muhammad as an epileptic persisting still in Tilman Nagel's recent scholarship, which seems to be out of step with the rest of the field on this particular point.[55] In any case, whether the historical Muhammad suffered from epilepsy or not is largely irrelevant and ultimately unknowable, and if certain medieval and modern scholars sought to discredit Muhammad with this diagnosis, in his own context such symptoms very likely served to confirm his status as a prophet.[56]

Political and Economic Lives

The political and economic life of Muhammad has certainly proven to be one of the most influential and durable types, particularly among western historians who frequently seek the explanation of religious culture in terms of social and economic conditions. The first exemplar of this genre would appear to be D. S. Margoliouth's *Mohammed and the Rise of Islam*, a work that stands out for its conscious effort to write a biography of Muhammad that would avoid both western polemic and Islamic piety. In so doing it

---

53. Buhl, *Muhammeds liv* (1903), 145–46; Buhl, *Das Leben Muhammeds*, 139; Margoliouth, *Mohammed*, 45–46.

54. Hirschfeld, *New Researches*, 20; Hurgronje, *Mohammedanism*, 46–47.

55. Nagel, *Mohammed: Leben*, 146, 849; Nagel, *Mohammed: Zwanzig*, 48; Nagel, *Muhammad's Mission*, 35.

56. E.g., Brodtkorb and Nakken, "Epilepsy and Religiosity."

builds on the basic criteria elaborated by Muir while also taking into account the more critical perspectives that had recently been offered by Goldziher's important work. Still, Margoliouth's portrait of Muhammad remains largely faithful to the basic framework of Muhammad's life as presented in his traditional biographies: apparently Goldziher's trenchant critique of the reliability of Islamic tradition had yet to sink in. Margoliouth also believed that Muhammad was likely an epileptic, and while in some sense this position links his biography with the Pathological Lives, it does not make for a defining quality in his presentation of Muhammad.[57] Instead, Margoliouth found Muhammad to have been first and foremost a clever and highly successful political figure. According to Margoliouth, then, the historical Muhammad was not so much an inspirational prophet as he was a gifted political organizer and leader. His great accomplishment was not the foundation of a world religion but rather his ability to unite the contentious tribes of Arabia into a single state, which enabled them to meet and exploit the challenges that they faced in late antiquity for political and economic gain.

In this regard one must note that despite Margoliouth's intention to avoid polemic, his work inevitably returns to the idea of a Muhammad who was, as a prophet, not entirely sincere. Nevertheless, one imagines that perhaps from Margoliouth's own point of view, he thought of this portrayal of Muhammad as flattering. Margoliouth's Muhammad saw religion as little more than an effective tool to be used in growing and galvanizing the new Arab polity that he sought to form under his leadership. Both well born and eloquent, Muhammad did not himself believe in his "prophesies," but using his epilepsy as a pretext, he employed them as an instrument to "mystify" others into following him. Muhammad's closest contemporary analogue, according to Margoliouth, was to be found in Joseph Smith, who like Muhammad employed "'revelations' as a political instrument." Indeed, the similarities between the rise of Islam and the Latter Day Saints, as well as the Qur'an and the Book of Mormon, are certainly deserving of further (non-polemical) study.[58] All in all, for Margoliouth Muhammad's movement was primarily about Arab nationalism and political power. While Muhammad clearly joined a religious message to his political agenda,

---

57. Margoliouth, *Mohammed*, 45–46.

58. Shoemaker, "New Arabic Apocryphon," 38–39, which appears also as the following chapter in this volume.

religious belief should be seen as ancillary, rather than principal, in the growth of his movement.[59]

The idea of Muhammad as a cunning political operative in prophetic garb would prove popular for much of the early twentieth century. Perhaps the most cynical expression of this interpretation of Muhammad's career came from Caetani: the title given to a brief excerpt from his *Studi di storia orientale*, "The Art of War of the Arabs, and the Supposed Religious Fervour of the Arab Conquerors," pretty much says it all.[60] Caetani saw the Arabs as perpetually restless, due to economic deprivation, finding them ripe for manipulation by Muhammad. Only for Caetani, unlike Margoliouth, Muhammad's followers seem to have been in on the plan, thirsting for worldly booty rather than heavenly salvation. Likewise, although Carl Becker was willing to allow that Muhammad started off with sincerity, "with success the politician in Muhammad awoke," and "by the time Muhammad first drew additional tribes under his banner, . . . the will for political power had long come to outweigh religious sentiment."[61] Thus, he concludes, "It would be incorrect for the most part to regard the warrior bands which started from Arabia as inspired by religious enthusiasm . . . The Muhammedan fanatics of the wars of conquest, whose reputation was famous among later generations, felt but a very scanty interest in religion and occasionally displayed an ignorance of its fundamental tenets which we can hardly exaggerate. The fact is fully consistent with the impulses to which the Arab migrations were due. These impulses were economic and the new religion was nothing more than a party cry of unifying power."[62]

Lammens too, who perhaps more than anyone else bears responsibility for creating the myth of Mecca as a wealthy center of trade in spices and incense (more on this below), nonetheless saw economic privation, driven by climate change and famine, as a principal cause for the rise of Islam.[63] Hubert Grimme took a slightly different angle on an economic interpretation, understanding the beginnings of Islam as a socialist response to the conditions of economic inequity in Muhammad' Hijaz, rather than as a genuine religious movement. Muhammad, therefore, was not a prophet but a political organizer, who led a peasant uprising against an exploitative

59. Margoliouth, *Mohammed*, e.g., vi–viii, 76–77, 82–91, 134, 136, 139, 156, 471–72.
60. Caetani, *Studi di storia orientale*, 355–71; Caetani, "Art of War."
61. Becker, "Der Islam als Problem," 7–8.
62. Becker, *Christianity and Islam*.
63. Lammens, *Le berceau*, 116–21, 174–77; Lammens, *La Mecque*.

wealthy class. Only in the aftermath of this revolution did the movement gradually transform into new religious community.[64] Although this interpretation of earliest Islam as a fundamentally political movement either stoked or cloaked by religious messages has become much less prevalent over the last century, it still persists even in recent scholarship, albeit without accompanying accusations of rapacious Arab greed. For instance, James-Howard Johnston maintains that religion played a primarily catalytic, secondary role in the emergence of "Islam," so that religion was not fundamental but instead "acted as a supercharger" and a "bonding agent" in the formation and expansion of the early Islamic polity.[65] Likewise, Robert Hoyland, while not saying anything specifically regarding Muhammad himself, has recently presented the rise of Islam as fueled primarily by political and economic interests, rather than religious conviction.[66]

Of course, it is notoriously difficult to separate religion from politics in Islamic culture, since, as Patricia Crone rightly notes, Muhammad was not "a prophet who merely happened to become involved with politics. His monotheism amounted to a political program." Indeed, Muhammad's success as a prophet (so his traditional biographies would tell us) owed itself almost entirely to his political success in Medina, whose feuding tribes agreed to recognize him as their chieftain and submit to his religious authority.[67] Accordingly, certain more recent political and economic interpretations of Muhammad and the rise of Islam have been willing to allow a more significant and positive role for religion in the formation of this new community. The highly influential work of Montgomery Watt perhaps best exemplifies this reconfiguration of the political and, most especially, economic interpretation of the historical Muhammad. Watt's Muhammad, however, is more in the vein of Grimme's socialist than Caetani or Becker's conniving politician, and he is nothing at all if not utterly sincere. Indeed, one of the hallmarks of Watt's work on Muhammad is a desire to somehow find a way to recognize his prophecy and prophetic stature within a Christian theological context: Watt didn't just think Muhammad was sincere in believing himself a prophet; Watt believed that he was in fact a true prophet.[68]

64. Grimme, *Mohammed*, vol. 1.
65. Howard-Johnston, *Witnesses*, 459–60; see also Lewis, *Arabs in History*, 55.
66. Hoyland, *In God's Path*, esp. 5, 16–30, 56–65.
67. Crone, *Meccan Trade*, 241, 244–45; Crone, *God's Rule*, 11; Cook, *Muhammad*, 51.
68. Tolan, *Faces of Muhammad*, 251–58.

As for the historical Muhammad, Watt presents him as a social and economic reformer, whose prophetic mission was directed primarily against an elite and oppressive merchant class that had recently taken control of Mecca and were exploiting Mecca's vulnerable and impoverished proletariat. Muhammad's movement of social reform therefore championed an underclass newly disenfranchised by the emergence of a capitalist economy, promising them with his religious message a new social order based on economic justice.[69] Unsurprisingly, some of Watt's contemporaries criticized his studies of Islamic origins as little more than a Marxist interpretation of both Muhammad and the rise of Islam. Interestingly enough, Watt himself did not entirely object, allowing that perhaps "an elementary knowledge of Marxism" had possibly influenced his analysis.[70] Nevertheless, at the same time, Watt was utterly convinced of the sincerity of Muhammad's religious preaching, which was always the solid foundation of his campaign for social and political justice and not just a means to an end.[71]

Watt's vision of Muhammad has proven to be enormously popular, to the effect that some version of his interpretation of Muhammad as a social and political reformer remains ubiquitous in contemporary scholarship on early Islam. It has become, in effect, something of a "secular vulgate" in Islamic studies.[72] For instance, one finds remarkably similar portraits of Muhammad as crusader for social and economic justice in the work of Rudi Paret, Maxime Rodinson, Alford Welch, F. E. Peters, Irving Zeitlin, and Tilman Nagel, just to name some of the most significant biographers of Muhammad since Watt.[73] Muhammad the reformer is even more popular, perhaps not surprisingly, in recent biographies aimed at a popular audience, most of which belong more properly in the category of Apologetic Biographies, to which we will turn in a moment.[74] A particularly striking

---

69. Watt, *Muhammad at Mecca*, 1–25; see also Watt, *Muhammad: Prophet and Statesman*, 7–13.

70. Watt, *Islam and the Integration of Society*, 2.

71. Watt, *Muhammad at Medina*, 146–47.

72. van Sivers, "Islamic Origins Debate Goes Public," 3.

73. Paret, *Mohammed und der Koran*; Rodinson, *Mahomet*; Rodinson, *Mohammed*; Buhl [and Welch], "Muḥammad"; Peters, *Muhammad and the Origins of Islam*; Peters, *Jesus and Muhammad*; Zeitlin, *Historical Muhammad*; Nagel, *Mohammed: Leben*; Nagel, *Mohammed: Zwanzig*; Nagel, *Muhammad's Mission*; also Mirza, "Muḥammad."

74. E.g., Armstrong, *Muhammad*; Armstrong, *Muhammad: A Prophet for Our Time*; Aslan, *No God but God*; Ramadan, *In the Footsteps*; Afsaruddin, *First Muslims*;

example of this trajectory is Juan Cole's *Muhammad: Prophet of Peace amid the Clash of Empires*, which seeks, rather astonishingly and unconvincingly, to present Muhammad as a prophet who stood athwart the violent empires of his day to found a community committed above all to peacemaking.[75] Yet as I have noted elsewhere, these portraits of Muhammad as champion of peace, the poor, and the oppressed bear a striking similarity to the Liberal biographies of Jesus that Schweitzer dismantled as based in nothing so much wishful thinking on the part of a Liberal intellectual elite, who wanted to find a more palatable Jesus who was relevant to their own contemporary circumstances.[76] One imagines that the same principles are at work in these biographies of Muhammad: their authors wish to find a more attractive and relevant Muhammad, instead of the militant and often ruthless leader that his traditional biographies regularly make him out to be.[77] Yet in this case, no less than with the Liberal Jesus, we must come to recognize these portraits of Muhammad as similarly wishful thinking.

Much more importantly, however, these biographies of Muhammad as a reformer fall far short in their uncritical acceptance of the traditional Islamic accounts of both Muhammad's life and the social and economic conditions in Mecca at the beginnings of Islam, when the relevant sources are in fact deserving of deepest skepticism from any truly critical historian. In reality, we know next to nothing at all about Mecca in the years before the rise of Islam: in fact, no pre-Islamic source so much as even mentions its existence.[78] Accordingly, this interpretation of Muhammad as an advocate of the poor and oppressed in the face of capitalist exploitation is built entirely on a historical house of cards. And not only does it require an unwarranted credulity in the traditional Islamic accounts of pre-Islamic Mecca, but as it turns out, according to the most reliable evidence available to us, Mecca was an extremely poor, remote hamlet with a subsistence economy based in herding goats and sheep. Although we will have more to say about conditions in Muhammad's Mecca below, for now it is enough

---

Safi, *Memories of Muhammad*; Brown, *Muhammad*; Hazleton, *First Muslim*; Jebara, *Muhammad*.

75. Cole, *Muhammad*. See, however, the critiques in Ibrahim, "Review of Juan Cole"; Shoemaker, "Imperial Qur'an."

76. Shoemaker, "Reign of God," 518–20; Shoemaker, *Apocalypse of Empire*, 118–20.

77. See Ibrahim, *Muhammad's Military Expeditions*.

78. Crone, *Meccan Trade*, 134–37; Crone and Cook, *Hagarism*, 22, 24–25. It is now quite clear that the Macoraba mentioned by Ptolemy is not to be identified with Mecca: see Morris, "Mecca and Macoraba."

to cite Patricia Crone's penetrating, corrective study *Meccan Trade and the Rise of Islam*.[79] Crone's work utterly dispels Watt's mirage of Mecca as a wealthy hub of high-value trade, eliminating any possibility of a wealthy merchant class that Muhammad could have sought to challenge. Indeed, it is truly astonishing that this understanding of Muhammad as a social reformer continues to persist so broadly, since Crone has completely falsified its economic basis.

Theological and Apologetic Lives

Almost as soon as more critical European biographies of Muhammad began to be published on the basis of the earliest Islamic sources, a response came from the Islamic world. Muslims read them with "amazed horror," and sought to defend Islam's prophet by placing him in the best possible light.[80] Of these early apologetic efforts, Margoliouth rightly observes that they "endeavor to discredit the biography of Ibn Ishaq where it shocks the European reader, and where this cannot easily be done, they suggest honorable motives, or suppose the course followed by the Prophet to have been the least objectionable of those that were open to him at the time."[81] One should note that the same tendency prevails in apologetic lives of Muhammad up until the present.[82] Among the most significant and successful of these early apologetic biographies came from the Paris-educated Egyptian modernist Husayn Haykal, who in 1935 published a biography of Muhammad in Arabic.[83] In many respects, Haykal should perhaps be classed with most of his European contemporaries among Muhammad's political biographers. His Muhammad, after all, was "an able commander and social reformer," whom Haykal held forth as "a consummate statesman and role model for leaders in modern times."[84] It is this final point, however, that hints towards Haykal's broader apologetic agenda: his version of Muhammad was intended to serve as the model for a modern Islam. Haykal's

---

79. Crone, *Meccan Trade*; see also Crone, "How Did the Quranic Pagans"; Crone, "Quraysh."

80. Schimmel, *And Muhammad Is His Messenger*, 228; Jeffery, "Quest," 344–46; Ali, *Lives*, 39–40, 53–55, 63–71.

81. Margoliouth, "Muhammad," 878.

82. E.g., Jebara, *Muhammad*, 11–12.

83. Haykal, *Ḥayāt Muḥammad*; Haykal, *Life*.

84. Brown, *Muhammad*, 126.

biography therefore aims not just to defend Muhammad against perceived European slights, but it also seeks to advance a modern vision of Islam, using Muhammad's life as the canvas on which to paint his vision of Islam for the present age.

In recent decades, the genre of apologetic biographies has proliferated, to the extent that they have all but crowded out serious historical studies of the historical Muhammad in the book market. Often, these biographies are the work of popular writers, with limited credentials as historians or academics,[85] yet one finds biographical apologies for Islam's prophet no less from scholars who have been trained and hold positions at elite universities. In both cases we witness a problematic symptom of the entrenched protectionist discourse that characterizes the study of Islamic religion, particularly in the North American academy but also in much of Europe, serving to shield the study of Islam from the rigors of historical critical analysis.[86] These biographies regularly lack any sort of critical stance with regard to the early Islamic sources, which they treat in the main as entirely unproblematic and reliable records of Muhammad's life and teaching. Likewise, as noted above, they generally either ignore or seek to whitewash the many more unsavory elements of Muhammad's behavior or his commendations of violence as reported in his traditional biographies. The aim of these works is undoubtedly to foster greater sympathy for Islam in the West at a time of high tension between the western and Islamic worlds, which has often sparked violence on both sides. It is an eminently laudable goal, to be sure, yet when these biographies are presented as works of history, rather than religious apology, it is disquieting, adding significant confusion to the public discourse about the nature and history of Islam while marginalizing and obscuring genuine historical scholarship on Muhammad and the beginnings of Islam. When such works are forthrightly presented as the theological apologetic works that they are, they serve an important purpose for Muslim believers or those interested in a certain kind of interfaith dialogue. Nevertheless, in most instances the boundaries between theology and history are made unclear in these works, even occluded, often to the great detriment of the latter.

---

85. E.g., Armstrong, *Muhammad: A Biography*; Armstrong, *Muhammad: A Prophet*; Peterson, *Muhammad*; Hazleton, *First Muslim*; Jebara, *Muhammad*.

86. Regarding "protectionism" in the study of religion, see Proudfoot, *Religious Experience*, 190–227.

In the case of those authors who are confessing Muslims, including Jonathan A. C. Brown, Omid Safi, and Tariq Ramadan, perhaps such an apologetic approach is to be expected.[87] Nevertheless, when these scholars burnish their academic credentials (whether intentionally or not) to present a confessionally and theologically derived portrait of Muhammad in the guise of a critical historical study, it is deeply problematic.[88] For comparison to such works, I regularly call attention to the three-volume biography of Jesus published by the late Pope Benedict XVI, formerly known as Prof. Dr. Joseph Ratzinger in earlier stages of his career.[89] No one would question that this biography is a work of Christian theology intended primarily for the edification Christian believers. Nevertheless, the Pope's biography routinely engages with critical scholarship on the gospels at every turn, not only Catholic but secular as well. Still, no one would mistake it for the equivalent of E. P. Sanders's *The Historical Figure of Jesus* or Bart Ehrman's *Jesus: Apocalyptic Prophet of the New Millennium*.[90] Yet by comparison the spate of recent biographies of Muhammad produced by confessing Muslim scholars of Islam generally do not meet the standards of historical criticism even as evidenced in Benedict's biography. This is no insult or slight, I wish to be clear, for it should not be forgotten that this pope was a professor of historical theology at Bonn, Münster, Tübingen, and then Regensburg (where he became vice president) before entering the Catholic Church hierarchy at the age of 50. Indeed, Benedict's biography of Jesus could serve as a useful model for critically engaged, theological biographies of Muhammad going forward, and indeed such works, when rightfully presented and read in the intended context, are highly welcome.

Eschatological Lives

At the time when Jeffery was writing his article on the quest for the historical Muhammad, eschatological interpretations of Muhammad's prophetic mission and message were not uncommon, scarce though they would

---

87. Ramadan, *In the Footsteps*; Safi, *Memories of Muhammad*; Brown, *Muhammad*.

88. Although in fairness to Brown in a more recent publication he is appropriately forthright in identifying the book as a work of apology rather that history: Brown, *Misquoting Muhammad*, e.g., xv–xvii, 236–37, 268–72, 288–90.

89. Benedict XVI, *Jesus of Nazareth: From the Baptism*; Benedict XVI, *Jesus of Nazareth: Holy Week*; Benedict XVI, *Jesus of Nazareth: The Infancy Narratives*.

90. Sanders, *Historical Figure of Jesus*; Ehrman, *Jesus*.

become soon thereafter. Seemingly the first scholar to advance an eschatological understanding of Muhammad was Snouck Hurgronje, who saw in Muhammad's traditional designation as "the seal of the prophets" a sign that he and his followers believed that the world was about to end. Indeed, Hurgronje was the first to propose that both Muhammad and his followers expected the world's end even before their own deaths.[91] The content of the Qur'an, which as it turns out is our best source for the earliest history of Islam, certainly lends itself to this interpretation. The impending judgment is, after all, the second most frequent theme of the Qur'an, surpassed only by its call to monotheism.[92] Hurgronje concludes that the divine judgment's imminence "haunted" Muhammad from start to finish: other elements of his message were "more or less accessories" to the fundamental theme of the world's imminent judgment and destruction, which always remained "the essential element of Muhammad's preaching."[93]

Inspired by Hurgronje's work, Frants Buhl would develop this understanding of Muhammad further in his influential life of Muhammad, not to mention his article on "Muḥammad" in the first edition of the *Encyclopaedia of Islam*. Buhl saw Muhammad's overpowering concern with the looming eschaton as the main impulse for his new religious movement.[94] Josef Horovitz also noted the ubiquity of eschatological warnings throughout the Qur'an, which he took as evidence that Muhammad and his followers believed the end of the world was nigh.[95] Tor Andræ likewise understood Muhammad as having been first and foremost an eschatological prophet, who warned his followers that world was about to end. According to Andræ, "the basic conviction of Mohammed's preaching, and the heart of his prophetic message . . . is the *last day*—the day of judgment and retribution. For him the Day of Judgment is not an occurrence far off in the hazy uncertain future, belonging to a different sphere from that of mundane events. It is a reality that is threateningly near."[96]

Nevertheless, it was Paul Casanova who developed this hypothesis most thoroughly and cogently in his astute yet unfortunately neglected

---

91. Hurgronje, "Der Mahdi," 26.

92. Bell and Watt, *Introduction to the Qurān*, 158.

93. Hurgronje, "Une nouvelle biographie de Mohammed," 149–51, 161–62.

94. Buhl, *Das Leben Muhammeds*, 126–27, 132–33, 144–45, 157; Buhl, "Muḥammad," 645–46.

95. Horovitz, *Koranische Untersuchungen*, 1–32.

96. Andræ, *Mohammed: The Man*, 53–63; Andræ, *Mohammed, sein Leben*, 43.

study *Mohammed et la fin du monde*. Casanova exposed the imminent eschatological belief pulsing across the Qur'an with a clarity and force that has rarely been equaled, adding important corroborating evidence from certain early eschatological hadith. Like Hurgronje before him, Casanova concluded that Muhammad and his early followers believed that the end of the world would arrive before Muhammad's death. Yet in his effort to explain those few passages in the Qur'an that seem to indicate a more patient eschatological timetable, Casanova seems to have severely damaged his cause and invited derision from his contemporaries. He proposed that the passages in question had been added to the Qur'an by Abu Bakr, Uthman, and others, who sought to "falsify" or "conceal" the true nature of Muhammad's original eschatological teachings.[97] In Casanova's day scholarly conviction in the absolute integrity of the Qur'an as the words of Muhammad himself was so paramount that his work was immediately and almost universally anathematized solely for his deviance from this academic orthodoxy.[98] As a result, Casanova's arguments for the locating imminent eschatological belief at the heart of early Islam never received the fair and full consideration that they richly deserved, and by consequence, apocalyptic understandings of Muhammad and early Islam were long sidelined in the aftermath.

The scholarly guild's rough dismissal and disavowal of Casanova's presentation of Muhammad as eschatological prophet was unfortunate, particularly since it forestalled an opportunity to bring greater unity to the study of the historical Jesus and the historical Muhammad, as well as to investigations of the beginnings of Islam and the beginnings of Christianity more broadly. Casanova's publications were contemporary with the pathbreaking work of Schweitzer and other scholars of early Christianity, which similarly discovered imminent eschatology at the heart of Jesus's preaching and the new religious community that he founded.[99] Almost immediately, this newly recovered apocalyptic Jesus brought an end to Liberal Protestantism's fantasy of Jesus as a social reformer in the mold of a nineteenth-century Social Democrat.[100] Casanova's work was a missed opportunity to make the same correction in the study of early Islam. To be sure, a primary

---

97. Casanova, *Mohammed*, 4.

98. E.g., Hurgronje, *Mohammedanism*, 15–18; Bergsträsser and Pretzl, *Geschichte des Qorāns III*, 6–8; Bell and Watt, *Introduction to the Qur'ān*, 53–54.

99. E.g., Schweitzer, *Von Reimarus zu Wrede*; Schweitzer, *Quest of the Historical Jesus*; Weiss, *Die Predigt Jesu vom Reiche Gottes*.

100. Baird, *History of New Testament Research*, 1:85–132.

message of impending divine judgment in no way precludes a prophet from also advocating for greater social justice or ordaining the structures of a new religious community, as for instance research on Jesus and the Jesus movement make clear.[101] Nor, in the case of Muhammad and Islam, is the aspiration to conquest and empire at odds with urgent eschatological expectation. Indeed, in late antiquity, visions of imperial conquest regularly went hand in hand with imminent eschatology.[102] Nevertheless, the experts on Muhammad and early Islam from this era (not to mention the present) were, in contrast to scholars of early Christianity, firmly committed accepting to the representations of Muhammad, his context, and his new religious community as found in the traditional Islamic sources—even as they had come to recognize the deeply artificial and unreliable nature of these same sources. By this time, it would seem, profoundly different assumptions regarding the reliability and use of traditional sources had separated the study of early Islam from the more critical perspectives that had emerged within early Christian studies, making any significant methodological influence from the latter all but impossible.

More recently, however, eschatological interpretations of Muhammad mission and message have begun to reemerge. The revival began quietly in several studies that treated specific texts and themes suggesting the presence of imminent eschatological belief as a driving force in the new religious movement that Muhammad founded.[103] A more prominent and forceful statement of Islam's apocalyptic origins came in Michael Cook and Patricia Crone's brilliant, controversial, and flawed study, *Hagarism*.[104] More recently, David Cook and Fred Donner have advanced this interpretation Muhammad's preaching and the faith of his early followers, albeit without pursuing it systematically.[105] Some of my own work has offered a more thoroughgoing presentation of the evidence that Muhammad and

---

101. Shoemaker, *Death of a Prophet*, 159–60.

102. Shoemaker, "Reign of God"; Shoemaker, *Apocalypse of Empire*.

103. Lewis, "Apocalyptic Vision"; Kister, "Booth like the Booth of Moses"; Bashear, "Title 'Fārūq'"; Bashear, "Apocalyptic"; Bashear, "Riding Beasts"; Bashear, "Muslim Apocalypses."

104. Crone and Cook, *Hagarism*, esp. 3–15.

105. Cook, "Muslim Apocalyptic and *Jihād*," 66; Cook, "Beginnings of Islam as an Apocalyptic Movement"; Cook, *Studies in Muslim Apocalyptic*, 30; Donner, *Narratives of Islamic Origins*, 30n78; Donner, "From Believers to Muslims," 10–13; Donner, *Muhammad and the Believers*, 79–82, 97; see also Ayoub, *Crisis of Muslim History*, 145–46; Hoyland, "Early Islam," 1066.

religious community that he founded believed themselves to be living in the last days. Indeed, I believe this to be one of the few things that we can know about the historical Muhammad and earliest Islam with a high measure of probability.[106] Muhammad was born into a world where eschatological expectations were running high and were focused the success of a divinely chosen empire that would arise and liberate Jerusalem and the Holy Land. His preaching and the religious polity that it birthed show clear marks of engagement and participation in this larger contemporary trend of late ancient religious culture in western Asia.

More Recent Developments: Syriac Sources and Solo Corano

In the final pages of his article, Jeffery briefly mentions the then soon to be published work of Richard Bell on *The Origins of Islam in its Christian Environment*, a work that Jeffery suggests "may provide us with the clue for getting back, at least as far as we can expect, in our quest for the historical Mohammed."[107] In this study, Bell argues that Muhammad's message, as reflected in the Qur'an, is a pastiche of traditions and ideas borrowed from Christianity, mostly from the Syriac tradition but also to some degree from Ethiopia as well. In the following year, Alphonse Mingana likewise published an article on "Syriac Influence on the Style of the Kur'ān" that more tersely and specifically identifies signs of the Qur'an's origins within a Syriac Christian cultural milieu.[108] Neither Bell nor Mingana, however, was the first to propose this hypothesis. That honor, it would appear, belongs instead to Andræ, who between 1923 and 1925 published an important monograph in three lengthy journal articles on "Der Ursprung des Islams und das Christentum."[109] It was, in effect, a sort of Christian equivalent to Geiger's work identifying the Qur'an's (and Muhammad's) debts, in this case, to late ancient Christianity. Focusing particularly on the homilies of Ephrem the Syrian, Andræ concluded that the Qur'an derives not only much of its eschatological content, but indeed the homiletic form from

---

106. Shoemaker, *Death of a Prophet*; Shoemaker, "Muḥammad and the Qur'ān"; Shoemaker, "The Reign of God"; Shoemaker, *Apocalypse of Empire*; Shoemaker, "Eschatological Reign" (reprinted as chapter 4 in the present volume); Shoemaker, "Portents of the Hour"; also Amir-Moezzi, "Muḥammad the Paraclete."

107. Bell, *Origin of Islam*, 348.

108. Mingana, "Syriac Influence."

109. Andræ, "Der Ursprung des Islams"; Andræ, *Les origines de l'Islam*.

the Syriac tradition. Although the Qur'an does not fit well the homiletic genre, as Andræ and others after him would maintain, clearly both it and the prophet and community behind it drew heavily on traditions found in contemporary Syriac Christian religious culture for much of its content.[110]

Over the ensuing century, and particularly in recent decades, the idea that the Qur'an, and by consequence Muhammad, drew deeply on Syriac Christianity has blossomed. Indeed, the sheer number of recent studies adopting this approach precludes any possibility of mentioning them all. Among the most radical hypotheses advanced along this trajectory stands the proposal that the Qur'an itself was in fact originally written in Syriac as a kind of Christian lectionary.[111] Nevertheless, this interpretation has been soundly rejected, and, with regard to our particular interests, it would sever the qur'anic text almost completely from the historical Muhammad. Numerous more convincing studies, however, have sought to identify certain Syriac traditions as the basis for elements of Muhammad's teaching—insofar as we may identify his teaching with the contents of the Qur'an. Some of the most notable examples of this approach include the work of Gabriel Reynolds and Emran El-Badawi, for instance, and more recently studies by Julien Decharneux and Paul Neuenkirchen.[112] Particularly important on this front is the still unpublished dissertation of Joseph Witztum, wherein he demonstrates persuasively that most of the Qur'an's "Jewish" content— that is, its treatment of figures and traditions from pre-Christian Jewish history—derives not from Jewish sources (as Geiger believed) but rather from Syriac Christianity.[113]

On the whole, this approach has proven to be highly productive, and it seems clear that much of the Qur'an's material indeed somehow derives from material present in the contemporary Syriac Christian tradition, as well as eastern Christian culture more broadly. The only potential problem, however, is the fact that (as we will see in more detail below) there is no evidence of Christianity whatsoever anywhere remotely near Mecca and Medina, where Muhammad is supposed to have taught the Qur'an to his followers. For Muhammad and/or the Qur'an to possess such deep

---

110. Shoemaker, "New Arabic Apocryphon," reprinted as the next chapter in the present volume.

111. Lüling, *Über den Ur-Qur'ān*; Lüling, *Challenge to Islam*; Luxenberg, *Syro-aramäische Lesart*; Luxenberg, *Syro-Aramaic Reading of the Koran*.

112. Reynolds, *Qur'ān and Its Biblical Subtext*; El-Badawi, *Qur'ān*; Neuenkirchen, "Late Antique Syriac Homilies and the Quran"; Decharneux, *Creation and Contemplation*.

113. Witztum, "Syriac Milieu of the Quran."

knowledge of Christian religious culture, the presence of a vibrant and sizeable Christian community seems necessary. Both is author(s) and its community would have to possess a fairly sophisticated knowledge of the Christian tradition. Consequently, this approach seemingly raises at least as many questions as it answers, revealing the Qur'an to be a text that does not seem very compatible with the historical milieu that supposedly gave it birth.

Nevertheless, the Qur'an still remains our single best source for pursuit of the historical Muhammad. For this reason, one of the most promising recent trends in the study of Islamic origins is to proceed solely on the basis of the Qur'an alone for our primary knowledge of Muhammad's message and the faith of his earliest followers. Jeffery also briefly introduces such an approach in his article under the rubric "Advanced Criticism," where he notes the inescapable consequences of Goldziher's, Caetani's, and Lammens's work for future research on Muhammad and the beginnings of Islam. Previous scholarship, he notes, from Weil even to Margoliouth worked "on the assumption that if a certain amount of careful sifting were done, a considerable body of reliable Tradition could be found on which reliance could be placed for biographical purposes." Nevertheless, by the beginning of the twentieth century it had become clear that this assumption was not only unwarranted but false, since, as Jeffery rightly observes, "even after the most careful sifting we find that the oldest traditions only take us back to the first century after Mohammed, and very much of this oldest tradition is of very uncertain character." Accordingly, the critical scholar can no longer naively rely even on a carefully excavated sketch drawn from Muhammad's traditional biographies, since, continuing to quote Jeffery, "as a basis for critical biography the Traditions are practically worthless." Instead, scholars must leave these traditions aside and turn "back to the Qur'an," since "in the Koran alone can we be said to have firm ground under our feet." Yet already almost a century ago Jeffery could see that even this new foundation would likely soon encounter problems of its own, since it had yet to be ascertained "how firm ground it provides," and "recent work, such as that of Casanova and Mingana, has raised serious doubts as to the trustworthiness of even this source."[114] As it turns out, Jeffery's concerns about the Qur'an would prove to be well founded and prescient.

Still, efforts to probe the beginnings of Islam and search for some credible approximation of the historical Muhammad based primarily on the

---

114. Jeffery, "Quest," 340, 342.

Qur'an continue to hold the most promise going forward. Régis Blachère was seemingly the first to attempt a biography of Muhammad based on the Qur'an alone, and the limited results of this endeavor attest to the inherent limitations of such an approach.[115] Nevertheless, Gerald Hawting and Crone have both demonstrated the usefulness of this approach, by showing, through careful reading of the Qur'an itself, that its traditions emerged within a context that seems to have been thoroughly monotheist, rather than, as the Islamic tradition would have it, dominated by Arabian polytheism. As Hawting and Crone persuasively argue, the Qur'an's criticisms of the so-called "associators," traditionally identified as "pagans," are directed at policing the limits of monotheism rather than condemning any actual polytheist belief in its immediate milieu.[116] Likewise, Fred Donner's recent excellent—if controversial—study *Muhammad and the Believers* shows the benefits of this back-to-the-Qur'an approach. Arguing primarily on the basis of the Qur'an, Donner concludes that in its earliest stages Muhammad's religious movement was an interconfessional, Abrahamic monotheist community that welcomed both Jews and Christians *as* Jews and Christians, so long as they would confess their belief in one God and the impending Last Day and accept Muhammad's leadership of the community.[117] Although there are some rough spots in Donner's hypothesis, as he himself will acknowledge, most notably in regard to the Qur'an's anti-Trinitarianism, his study remains the single best historical reconstruction of earliest Islam.[118] Without question Donner's work far surpasses the many other accounts of Muhammad's life and the rise of Islam that continue to be produced on the basis of Muhammad's now discredited traditional biographies. For the moment, then, relying primarily on the Qur'an appears to hold the most promise for discerning what little we may know about the historical figure of Muhammad and understanding the rise of Islam, even despite the many questions that remain about the status of the Qur'an and its origins.

---

115. Blachère, *Problème de Mahomet*.

116. Hawting, *Idea of Idolatry*; Crone, "Religion of the Qur'ānic Pagans"; Crone, "Quranic Mushrikūn I"; Crone, "Quranic Mushrikūn II."

117. Donner, *Muhammad and the Believers*. See also in favor of this hypothesis Lindstedt, "Who Is In?"; and Lindstedt, "Surah 5."

118. But on the matter of the Qur'an's anti-Trinitarianism see Shoemaker, "Jewish Christianity."

In Search of the Historical Muhammad: The Sources

By now we have hopefully already made the point that Muhammad's traditional Islamic biographies, even as preserved in the earliest recoverable collections, are effectively useless for any effort to recover the historical figure of Muhammad in a critical manner. While there is no need to belabor the fact, suffice it to say that any modern studies of Muhammad's life and the beginnings of Islam that make significant use of these sources—and unfortunately there are many—are not truly critical. What these traditionally derived biographies of Muhammad reveal is not so much the historical figure of Muhammad. Instead, they reproduce highly mythologized narratives of Muhammad's life and the beginnings of Islam that were filtered through the Islamic collective memory over generations—at least a hundred years, if not two hundred—before they were eventually written down.[119] Such biographies can perhaps be useful for teaching (although problematic nonetheless) or for knowledge of what the Islamic tradition believes about Muhammad. Yet they cannot be considered critical studies, inasmuch as they are based almost entirely in uncritical acceptance of sources known to be thoroughly unreliable. The persistent repetition of this scholarly misstep can make it seem to the uninitiated as if no such problem exists, further compounding the problems inherent in this collective misuse of the sources. Nevertheless, scholars who continue to use such studies of Muhammad and the beginnings of Islam should know what they are getting: a replica of the Islamic tradition with some western inflections.

Horovitz, who would emerge as the first critical historian of these biographical traditions, is unflinching in his judgment that "modern scientific investigation" of Muhammad and the Qur'an must "leave Islamic tradition entirely out of consideration."[120] And yet scholars such as Watt casually persist in reproducing the basic narrative of these traditional biographies despite their well-known artificiality and unreliability. Watt and others regularly invoke in defense of their approach—but never demonstrate—the existence of a supposedly reliable "kernel" at the core of these biographies.[121] With this unwarranted assumption, Watt and others take license to reproduce essentially unaltered the traditional Islamic accounts

---

119. Shoemaker, "In Search of 'Urwa's Sīra," 257–61; Anthony, *Muhammad*, 2–11.

120. Horovitz, "Jewish Proper Names," 146; see also Horovitz, *Earliest Biographies of the Prophet*.

121. Watt, "Materials Used by Ibn Ishaq"; Watt, "Reliability of Ibn Ishaq's Sources," 32; also Andræ, *Mohammed: The Man*, 31.

of Muhammad's activities at Mecca and Medina, creating the illusion that we know far more about Muhammad and the beginnings of Islam than we actually do. Yet such studies are grounded in a fatal credulity that fails to confront significant problems with the source material, decisively undermining their value for understanding the historical figure of Muhammad or the beginnings of Islam.[122]

Of course, one must acknowledge that these early biographical memories of Muhammad were not simply produced out of thin air over a century after his death. There was, after all, an actual historical figure named Muhammad whose life and teaching ultimately inspired these later memories. Yet after a century of oral transmission from memory, there is little reason to place any confidence in even the most basic outline of these memories, given the extremely unstable qualities of oral transmission and human memory, both individual and collective.[123] At the same time, however, it certainly is not impossible that in some specific instances Muhammad's traditional biographies may preserve reliable information regarding events and individuals from the early seventh century, albeit with a heavy overlay of medieval mythologization of Muhammad and the beginnings of Islam. Yet in each such instance the tradition in question must be rigorously interrogated using the tools of historical criticism in order to validate whatever information therein may be judged to be reliable. Since it is well known that the invention of new traditions about Muhammad was rampant in early Islam, one must always begin, as Schacht rightly insists, from a position of extreme skepticism when approaching any particular tradition in these medieval collections, initially assuming the tradition to be an invention of pious imagination "until the contrary is proved."[124] And even in those instances where we may find an individual tradition to be more or less credible, the results often turn out to be quite meager, with little relevance for pursuit of the historical Muhammad.

Some scholars have recently proposed a method for identifying early (although not necessarily trustworthy) traditions through critical study of their *isnāds*, that is, the alleged chains of transmission that accompany many (but not all) early traditions. The purpose of these pedigrees is obviously to validate the tradition in question by assigning it to an early authority through an unbroken chain of transmission by individuals who

---

122. Cf. Schacht, "Revaluation of Islamic Traditions," 146–47.
123. See, e.g., Shoemaker, *Creating the Qur'an*, 117–203.
124. Schacht, *Origins of Muhammadan Jurisprudence*, 149; Cook, *Muhammad*, 67.

were believed to be reliable. Nevertheless, since the work of Goldziher and Schacht, it has become widely acknowledged that these *isnād*s were readily and regularly forged no less than the traditions that they purport to guarantee, so that they can be taken at face value no more than the traditions that they aim to validate.[125] Yet there are means of deriving historically useful information, which can sometimes date the introduction of a particular tradition, through critical analysis of these chains of transmission. For instance, if one were to take a widely circulated tradition and compare all of its various *isnād*s, in many cases they may eventually converge on a single transmitter, the so-called "common link" on which all subsequent transmissions seem to depend. In cases where the networks of transmission from this common link are sufficiently varied and dense, one can take indeed some confidence in identifying this person as the figure who most likely placed a given tradition into circulation, following a method first devised by Schacht and then further refined by G. H. A. Juynboll.[126]

Unfortunately, this method of common link analysis is not as failsafe as it might seem, as Schacht was the first to acknowledge, since many factors inherent to the process of transmission can result in the identification of a false common-link, and therefore an inaccurate dating.[127] Still, the method is frequently a useful means of dating, particularly for widely circuited traditions with complex transmission histories. Nevertheless, with some regularity, this method confirms that even the earliest elements of Islamic tradition—with the exception of the Qur'an—cannot be dated prior to the turn of the second Islamic century, when the very earliest common links start to appear. Any transmissions ascribed to figures before the common link, from the first century, are as a general rule to be disregarded by the critical historian. As Schacht persuasively demonstrated, these tradents reflect artificial attempts to enhance the authority of a tradition by elevating it to Muhammad himself or one of his companions.[128] Accordingly, one should additionally note that these findings of *isnād* criticism serve to confirm what we otherwise learn from the Islamic tradition itself: that

---

125. Cf. Goldziher, *Muhammedanische Studien*, 80–83; Goldziher, *Muslim Studies*; Schacht, "Revaluation of Islamic Traditions"; Schacht, *Origins of Muhammadan Jurisprudence*.

126. Schacht, *Origins of Muhammadan Jurisprudence*, 163–75; Juynboll, *Muslim Tradition*, 206–17.

127. Cook, *Early Muslim Dogma*, 107–16; Crone, *Roman, Provincial and Islamic Law*, 27–34; Calder, *Studies in Early Muslim Jurisprudence*, 236–41.

128. Schacht, *Origins of Muhammadan Jurisprudence*, esp. 5, 30, 33, 166.

it was only in the early and mid-eighth century that the earliest memories of Muhammad and the beginnings of Islam began to be written down after nearly a century of purely oral transmission.

Some scholars have attempted to apply this method of dating to traditions from the corpus of Muhammad's Islamic biographies, albeit without much success. The problem is that the transmission of these biographical traditions is often very narrow, focusing on only a handful of early transmitters and the few early sources mentioned above. For whatever reason, it would appear that only a few individuals were remembered as active in collecting and transmitting biographical traditions during the eighth and ninth centuries, so that it is often not possible to establish a common link with any confidence on the basis of a sufficiently dense and complex pattern of transmission. In the best-case scenarios, we can often date a number of biographical traditions to the career of an early eighth-century scholar named al-Zuhrī, who was the teacher of Ibn Isḥāq (and Maʿmar), but then we are still only at the beginning of the second Islamic century. Nevertheless, several scholars have sought to argue on the basis of *isnād*s for an even earlier dating of certain traditions about Muhammad, reaching back into the late first century.[129] To do so, however, they must regularly engage in special pleading on behalf of both the traditions and their tradents, with largely unconvincing results.[130]

Yet even if we were to grant not only the relative antiquity but even the accuracy of all the traditions that these scholars have sought to anchor to the first Islamic century, the resulting knowledge about Muhammad is exceedingly minimal, as even the main advocate of this approach will acknowledge.[131] In each case the allegedly authenticated tradition generally describes some event from Muhammad's life that could otherwise be judged as probable simply on the basis of the content itself. Some traditions are fairly obvious, for instance, such as the report of Muhammad beginning to receive revelations: after all, his followers did believe he was a divinely inspired prophet, and one imagines that he did as well. One would expect such a tradition, particularly in the highly generic form that *isnād* criticism has been able to validate, to be both early and authentic. So too early

---

129. Schoeler, *Charakter und Authentie*; Schoeler, "Character and Authenticity"; Schoeler, "Foundations for A New Biography"; Görke, "Historical Tradition about al-Hudaybiya"; Görke and Schoeler, "Reconstructing the Earliest *Sīra* Texts"; Görke and Schoeler, *Die ältesten Berichte*; Motzki, "Murder of Ibn Abī l-Ḥuqayq."

130. Shoemaker, "In Search of 'Urwa's Sīra."

131. Motzki, "Murder of Ibn Abī l-Ḥuqayq," 234–35.

memory of a tradition of some sort of migration by Muhammad finds confirmation more easily than through *isnād* criticism: from early on Muhammad's followers anchored their calendar to the memory of this migration, the *hijra* in Arabic.¹³² In other cases, the content of a particular tradition is sufficiently embarrassing or contradictory in one way or another to the consensus of the later Islamic tradition. On this basis we may establish a high degree of probability that the tradition in question is likely to be early if not authentic since its invention at a later time would be hard to reconcile the community's evolving beliefs about Muhammad and his early followers and their character. In such cases, the reasoning follows the "criterion of dissimilarity" or "criterion of embarrassment," a foundational principle of historical Jesus research: material at odds with or embarrassing to the later tradition is more likely to be early or even authentic.¹³³ And so on this basis we might reasonably believe that there were early memories of a scandal regarding the chastity of Muhammad's wife Aisha; of Muhammad arranging a surrender on unfavorable terms; and of Muhammad ordering his followers to assassinate a political opponent. All of these things seem entirely plausible, even as not they are not especially helpful for understanding either the historical Muhammad or the beginnings of Islam.¹³⁴

Indeed, most importantly, the traditions in question reveal almost nothing about the nature of Muhammad's religious teachings, the beliefs of his religious community, or its early history. In these areas, the *sira* traditions remain not only unproven but also highly suspect, so that the critical scholar must leave them well to the side. Accordingly, in searching Muhammad's traditional biographies for information that could shed light on the historical Muhammad, *isnād* criticism does not seem to hold much potential even under the most optimistic conditions.¹³⁵ Instead, we must approach their contents using the methods of "*matn* criticism," an approach initially outlined by both Goldziher and Schacht that focuses analysis on the content—the *matn*—of a particular tradition in order to determine the context in which it likely arose.¹³⁶ Indeed, the principles of *matn* criticism

---

132. E.g., Crone and Cook, *Hagarism*, 7, 157n39; Humphreys, *Islamic History*, 19.

133. E.g., Porter, *Criteria for Authenticity*, 82–89.

134. Shoemaker, "In Search of 'Urwa's Sīra," 339–44. Nevertheless, given Muhammad's violent portrayal in his earliest biographies, perhaps the final example was not particularly "embarrassing" to the early Muslim transmitters.

135. Shoemaker, "In Search of 'Urwa's Sīra," 340–43.

136. Goldziher, *Muhammedanische Studien*, 2:22–130; Goldziher, *Muslim Studies*, 2:33–125; Schacht, *Origins of Muhammadan Jurisprudence*, 176–89.

bear useful and reassuring resemblance to the well-established practices of form criticism and redaction criticism in biblical studies, valuable tools whose application is sorely wanted in the study of early Islam. When Muhammad's traditional biographies are approached in this manner, examining each tradition carefully and critically on a case-by-case basis, it may indeed be possible to identify material that could be early and even authentic. But with the exception of such painstakingly validated individual cases, the critical historian must abandon these pious medieval memories of Muhammad for reconstructing events of the early seventh century.

In the Qur'an, however, we have a source that is, by near universal agreement, from the first century of Islam. Yet beyond that point of easy consensus, much debate persists regarding the origins of the Qur'an: When during the first century did the Qur'an reach its final canonical state? How did the traditions develop before that point? What relation do its contents have with the historical figure of Muhammad? These questions have gone largely unanswered, even unaddressed, as most scholars of early Islam have decided to resolve them through deference to the Islamic tradition. As a result, these issues remain no more settled today than they were when Jeffery expressed similar concerns about the Qur'an's historical value nearly a century ago.[137] Even more problematic for our purposes, however, is the nature of the qur'anic text itself: as already noted, it is not about Muhammad and the early Islamic community. Instead, its focus is the prophetic history of the past and an urgent call to piety in advance of an imminent final judgment. As Andrew Rippin rightly notes, the Qur'an serves primarily to "bring strands of earlier biblical and Arabian traditions together through the person of Muhammad," while remaining altogether indifferent to the incidentals of time and space, with the exception, of course, of the impending eschaton. Consequently, Rippin concludes, "In no sense can the Qur'ān be assumed to be a primary document in constructing the life of Muhammad. The text is far too opaque when it comes to history; its shifting referents leave the text a historical muddle for historical purposes."[138] At the same time, however, despite these serious limitations, the Qur'an remains our single best witness to the earliest beliefs of Muhammad's new religious community and their memories of what he taught. If we have any hope at all of reaching back to the historical figure of Muhammad, our best

---

137. Jeffery, "Quest," 342.

138. Rippin, "Muḥammad in the Qur'ān," 307; Wansbrough and Rippin, *Quranic Studies*, xvii; see also Donner, *Narratives of Islamic Origins*, 84.

prospect is to find our way through the complex history and content of the qur'anic text, while keeping our expectations necessarily low.

Although most modern scholars accede to the Islamic tradition in assigning the Qur'an's collection and standardization to the caliph Uthman around 650 CE, following the received account, a final redaction and canonization of the text sometime around 700, under Abd al-Malik, seems historically more likely.[139] For most of the seventh century, then, from the end of Muhammad's life in the 630s until the final authorization and promulgation of the qur'anic *textus receptus*, its traditions were in a persistent state of transmission and, inescapably, transformation. Initially recollections of Muhammad's teachings circulated among his followers by oral transmission from memory, both notoriously unstable vessels, seemingly for several decades. In the process, memories of what Muhammad taught would regularly change to meet the circumstances of those who were remembering, telling, and listening to them. New beliefs would be spontaneously remembered as something that Muhammad must have said, while other teachings deemed no longer relevant would quickly be forgotten.[140] New sacred traditions learned from the Jews and Christians of the Near East touching upon themes and figures of the Qur'an would seamlessly come to be remembered as things Muhammad had taught from the very start.[141] Yet none of this, it must be emphasized, requires any kind of elaborate conspiracy or deliberate deception: such transformations are simply inherent to the nature of memory and oral transmission alike. Moreover, even for those who would accept the traditional account of the Qur'an's formation two decades after Muhammad's death on the basis of an oral tradition, it remains the case that these same dynamics would have invariably effected changes in the Qur'an's content. The Qur'an, then, is not a record of Muhammad's teaching, but rather his followers' orally transmitted memories of his message.

Eventually individuals and local communities began to write down some of the traditions that they wanted to be sure not to forget, a transition, one must emphasize, that did not immediately bring an end to oral transmission, which nonetheless continued alongside the move to writing. Nor did the gradual shift to writing bring an end to changes in the tradition.

---

139. De Prémare, *Aux origines du Coran*; Robinson, *'Abd al-Malik*; Shoemaker, *Creating the Qur'an*.

140. Shoemaker, *Creating the Qur'an*, 148–203.

141. Shoemaker, "Christmas in the Qur'ān"; van Bladel, "Alexander Legend"; Tesei, "Prophecy."

Although written traditions are more stable than oral traditions told from memory, until we have the Islamic state policing a strictly standardized wording for the Qur'an, change is almost inevitable, and its contents would continue to be adjusted to meet changing circumstances. Indeed, according to the traditional Islamic account of the Qur'an's formation, it was the existence of several local, divergent collections of Muhammad's revelations that compelled the ruling authorities to step in and establish a single authoritative version. Whether this standardization happened after seventy years of oral transmission from memory or only twenty, the effect of memory and orality in transforming these traditions must have been significant. Therefore, despite a prevalent and deeply misplaced confidence among many modern scholars of the Qur'an, there is simply no chance that, to quote one among many examples, "our copy of the Qur'an is, in fact, what Muhammad taught, and is expressed in his own words."[142] To believe otherwise at this point is a matter of faith, for the believing Muslim, or, quite frankly, for the modern historian, a delusion.

For these reasons, in using the Qur'an to search for the historical Muhammad, we must constantly filter its contents with active concerns for how these memories of Muhammad's teachings are no less—indeed, perhaps even more—a product of the faith and reminiscence of his earliest followers across the decades of the seventh century. The Qur'an is hardly the direct pipeline into the historical Muhammad's religious thinking that was once imagined. Instead, we must approach it as a communally shaped repository of memories of sacred tradition believed to derive from Muhammad's revelations to his earliest followers. To quote Michael Pregill, who nicely summarizes the status of the Qur'an in this early period, "we should think of 'Qur'an' in the first Islamic century as a genre of early Islamic historical remembrance and not a singular artifact of prophetic revelation."[143] At the same time, however, there are also signs that at least some parts of the Qur'an may predate Muhammad, having been appropriated by a prophet and his community as a sort of sacred textual artifact that was not always perfectly understood by Muhammad and his followers.[144] Consequently, we may not use the Qur'an naively as some sort of window into Muhammad's

---

142. Peters, "Quest of the Historical Muhammad," 293–95; more recently, see, e.g., Neuwirth, "Structural, Linguistic and Literary Features," 100; Neuwirth, "Locating the Qur'an," 193.

143. Pregill, "Review of *Creating the Qur'an*."

144. See the discussion in Shoemaker, *Creating the Qur'an*, 234–45, as well as my forthcoming article Shoemaker, "You Pass by Them."

mind, as if it offered an unmediated and accurate record of his teaching. Indeed, even if some scholars may no longer insist that the Qur'an preserves Muhammad's words verbatim, it remains widely assumed that somehow the text can transparently provide modern scholars with direct access to Muhammad's thoughts, words, and world, revealing the historical man through his message.[145] Yet given the Qur'an's formation over a period of several decades within the sectarian milieu of late ancient western Asia, we must acknowledge that Muhammad is not the Qur'an's author so much as its inspiration, even as we recognize that the text as we have it today surely bears traces of his actual teaching in the mix. Therefore, we must approach the Qur'an first and foremost with the community's role in shaping the text in mind, searching carefully for any characteristics and clues that might lead back to Muhammad himself.

Finally, in addition to Muhammad's traditional Islamic biographies and the Qur'an, we possess another set of invaluable sources that are all too often overlooked in the study of early Islam: the contemporary—in some instances eyewitness—accounts of non-Muslim writers who were observers to the rise of Islam during its first century, mentioned already above. Although many of these sources had long been available to scholars of early Islam, who largely ignored them, only in the later 1970s did they begin to receive the attention that they truly deserve. This development in the study of early Islam emerged in concert with a renewed attention to the Christian communities of the late ancient Near East, who often wrote in Syriac, Georgian, Armenian, and other languages in addition to Greek and Latin. The key moment seems to have come in 1975 at an Oxford University conference on first-century Islam, where Sebastian Brock delivered a paper on "Syriac Views of Emergent Islam," which first introduced the importance of these long neglected sources to specialists on Islam.[146] Although many scholars would subsequently choose to ignore the significance of these sources, henceforth no truly critical study of Islamic origins can avoid engaging with these contemporaneous reports.

Michael Cook and Patricia Crone were the first scholars to take seriously the witness of these non-Islamic sources, in their path-breaking work *Hagarism* which initially took shape at this same conference.[147] It is fair to say that *Hagarism* went a bit too far in writing a history of earliest Islam

---

145. E.g., Sinai, *Qur'an*, 47–52; Anthony, *Muhammad*, 11–18.
146. Brock, "Syriac Views."
147. Crone and Cook, *Hagarism*.

based solely on these non-Islamic sources while excluding evidence from the Islamic tradition almost entirely. Nevertheless, the overarching genius behind the work and its transformative effect on the subsequent study of early Islam must not be overlooked, despite frequent efforts to marginalize and malign both the book and its authors, which unfortunately continue. Indeed, still as recently as just a few years ago Aziz al-Azmeh posted an article decrying "revisionist" scholarship—and Crone's work and legacy in particular—as "Islamic origins for Neo-Conservatives."[148] Nevertheless, despite such overheated rhetorical attacks, *Hagarism*'s challenge has undeniably changed the field, so that, among other things, these invaluable sources have now become widely known and accessible, even as their usage remains disappointingly spare in many studies of formative Islam.[149] These contemporary non-Muslim accounts of the rise of Islam hold unique value for the historian, particularly in light of the failings of the traditional Islamic materials for reconstructing the rise of Islam. It is true that they may not be taken simply at face value and must be subject to careful historical criticism no less than any other source. But the simple fact that they relate information from witnesses external to the early Islamic community is no reason to disregard their evidence. Indeed, it has long been routine in study of early Christianity to prioritize and even privilege reports from contemporary non-Christian writers about the beginnings of Christianity.[150] In making use of such sources, one must take into consideration any potential biases or ideological tendencies in a particular author's account as well as the source of the information in question—no less than one must do so for the Islamic sources as well. Having been duly scrutinized, however, these non-Islamic sources stand without equal for their contemporary reports of events that were unfolding around their authors as the wrote. Accordingly, these sources must figure prominently in any reconstruction of the historical Muhammad, even as they remain frustratingly reticent, telling us much less than we would like to know.

---

148. Al-Azmeh, "Islamic Origins for Neo-Conservatives."

149. Hoyland, *Seeing Islam*; Penn, *When Christians*; Shoemaker, *Prophet Has Appeared*. A welcome exception to this tendency is Anthony, *Muhammad*.

150. E.g., Wilken, *Christians*.

In Search of the Historical Muhammad: The Context

By all indications it would appear that Muhammad and his earliest followers came from Mecca, on the western coast of the Arabian Peninsula. It is true that occasionally scholars have proposed that we should locate the beginnings of Islam elsewhere—somewhere in the Nabataean world on the borders of the Roman Empire has been a popular alternative—but so far, none of these hypotheses has gained much traction. Among the primary reasons that scholars have sought an alternative home for the rise of Islam is that the cultural sophistication of the Qur'an seems to require a more cosmopolitan and cultivated milieu than the traditional cradle of Islam, Mecca and Medina in the central Hijaz, could provide. Indeed, the Qur'an's incompatibility with the simplicity of both Mecca and the Yathrib oasis in late antiquity effectively requires the historian to identify an alternative matrix for much of its content in one fashion or another. One solution to this problem, obviously, is to relocate the Qur'an, along with Muhammad and the beginnings of Islam as a whole to a more culturally compatible locale. Thus, Cook and Crone, for example, posited in *Hagarism* the origins of Islam somewhere in northwestern Arabia, on the fringes of the Roman Empire and in the cultural sphere of the Nabateans.[151]

Yet as attractive as such a migration may be for solving the problem of the Qur'an's sophistication (among other things), it fails to explain convincingly why Mecca and Medina would figure so prominently in later Islamic memories of Muhammad and the beginnings of their faith tradition. In the early seventh century, both settlements were small, insignificant, and remote hamlets that were effectively unknown to the rest of the ancient world. Why, then, one must ask, would Islam eventually come to center its sacred landscape on these obscure and isolated villages if they did not have some sort of ancestral link with Muhammad's new religious movement? There seems little inherent significance to either place that could explain their eventual adoption as the twin sacred cities of Islam other than a genuine connection to Muhammad and the beginnings of the community. The argument proposed by Crone and Wansbrough, that the origins of Islam were reimagined entirely against a Hijazi backdrop to insulate Muhammad from claims of Jewish and Christian influence, does not seem sufficient.[152] Moreover, Mecca is named, albeit only once, in the Qur'an (48:24), again

---

151. Crone and Cook, *Hagarism*, 21–24.
152. Wansbrough, *Quranic Studies*, 50–58, 179; Crone, "What Do We Actually Know."

raising the question of its inclusion absent some actual genetic link to this impoverished, remote Arabian outpost. The Qur'an's notice elsewhere of a place named Bakka (3:96) is not, one should note, a reference to Mecca, as the Islamic tradition would have it, but almost certainly to Jerusalem instead.[153] Indeed, by all indications, it would seem that Jerusalem was actually the original *locus sanctus* of Muhammad's new religious movement, only to be gradually displaced by Mecca and Medina over the course of the seventh century, as Islam increasingly required its own distinctive holy land. Presumably, Mecca and Medina were selected for this preeminent status on the basis of some historical connection with Muhammad and the foundation of his community of the Believers.[154]

Muhammad, therefore, as well as his earliest followers, most likely hailed from Mecca, where his new religious movement first began to take shape, before eventually relocating to the Yathrib oasis, now Medina, which also seems to be highly probable. With this recognition we now have the first building blocks for reconstructing the historical Muhammad, since we can draw some important conclusions based on the status of these settlements within the broader world of West Asian late antiquity. Firstly, we may look to the climate and geography of Mecca and Medina, which do not seem to have changed much at all over the past 1,400 years. Mecca and Medina both lie in a highly arid and hot desert region, with an average annual rainfall of just 60–70 mm (2–3 inches). Moreover, most of this rainfall comes as a deluge in the winter months, so that before flood control measures were implemented, in Muhammad's lifetime these annual rains would regularly bring devastating floods for both Mecca and the Yathrib oasis. During the summer, average high temperatures hover around 43 C (110 F) in both places, while average winter highs cool down to 31 C for Mecca (87 F) and 25 C (75 F) in Medina, a difference due to the latter's higher elevation.

Mecca lies in a valley surrounded by barren mountains and has extremely limited natural water sources, amounting to only a few brackish wells and a small spring. As should be entirely obvious, such conditions cannot sustain either significant agricultural activities or, consequently, a large population: as Crone rightly observes, Muhammad's Mecca was "devoid of food and other amenities that human beings and other animals

---

153. Shoemaker, "Jerusalem Temple," reprinted in the present volume as chapter 3.
154. Shoemaker, *Death of a Prophet*, 218–65.

generally require to engage in activities of any kind."[155] Its economy could only have been based in subsistence level pastoralism—making it all the more peculiar that the Qur'an's opponents are regularly identified as agriculturalists who grew wheat, grapes, olives, and other things that were impossible to grow in Mecca's hot, arid climate.[156] Likewise, the region possessed no natural resources of any value or really any significant economy to speak of, so that we should not be surprised at all to learn that, according to a convincing recent study, in the early seventh century Mecca had a population of around 500, of whom only about one-third (130) would have been free adult men.[157] Its dwellings in this period were, as Michael Cook notes, "still mere huts constructed of palm-branches."[158] Circumstances were not all that different in the Yathrib oasis, where Muhammad and his initial followers would first come into power. It too lay in a valley surrounded by barren mountains, with a vast desert lying beyond their ridges: in the words of Watt, "it was not so much a city as a collection of hamlets, farms, and strongholds scattered over an oasis. . .surrounded by hills, rocks, and stony ground—all uncultivable."[159] Yet, as an oasis, Yathrib had better natural water resources than Mecca and was therefore capable of sustaining some agricultural activities, even as water remained scarce.

Therefore, although figures are hard to come by, Yathrib no doubt had a larger population than Mecca, probably amounting to around 1,000 or so inhabitants. Nevertheless, one should not mistake Yathrib for a small town of this size. Prior to the beginnings of Islam, as Watt notes, Yathrib was not the name of a particular village, but rather the name given to the oasis itself, which encompassed altogether approximately fifty square kilometers (roughly 20 square miles). Within this region there was no single organized or dominant settlement, but instead the oasis was comprised of a group of loosely connected and disparate settlements, around eighteen in total.[160] These hamlets and homesteads were scattered across the oasis' fifty square kilometer expanse and clustered around the valley's main water sources, where their inhabitants relied on this precious resource to engage in

155. Crone, *Meccan Trade*, 160.

156. Crone, *Meccan Trade*, 159; Crone, "How Did the Quranic Pagans," 393–94; Waines, "Agriculture," 40.

157. Robinson, "Population Size."

158. Cook, *Muhammad*, 13.

159. Watt, *Muhammad at Mecca*, 141.

160. Makki, *Medina*, 29.

limited agriculture.¹⁶¹ Undoubtedly, no single one these hamlets was even as big as Mecca, and presumably no individual settlement in Yathrib had a population of more than a couple of hundred people, while most of them probably had less than one hundred inhabitants. And of these inhabitants, one should note, only around one-third would have been free adult males. Moreover, there was not, one should emphasize, any sort of overarching central authority in the oasis that united these disparate settlements, nor was there any central town that could have served an administrative center or the location of a central marketplace for exchange. Quite to the contrary, all evidence suggests that there was great disunity and discord among these various homesteads and hamlets prior to Muhammad's arrival, which, indeed, provided the occasion for his invitation to settle there and unite the settlements under his political and religious authority.¹⁶²

Given the continued prominence of political and economic lives of Muhammad, as noted above, we certainly must consider the economic conditions of both locales, which, as it turns out, were extremely meager in both cases. Mecca, of course, has long been famously known in the scholarly literature on early Islam as a major center of long-distance, high-value, intercontinental trade. As such, Muslims and modern scholars alike have been wont to imagine it as a thriving, wealthy, and cosmopolitan entrepot. According to this myth of Meccan trade, Muhammad's hometown was the hub of a lucrative network of spice and incense trade coming northward from the south of Arabia and points beyond across the Indian Ocean to the east. As these high-value commodities passed through Mecca on their way to the Mediterranean world, so many scholars have fancied, Mecca's inhabitants grew wealthy as brokers for the exchange of these luxury goods. At the nexus of this vast financial empire was the Quraysh tribe, Muhammad's tribe and also the dominant tribe in pre-Islamic Mecca, according to the Islamic tradition. And so modern scholars, in concert with the Islamic historical tradition, fashioned Muhammad's Mecca as an important commercial center, where "financial operations of considerable complexity were carried on."¹⁶³ It is as if something resembling modern Dubai was conjured out of the barren desert of late ancient Arabia.

161. Munt, *Holy City*, 49–50.
162. Watt, *Muhammad at Medina*, 4–10; Crone, *Slaves on Horses*, 22–26; Hoyland, *Arabia and the Arabs*, 113–17.
163. Watt, *Muhammad at Mecca*, 3; Watt, *Muhammad at Mecca*.

Margoliouth seems to have been the first to develop this modern myth of Mecca as a wealthy center of trade in luxury goods, primarily on the basis of the early Islamic historical tradition.[164] Yet it was his contemporary Lammens who would supercharge this invention and ensconce it, while Watt would sacralize it, establishing its unimpeachable canonical status, still to this day in many quarters.[165] Nevertheless, this orientalist mirage has since been thoroughly dispelled by Crone in her *Meccan Trade and the Rise of Islam*, where she dismantled the fiction of Meccan trade in luxury goods for lack of any sufficient evidence.[166] One should note, however, that well over a century before Crone wrote her book, Muir had already convincingly made the same case using many of the same arguments, only to be ignored, unfortunately, by subsequent scholarship.[167] Indeed, although this myth of Mecca as a major mercantile center of considerable wealth and with a far-reaching network is fundamental to the Islamic tradition's memory of its origins, it bears little resemblance whatsoever to the conditions in Mecca in the early seventh century.[168] The truth of the matter is that, even if there may have once been caravan traffic that passed through Mecca on its way from South Arabia to the Mediterranean world, by Muhammad's lifetime such overland trade was centuries in the past. And even when it existed, long before Muhammad was born, it almost certainly completely bypassed Mecca, which "only by the most tortured map reading can be described as a natural crossroads."[169]

By no later than the first century CE, trade between South Arabia and the Mediterranean world shifted completely from overland transit to seaborne transport via the western coast of the Red Sea, as our classical sources make abundantly clear.[170] The spice and incense trade thus completely passed the Hijaz by as it wound up and down the coast of Egypt and Ethiopia between Yemen and Sinai, and accordingly, it did absolutely nothing to enrich Mecca or its inhabitants. More recently, some scholars have sought to salvage the riches of Mecca by positing that it had become relatively wealthy in Muhammad's lifetime through exchange in locally

---

164. Margoliouth, *Mohammed*, 4–15.
165. Lammens, *La Mecque*; Watt, *Muhammad at Mecca*.
166. Crone, *Meccan Trade*.
167. Muir, *Life of Mahomet*, 1:cxxx–cxlii.
168. Anthony, *Muhammad*, 78.
169. Bulliet, *Camel*, 105.
170. E.g., Casson, *Periplus Maris Erythraei*.

mined precious metals that were traded with the Roman and Sasanian Empires to the north. It is true that we possess archaeological evidence for ancient gold, silver, and copper mining at various locations in the Arabian Peninsula. Nevertheless, according to that same archaeological evidence, none of these mines was active during Muhammad's lifetime, and the closest sources of precious metals to Mecca and Medina were either 250 km or 450 km distant (150 or 280 miles), and deep within the desolate deserts of the central Arabian interior. Even if these mines had been functional in late antiquity, which by all indications they were not, it is extremely unlikely that they would have had any impact on or interaction with the local economies of Mecca and Yathrib.[171] Therefore, simply put, in Muhammad's lifetime, Mecca was not a major center of international trade in high-value luxury goods. It was a far more humble and insignificant place, so that it is hardly any wonder that no ancient source so much as even mentions its existence before its single appearance in the text of the Qur'an.[172] Despite these facts, however, the orientalist myth of Mecca as a wealthy and cosmopolitan center of international exchange has proven difficult to dislodge, and likely will continue to be so.

What about the tradition that pre-Islamic Mecca possessed an important pilgrimage shrine, revered across Arabia as an important religious center in its polytheist cults: could that have possibly raised its significance within the central Hijaz at least and given it an economic lift? The Islamic historical sources certainly remember Mecca as having been a major pilgrimage destination in the age of Muhammad, with devotees traveling from near and far to worship at its Holy House. This shrine and its attendant pilgrimage made Mecca, according to the Islamic tradition, a kind of sanctuary city or *haram*—a place that was religiously inviolable and in which no violence or bloodshed could be committed. Not only, then, did Mecca's regular pilgrimage traffic bring considerable wealth to town, as is commonly supposed, but the city's sanctuary status also encouraged people, particularly merchants, to settle there and brought visitors year-round, on account of the safety afforded by the inviolability of its precincts. Thus, Mecca's sanctuary status formed the basis, so it is maintained, for its emergence as a major center of international trade in luxury goods, since, as Watt avers, there people could come to trade "without fear of

---

171. Shoemaker, *Creating the Qur'an*, 100–106.
172. Morris, "Mecca and Macoraba."

molestation."[173] Nevertheless, as it turns out the image of Mecca in so much modern scholarship and in the early Islamic tradition as both a major pilgrimage center and a haven from violence is no less of a scholarly mirage than the imagined Meccan spice trade to which these notions have become so closely bound.

Already in the late nineteenth century, Julius Wellhausen demonstrated convincingly that in late antiquity Mecca simply was not a major pilgrimage center of any sort, a finding that has since been solidly confirmed by Crone.[174] There were perhaps pilgrimages and pilgrimage shrines in the central Hijaz, it would seem, but Mecca itself was not the object of any such pilgrimage, nor did it possess a shrine of significance to anyone beyond its 500 or so inhabitants. Memories in the early Islamic tradition suggesting otherwise are simply projections of later Islamic practices back onto the blank canvas of pre-Islamic Mecca. So did Mecca even have some sort of a shrine in late antiquity? I think it is entirely reasonable to assume on general principles that the herdsmen of this small, remote village and their families would have had some sort of sacred shrine, as is customary in most cultures. Just what the nature of this shrine may have been, however, is a difficult question that is not easily answered based on the much later information that we have from the Islamic tradition, which overlays later practices onto the memory of origins, as both Crone and Hawting have made clear.[175] The Qur'an cannot help us, since, as Hawting rightly discerns, its content already reflects the process of Islamicizing certain pre-Islamic pilgrimage practices, which originally were not focused on Mecca, by linking them directly with Mecca and establishing Muhammad's hometown as

---

173. Watt, *Muhammad at Mecca*, 3.

174. Wellhausen, *Reste arabischen Heidentums*, 80–89; Crone, *Meccan Trade*, 168–77.

175. Crone, *Meccan Trade*, 185–95; Hawting, "Origins of the Muslim Sanctuary." Note that recently Peter Webb has proposed to establish the existence of a pre-Islamic Meccan pilgrimage on the basis of memories appearing in the corpus of so-called "pre-Islamic" Arabic poetry: Webb, "Hajj." Nevertheless, the poems all circulated orally for centuries before being committed to writing long after the Hajj had been well established and observed for generations. Such witnesses, which were transmitted orally from memory for hundreds of years in a context in which the Hajj was a "pillar" of the Islamic faith, can hardly be relied upon as evidence for practice in the fifth and sixth centuries, particularly in the absence of any corroborating evidence from better sources. The same holds true for the parallel article, Webb, "History and Significance." Note also the recent article by Suleyman Dost that identifies epigraphic evidence for parallels to the Islamic Hajj with inscriptional evidence related to pilgrimages *elsewhere* in the Arabian Peninsula, notably in South Arabia, at considerable distance from Mecca: Dost, "Pilgrimage."

a distinctively Islamic holy place. It was a process that was still ongoing at the time when the Qur'an itself was being composed, which explains the messiness of the Qur'an's representations of the pre-Islamic pilgrimage and sanctuary.[176] Likewise, the existing structure of the Meccan Ka'ba does not help us much in this quest, since it is not only off limits to investigators, but this shrine was destroyed and rebuilt twice in close proximity at the end of the seventh century.[177] Therefore, what survives today is not the shrine of pre-Islamic Mecca but a product of competing sectarian interests during the second Islamic civil war, at a time when Mecca became newly incorporated into the older pilgrimage practices and was increasingly identified as Islam's premier sacred city.

With such desolate environs, no spice trade, and no pilgrimage shrine, Mecca certainly could not have supported itself through agriculture alone, so that it must have had an economy driven largely by some sort of exchange—the only question is, what did they trade? Certainly, they were not wealthy brokers in the international spice trade nor were they exporting precious metals, that much is settled. The only sort of economic activities that Mecca's barren landscape could sustain was some sort of pastoralism, which presumably formed the basis of its subsistence level economy. Therefore, we must assume that the Meccans traded the produce of their flocks—animals, leather, and perhaps clarified butter, in exchange for the other foodstuffs that they needed to survive, along with fodder for their stock and materials for tanning their hides: left on their own the Meccans probably would have starved.[178] Such trade was almost certainly local, limited to other nearby settlements in the western Hijaz, such as Taif, less than forty miles (60 km) to the east, which, thanks to its much higher elevation (5000 ft / 1600 m) could produce some fruits and vegetables, which the Meccans desperately needed. Indeed, Meccan trade was not driven by a thirst for wealth but rather by the need to avoid starvation. Moreover, with such ordinary and low value commodities involved, it seems out of the question that the Meccans would have set out for faraway places across the desert for trade. The only possible, albeit unlikely, exception would have been for leather, which, as Crone has noted, was in high demand by the Roman army.[179] Yet given its size, Mecca could not have produced large quantities of

176. Hawting, "Sanctuary and Text," 106, 109.
177. Hawting, "House and the Book," 16.
178. Crone, *Meccan Trade*, 160.
179. Crone, "Quraysh."

leather that would have made such an arduous journey worth undertaking, particularly when securing food would have been the much higher priority. And even if Meccan leather was destined for the Roman army, one strongly suspects that, rather than traveling all the way to the Roman frontier, any Meccan traders would have discharged their wares to a broker in one of the major caravan centers in the north of the Hijaz.

As for the Yathrib oasis, its waters enabled it to grow an abundance of food, although by all indications cultivation in Yathrib was monocultural, devoted almost entirely to producing dates, as was typical of most Arabian oases. Yet this crop would not have brought Yathrib any wealth. Dates were—and are—ubiquitous across western Asia. Accordingly, their exchange between settlements that were more than 800 kilometers apart (500 miles), separated by a harsh desert that required a two-month round trip journey, is improbable in the extreme. Dates were no exotic treat but instead a basic food staple, the "bread of the desert" as they have famously been called. And so while dates were in high demand, there was also no shortage of supply. No one would pay the exorbitant costs it would require for the farmers of Yathrib to trade their fruit with those living on the margins of the Roman Empire. They would have had their own local dates in abundance. Nor was Yathrib, any more than Mecca, at a crossroads along major overland trade routes, and without any sort of main town it lacked an obvious center for trade. Any local traders that might happen to pass through would have been in transit elsewhere; if they bought anything in Yathrib it was surely no more than sufficient provisions to get them to their next destination.

In addition to these economic privations, the central Hijaz also possessed certain significant cultural limitations. According to the reigning consensus among specialists on the early history of the Arabic language, "both before and immediately after the rise of Islam, Arab culture was in all important respects fundamentally oral." Writing, by comparison, "was hardly practiced at all in the time of Muhammad."[180] One may wonder, how could this possibly be so, given the abundance of inscriptions in various writing systems that have recently come to light from various places in the Arabian Peninsula? As it turns out, the mere existence of writing and its occasional use do not automatically make a society literate, as strange as that may seem. Anthropologists have identified and studied a number of

---

180. E.g., Macdonald, "Ancient Arabia and the Written Word," 22; Robin, "Development of Arabic," 1.

cultures in which writing exists even as they have remained fundamentally nonliterate: that is, despite the availability of writing, these societies do not make use of writing as a tool for activities that are fundamental or even essential for daily living, such as governance, commerce, literature, or religion. What, then, was writing used for? Comparison with these contemporary cultures, as well as the nature of the early Arabian inscriptions themselves indicates that writing was a form of recreation, a diversion. As Michael Macdonald explains, "literacy was therefore of little practical use in these societies and would not have displaced speech and memory as the means of communication and record. Instead, writing seems to have been used almost entirely as a pastime for those doing jobs which involved long hours of enforced, usually solitary, idleness in the desert, such as guarding the herds while they pastured, or keeping watch for game or enemies."[181] Indeed, if we look to these ancient Arabian inscriptions themselves, there is effectively nothing of any cultural, social, or political significance. Rather, there is a lot of "Kilroy was here" defacing the rocks of the Arabian desert. And while these pre-Islamic scrawlings may be a treasure trove for historical linguistics, for the religious historian, they are unfortunately largely worthless.

---

181. Macdonald, "Uses of Writing in Ancient Arabia," 8–9. In a recent article Marijn van Putten rejects this consensus, although without any basis. In doing so, he also significantly misrepresents the content of Macdonald's "Ancient Arabia and the Written Word," wrongly maintaining that in the article Macdonald does not discuss literacy in western Arabia but only in regard to "Nomadic writers in the South Arabian scripts": van Putten, "Development of the Hijazi Orthography," 126n70. It is unfortunate to have to point this out, but I honestly do not see how any reasonable person could come to this conclusion after having read the article in question: perhaps he has in mind something else entirely? To the contrary, one need only glance at the last sentences of the article's abstract, which summarize the portion of the article that covers late antiquity: "In late antiquity, the Nabataean Aramaic script gradually ceased to be employed to write Aramaic and came to be used for Arabic, which thus at last came to be a habitually written language. However, writing appears to have been used only for notes, business documents, treaties, letters, etc., not for culturally important texts [i.e., religious texts, the Qur'an], which continued to be passed on orally well into the early Islamic period." Macdonald, "Ancient Arabia and the Written Word," 5. In any case, readers interested in this matter would do well to read Macdonald's article for themselves before trusting van Putten's inaccurate summary of its conclusions. Lindstedt too has recently protested against the reigning consensus that the cultures of Mecca and Yathrib were nonliterate in Muhammad's lifetime, insisting instead that they were just as literate as anywhere else in the late ancient Near East, although offering only his own authority for this judgment: Lindstedt, *Muḥammad and His Followers*, 22.

Therefore, the divide between literate and nonliterate cultures is not simply the existence of an alphabet but instead the status that writing holds within a given culture for achieving its most important collective endeavors. In the case of the late ancient Hijaz, all the evidence indicates that we are dealing with societies that had multiple writing systems readily available, which, for whatever reason, they did not use for political, cultural, and economic activities. In these arenas, orality remained the privileged medium, so that we must consider these societies as nonliterate (but not illiterate), despite the existence of writing. Like its modern analogues, the society in which Muhammad lived "continued use of memory and oral communication in their daily lives," while maintaining "an extremely rich oral literature in which writing, even in their own script, plays no part."[182] On this basis we must conclude that Muhammad, his earliest followers, and the other inhabitants of both Mecca and the Yathrib oasis lived in a society where writing was available, but it was not used for, among other things, writing cultural and religious texts. Thus, we must constantly bear in mind that Muhammad's new religious movement and its sacred traditions initially took shape in a milieu that was fundamentally oral and nonliterate.

Closely linked with the absence of literacy in the central Hijaz, one suspects, is the absence of any evidence whatsoever for a Christian presence of any meaningful significance anywhere remotely near the two Arabian settlements that are supposed to have birthed Muhammad's new religious movement and the Qur'an. According to later Islamic tradition, there were some Jewish tribes in the Yathrib oasis, and on the basis of the so-called Constitution of Medina and its sharp dissonance with the later tradition, one is strongly inclined to give these memories the benefit of the doubt. Yet there is no evidence whatsoever, in the Islamic tradition or elsewhere, for any Jewish presence in Mecca, and none at all for Christians in either Mecca or the Yathrib oasis. This Christian void is deeply problematic for any understanding of the Qur'an that would place the genesis of its traditions in the central Hijaz. The Qur'an demonstrates a deep knowledge of Christian culture and sophisticated engagement with it, qualities that are simply irreconcilable with the cultural and religious landscape of the central Hijaz, where there does not seem to have been any Christian presence at all. Likewise, the complete absence of Judaism from Mecca is no less troubling for the traditional memories of Islamic origins, since the Qur'an is deeply infused and engaged with Jewish religious culture. Yet according

---

182. Macdonald, "Ancient Arabia and the Written Word," 7.

to the Islamic tradition, a considerable amount of the qur'anic text was produced in Mecca, much of which contains Jewish content: the Jewish tribes of Yathrib cannot account for this material.

Accordingly, one must ask: where did the Qur'an's author(s), not to mention its audience, attain the very broad and sophisticated knowledge of the Jewish and Christian tradition that the composition and comprehension of this text clearly demand? Although Muhammad's traditional biographies remember a Christian uncle in Muhammad's family, Waraqa, we have already learned not to trust these sources. Moreover, in this case Waraqa's presence clearly serves the ideological agenda of offering Christian confirmation of Muhammad's prophecy: undoubtedly that is why this solitary Christian came to be remembered at the beginning of Muhammad's revelations.[183] Otherwise, on the whole the early Islamic historical tradition consistently recalls the central Hijaz as devoid of any Christian presence during Muhammad's lifetime. Yet even if Muhammad had a Christian uncle, a stray Christian convert or three among Mecca's several hundred inhabitants cannot explain the depth of Jewish and Christian culture evident in the Qur'an. The Qur'an's suffusion with Jewish and Christian traditions would only make sense if we were to assume a sizeable Christian presence in Mecca, probably amounting to the majority of its inhabitants, in Muhammad's lifetime. But this does not seem to have been the case.

And even if it were, these hypothetical Meccan Christians would have been simple believers in the extreme, to borrow a term from Jack Tannous's recent work.[184] Their remote location kept them segregated from the broader Christian world, and their nonliterate culture profoundly limited, if not altogether excluded, their ability to absorb the sophisticated traditions of Christian culture as it had developed far to the north in the Roman Near East and in Mesopotamia—or, for that matter, at roughly equal distances in Ethiopia or South Arabia. Still more problematic, however, the Bible did not even exist in their language yet according to the current consensus, depriving any and all inhabitants of the Hijaz of direct knowledge of the biblical traditions.[185] Accordingly, we must conclude that any possible knowledge these unlikely Meccan Christians could have had about their faith must

---

183. Shoemaker, "In Search of 'Urwa's Sīra," 303–21.

184. Tannous, *Making*. Nevertheless, in my opinion Tannous's portrayal of these "simple" believers as theologically illiterate occasionally goes to far: see the response in my forthcoming article, Shoemaker, "Religious Literacy."

185. Griffith, *Bible in Arabic*, 47–53, 106–27.

have been incredibly basic and imprecise. Nor will it suffice to imagine that somehow Muhammad picked these Jewish and Christian traditions up during his travels in Syria as a merchant (more on that in a moment). Casual contact with Christians in some Middle Eastern souk would not provide the requisite level of knowledge. Moreover, the Qur'an demands not only an author but also an audience already steeped in these traditions so that they would have any chance of understanding its highly elliptic references to Jewish and Christian traditions: a single learned individual simply is not enough.[186] Of course, the Qur'an's suffusion with oblique allusions to Jewish and Christian religious culture is a historical problem more strictly relevant to the origins of the Qur'an than to the historical figure of Muhammad, yet insofar as there is any understanding that the two may be closely connected, it is relevant.

Although Christianity had literally encircled the central Hijaz by Muhammad's lifetime, there is no indication whatsoever of a Christian community in either Mecca or Medina, or anywhere in their vicinity for that matter.[187] It is of course true that absence of evidence is not always evidence of absence, and yet, we possess ample evidence indicating the presence of sizeable Christian communities almost everywhere else in the Arabian Peninsula.[188] It certainly historically significant that south of the latitude of Aqaba there is simply no evidence whatsoever for Christianity in western Arabia until one reaches modern day Yemen at the southern tip of the peninsula.[189] To be sure, there is clear and abundant evidence of Christianity in Roman Arabia north of this line, but south of this latitude scholars have

---

186. Shoemaker, *Creating the Qur'an*, 245–57.

187. Bell, *Origin of Islam*, 1; Trimingham, *Christianity*, 258, 266; Beaucamp and Robin, "Christianisme dans la péninsule Arabique," 45–46; Peters, *Mecca*; Hainthaler, *Christliche Araber*, 137–40; Hainthaler, "Christian Arabs," 42–43.

188. Ilkka Lindstedt, however, has recently averred that there nevertheless must have been a Christian presence in Mecca and Medina, but the argument is not convincing: Lindstedt, *Muḥammad and His Followers*, 117–18. Lindstedt concludes that there were Christians in both settlements based almost entirely on the observation that these regions have not been studied archaeologically. Such invocation of the absence of evidence as somehow providing an argument for presence is not very persuasive, and on the whole Lindstedt's brief treatment of the issue seems to miss the full weight of the total absence of any indication of a Christian presence from any sort of source, anywhere remotely near Mecca and Yathrib, from Aqaba all the way to Yemen, coupled with the reports from the Islamic tradition that there was no Christian presence in either locale.

189. Villeneuve, "La résistance des cultes bétyliques," 227–28. See also on this point Trimingham, *Christianity*, 258, 266; Hainthaler, "Christian Arabs," 42–43; Hainthaler, *Christliche Araber*, 137–40.

so far only been able to grasp at two undated Greek inscriptions, neither of which is clearly Christian in nature and both of which are found some 1000 km (600 miles) north of Mecca: as such, they can hardly stand as evidence for a Christian presence in Muhammad's Mecca.[190] Even in the southern Nabataean capital of Hegra (Madā'in Ṣāliḥ), which knew a long history of literacy and had been part of the Roman Empire for several centuries in late antiquity, there is no indication at all of any Christian presence. As the lead excavator of the site, Laïla Nehmé, tersely observes in an overview of the site published just a couple of years ago: "There is no trace of Christianity at Hegra."[191] Accordingly, it hardly comes as a surprise, then, to find that in the smaller, more isolated locales of Mecca and the Yathrib oasis much further to the south, Christianity was similarly absent. Muhammad's world,

---

190. Lindstedt, as one recent example, adduces these two Greek inscriptions discovered approximately 1000 km NW of Mecca, around 100 km south of Tabuk and about 250 km SE of Aqaba, as evidence for a Christian presence in Muhammad's milieu: Lindstedt, *Muḥammad and His Followers*, 108–11. It is true that one of these inscriptions seems to include the name Petros: "ΘΗΠΕΤΡΟΣ" is the complete inscription. Perhaps this name may somehow derive from a Christian cultural context, although this is hardly sufficient evidence for Christians in Mecca and Yathrib. Likewise, Lindstedt claims that the presence of a cross in another of these inscriptions marks it as Christian, although, the "cross" in question is identical to a modern plus sign and the text of the inscription is complete nonsense: "+ΣΟΝΛΕ." I do not think that the mark + can be identified with any certainty in this case as a Christian symbol absent other signifiers or context; it could easily be instead a simple ornament or punctuation of sorts. The same holds true of a third inscription in Arabic adduced by Lindstedt, this one at Dūmat al-Jandal, also about 1000 kilometers due north of Mecca and about 450 kilometers due east of Aqaba (and just to the north of its latitude), and in this instance the alleged presence of a Christian cross seems equally dubious absent other indicators. For examples of a wide range of cruciform and other signs that do clearly indicate a Christian identity, see Garipzanov, *Graphic Signs*. Nevertheless, even if all three of these inscriptions could provide solid evidence of three Christians who traveled through these areas and paused to make their mark, in no way can they be considered as evidence for Christianity in Mecca and Yathrib. They are located far distant to the north, and while the Arabic inscription gives a date of 548–49, the Greek inscriptions are undated. A paleographic dating of second through fourth centuries is proposed for the Greek inscriptions, at which time, one should note, this region was a part of the Roman Empire. For the inscriptions in question, including photographs, see Nehmé, *Darb al-Bakrah*, 285, 291; and Nehmé, "New Dated Inscriptions," 124–31. Furthermore, the inscription published in Al-Jallad and Sidky, "Paleo-Arabic Inscription on a Route North of Ṭā'if," which Lindstedt also mentions, shows no signs at all of being Christian. Admittedly it seems to express belief in one God, and I do not question at all the presence of general monotheist ideas in this region: but there is nothing Christian about this inscription.

191. Nehmé, *Guide to Hegra*, 66.

therefore, was one without Christians, and for that matter Jews as well, at least until he reached Yathrib.

Therefore, we may conclude with some certainty that Muhammad and his new religious community were both formed in a barren, remote, and impoverished hamlet without any meaningful connections to the broader worlds of Mediterranean and Mesopotamian late antiquity. According to the Islamic tradition Muhammad was illiterate, and the social and cultural conditions in the central Hijaz of his age appear to confirm this. Both Muhammad and his early followers would have been nonliterate, even in the unlikely chance that they had somehow learned a script for doodling on desert rocks. Furthermore, the historical Muhammad, as well as his early followers, lived their lives in the complete absence of any significant Christian community anywhere near their environs. The same holds true of Judaism for Mecca, where much of the Qur'an—at least according to tradition—was composed. Therefore, the historical Muhammad and his earliest followers possessed no detailed knowledge of Christianity and its traditions, beyond only the most basic outlines: certainly, they would not have had the depth of knowledge about Christian culture that one finds in the Qur'an. Muhammad also would not have had any access to the biblical texts. Not only does the absence of literacy in the central Hijaz preclude this, but according to a broad scholarly consensus, the Bible was not translated into Arabic until well after he had died, only in the eighth century.[192] Therefore, the only way that the historical Muhammad could have possessed a broad knowledge of Christianity and its Scriptures at the beginning of his prophetic mission would be if Mecca had been a highly Christianized settlement with some level of literacy in Aramaic. Since these conditions seem unlikely in the extreme in the present state of our evidence, we must conclude that the historical Muhammad was largely ignorant of both Christian and Jewish religious culture, again beyond the most basic broad themes and outlines.

A Historically Plausible Muhammad

I suspect that many readers may be surprised at how brief this crucial, final section is in comparison with the rest of this study. But such is the nature of the quest for the historical Muhammad. Even more so than the historical Jesus before him, "he comes to us," in the words of Schweitzer,

---

192. Griffith, *Bible in Arabic*, 47–53, 106–27.

"as one unknown."[193] Firstly, what can we say about the basic chronological framework of Muhammad's life? Not much, other than that he was active in the first decades of the seventh century. According to a widely attested Islamic tradition, he began to receive his revelations and to share them at around the age of forty. Since his migration, most likely to the Yathrib oasis, can be dated to 622 CE—and this is as solid of a date as we have in regard to Muhammad's life—the tradition worked backwards to create some other dates.[194] On the basis of around ten years actively preaching to the Meccans before the *hijra*, according to a common tradition, Muhammad's prophetic call would have been sometime around the beginning of the 610s, so that his birth would have been around 570, which is the most commonly given date. With the exception of a migration of some sort in 622, however, most of this chronology does not warrant much, if any, credence, since the *sira* tradition's chronology is among the least reliable and most artificial elements of an already highly suspect corpus.[195]

There seems little reason to doubt that Muhammad had multiple wives, and that we may know the names of some of them, particularly those whose memories were prominent in the later tradition, such as Aisha. Likewise, he undoubtedly had progeny, through his daughter Fatima, who was born from his first wife Khadija. Fatima married Muhammad's cousin Ali and birthed a line of descendants that many in the early community believed were Muhammad's rightful successors. The violent and convulsive controversies over their status in Islam's early history leave little doubt on this matter. Likewise, there is a high probability that Muhammad formally adopted a man named Zayd who was one of his earliest followers and later married his divorced wife. The entire matter is sufficiently awkward in the eyes of the later tradition that its invention seems unlikely, not to mention that the events of Zayd's divorce and Muhammad's marriage to his ex-wife are obliquely referenced in Qur'an 33:37.[196] As for the date and circumstances of Muhammad's death, these too are more or less unknown. According to a widely attested early tradition, Muhammad survived to lead the invasion of Palestine, beginning in 635, which contradicts the collective

---

193. Schweitzer, *Von Reimarus zu Wrede*, 401; Schweitzer, *Quest of the Historical Jesus*, 401.

194. Crone and Cook, *Hagarism*, 7, 157n39; Donner, *Narratives of Islamic Origins*, 237.

195. Shoemaker, *Death of a Prophet*, 99–106; see also Conrad, "Abraha and Muḥammad," 230–39; Rubin, *Eye of the Beholder*, 203–9.

196. Powers, *Muḥammad is Not the Father*; Powers, *Zayd*; Powers, "Sinless, Sonless."

memory of the later Islamic tradition that remembers his death at Medina in 632. Thus, we can only say that Muhammad likely died approximately sometime around 632–635, perhaps in Medina, perhaps in Palestine, perhaps somewhere else altogether.[197]

Muhammad's life prior to his prophetic calling is almost entirely unknown, a point on which even the most sanguine of modern scholars and the Islamic tradition will both agree (the same holds true, interestingly enough, for Jesus, who was called at around the age of 30 according to tradition). Nevertheless, there is one question relevant to this period that we can answer to a certain degree, namely, what was Muhammad's profession before he took up the mantle of a prophet? Two possibilities present themselves, neither of which is inherently unlikely, and both of which may have been trades held by Muhammad simultaneously. The Islamic tradition preserves two different memories of Muhammad's pre-prophetic profession: that he was a shepherd or a merchant. The tradition of Muhammad as a traveling merchant is perhaps the most widely known, a fact that owes itself primarily to the orientalist myth of Mecca as a major center of international trade. Yet if we look to the early Islamic biographies of Muhammad, for instance, these sources remember him overwhelmingly as having been a shepherd rather than a merchant. On the one hand, it is true that Muhammad's identification as a shepherd serves to fulfill a trope of the Abrahamic prophetic tradition: that prophets have always been shepherds. For this reason, despite the ubiquity of this memory of Muhammad across the early biographical traditions, many scholars have suggested that we should dismiss Muhammad the herdsman as a mere prophetic topos, with no basis in historical reality.[198] Yet on the other hand, given what we know of Mecca's economy and ecology, a career as a shepherd actually makes a great deal of sense, much more so than a merchant it would seem. For this reason alone, there is an inherently high probability that Muhammad was a shepherd.

The traditions of Muhammad as a merchant in the Islamic tradition, by comparison, are relatively few, and, as other scholars have noted, these accounts are so fanciful and artificial that they do not inspire much confidence at all. The most credible such accounts concern traditions of Muhammad's marriage to his first wife, Khadija, who was herself a leather merchant, according to tradition. Yet even these reports do "not explicitly depict him as a merchant by trade—at least not in the same emphatic

---

197. Shoemaker, *Death of a Prophet*.
198. Anthony, *Muhammad*, 65–67.

manner that [the tradition] depicts him as a shepherd."¹⁹⁹ Moreover, in all the accounts where Khadija employs Muhammad as a hired agent, in each instance Muhammad trades in leather and secures only a meager profit. And his trading expeditions bring him not to the edge of the Roman Empire—let alone to the cities of Syria and Palestine—but to local Arabian markets: Hubāshah and Jurash to the south of Mecca. On the whole, the few reports of Muhammad trading further afield "are scattered and not well attested," and the earliest such accounts seem to have arisen only in the early eighth century. According one of the earliest versions, Muhammad, while still only a youth, accompanied his uncle Abū Ṭālib on a journey to Bostra in Syria for trade. They never made it to Syria, however. When they reached the northern oasis town of Taymā', a rabbi there warned them that if they continued on to Syria, Muhammad would be murdered. And so they immediately returned home, without reaching Syria or completing any trade at all. Indeed, the composite that emerges from the earliest reports of Muhammad's trading activities in the Islamic tradition indicates with unwavering consistency, as Sean Anthony concludes, "that Muḥammad never left the geographical confines of the Arabian Peninsula."²⁰⁰

More recent versions of these tales of Muhammad's mercantile travels merely elaborate on their older models, adding to them lavish but completely ahistorical details. It is only in these later embellished accounts, one must note, that Muhammad actually manages to leave the Arabian Peninsula. Yet as Crone rightly observes of these later legends of Muhammad's trading voyages, collectively they amount to nothing more than "fifteen equally fictitious versions of an event that never took place." Her conclusion, in this instance at least, may not be accounted to any radical skepticism of the tradition, but, as Anthony notes, "even by the standards of medieval Muslim ḥadīth criticism, she seems to have been in good company."²⁰¹ According to the Islamic tradition, Muhammad's tribe, Quraysh, made a living as traders, which could perhaps be taken as an indication that he too may have been a merchant. Nevertheless, the legend of these Qurayshi traders is itself a part and parcel of the myth of Mecca as the wealthy center of a vast network of international spice trade, and so we must view it equally with extreme skepticism, if not outright disbelief. Once we turn to look at the purported journeys of the Meccan merchants, immediately

---

199. Anthony, *Muhammad*, 68.
200. Anthony, *Muhammad*, 69–70.
201. Crone, *Meccan Trade*, 220; Anthony, *Muhammad*, 73.

such disbelief is fully validated. The stories themselves are so fanciful that they strain all credibility.[202] And despite numerous efforts to read such a mercantile context into the Qur'an, there is nothing in the Qur'an that can only be explained through the existence of an opulent tribe of merchants in Mecca. Thus, it would appear that, like the Meccan spice trade that was supposedly the source of their riches, the spice brokers of Mecca too are almost certainly a product of the later Islamic imagination and its salvation history.

As things stand so far, the evidence of both the early Islamic tradition and the economic situation of Mecca would seem to strongly favor Muhammad's career as a shepherd. There is, however, one significant, high-quality source that does not allow us to simply rest with this conclusion: an anonymous Armenian chronicle written around the middle of the seventh century known as the *Chronicle of Sebeos*. By every measure, this chronicle stands out as one of the best sources available for knowledge of West Asian history in the early and middle seventh century, and its witness to the rise of Islam does not disappoint, providing one of the most important and informative accounts of the beginnings of Muhammad's new religious movement. Among the wealth of information afforded by this unequaled source is its notice Muhammad had been merchant or tradesman (*t'angar*) before he became a prophet.[203] Based on the extremely high quality of this account and its sources, it seems we must acknowledge that Muhammad was known among his contemporaries for having been in some sense a merchant or tradesman before turning to prophecy.

But the chronicle is rather sparse on this point. All we can know from it is that Muhammad must have earned a living by selling some sort of goods or that he practiced a trade. Exactly what these goods were or where he sold them, or what trade he practiced, we simply are not told. If we understand Muhammad to have been a tradesman, then in light of Mecca's pastoralist economy, a tanner would seem to be the most likely trade for him. Yet if he was instead a merchant, for reasons that we have already seen, there is no historical basis for imagining Muhammad as an international broker who traveled throughout the late ancient Near East trading in luxury goods, whether they be spices, gold, or anything else for that matter. Rather, if he was a merchant, we should expect to find him selling

---

202. Anthony, *Muhammad*, 79.

203. Abgarian, Պատմութիւն Սեբէոսի, 135; Thomson and Howard-Johnston, *Armenian History*, 1:94–103; Shoemaker, *Prophet Has Appeared*, 62–72.

more modest goods and on a more local scale.[204] Surprisingly, in this case it seems that we find the most probable solution to our problem in the earliest memories of Muhammad from the Islamic tradition.

Since the early Islamic tradition overwhelming remembers Muhammad as herdsman, a profession that is one of very few compatible with the economic and ecological conditions of Mecca in his lifetime, one must ask: is there perhaps some way, then, in which we could understand Muhammad as having been both a herdsman and a merchant? Indeed, there is, and if we look at the earliest traditions of Muhammad's mercantile activities, few though they are, a consistent pattern emerges. They remember Muhammad as having sold leather, which on a few occasions he is said to have peddled in other nearby settlements along the western edge of the Arabian Peninsula, mostly within a few days journey of Mecca. The Islamic tradition's indication that he traveled to the south occasionally to sell these wares fits with the superior economic development of southern Arabia: perhaps it was worth the journey to fetch a higher price there or to trade for other agricultural products that were scare and needed in Mecca.

This image is in fact fully consistent with Muhammad also being a herdsman, who sold the leather and perhaps other pastoralist products

204. It is true, one must note, that a report from Jacob of Edessa's *Chronological Charts*, written at the very end of the seventh century, remarks at the year 617/18 CE that "Muhammad goes down on commercial business to the lands of Palestine and of the Arabias and of Phoenicia of the Tyrians." Brooks et al., *Chronica minora III*, 326; Palmer, *Seventh Century*, 39. Nevertheless, it is clear that the Meccans were not involved in the long-distance trade of high-value commodities, and any goods that they had available for trade were the produce of their small herds of livestock. Now, if Muhammad were merely peddling leather from the flocks of Mecca, his own and perhaps those of others as well, it is difficult to imagine him traveling so far abroad to tout what was, after all, a very locally common commodity. Perhaps, as Crone has suggested, he may have traveled to the borders of Roman Arabia to trade leather there for the higher prices that the Roman army may have been willing to pay, and perhaps we should understand Palestine in the broader sense as including this region. But even this proposal is, again, merely hypothetical. Tyre and Phoenicia, however, seem completely out of the question. I find it entirely improbable to imagine that Muhammad actually traveled to the coast of Lebanon to trade in leather. Indeed, I more than suspect if any Meccan hides were ever destined for the Roman army, they would more likely have been sold to brokers in the oasis towns of the north, rather than sold directly to the Roman army itself on the *Limes Arabicus*. Perhaps Jacob's tradition reflects on this point the emerging traditions of Muhammad as a trader that would eventually find their way into his traditional biographies: for evidence of such influence, see Conrad, "Theophanes and the Arabic Historical Tradition." It is hard to imagine this report having any basis in the life of the historical Muhammad, and Jacob's witness on this point is certainly not of similar quality to the *Chronicle of Sebeos*' report that he was some sort of trader or tradesman.

from his flock at nearby markets in order to support himself and his community. One suspects, then, that Muhammad was a herdsman who was also a petty merchant, selling the wares produced from his herd (and possibly those of his neighbors), including leather especially, within the broader region around Mecca. This solution makes perfect sense and is fully consistent not only with the state of the Meccan economy and its landscape, the early Islamic tradition, and our Armenian chronicler, but also with the important conclusions that Crone draws regarding the Meccan economy and trade in both her monograph and her more recent article on this topic. Thus, the most historically probable profession for Muhammad before he became a prophet was a herdsman who also was a leather peddler, selling the hides of his stock for a profit in the region around Mecca. Yet at the same time, we should not completely exclude the possibility that he may instead have been a tradesman, a tanner and leather vendor who sold his wares locally, as the report from Sebeos also could indicate.

As for the historical Muhammad's career as a prophet, what little we know must be determined primarily on the basis of the Qur'an, the contemporary non-Islamic witnesses, and whatever isolated elements of his traditional biographies can be validated through critical analysis on a case by case basis. From the Qur'an alone, we know extremely little about the historical Muhammad. As Michael Cook nicely summarizes, relying on the Qur'an alone, "we could probably infer that the protagonist of the Koran was Muhammad, that the scene of his life was in western Arabia, and that he bitterly resented the frequent dismissal of his claims to prophecy by his contemporaries. But we could not tell that the sanctuary was in Mecca, nor that Muhammad himself came from there, and we could only guess that he established himself in Yathrib. We might indeed prefer a more northerly location altogether, on the grounds that the site of God's destruction of Lot's people (i.e., Sodom) is said to be one which those addressed pass by morning and night (K 37.137–38)."[205] That is it. Presumably, also on the basis of the Qur'an, we can safely conclude that Muhammad preached an ethical monotheism to his followers: an obligation to worship the one true God and to live in righteousness according to the divine law. Yet while the Islamic tradition recalls Muhammad as proclaiming his monotheist call in an environment that was suffused with polytheism, if we look to the Qur'an alone, by all indications the Qur'an's (and thus Muhammad's?) opponents were, as noted above, actually monotheists whose monotheist faith was

---

205. Cook, *Muhammad*, 70.

insufficiently austere in the Qur'an's view. The Qur'an's opponents, it would seem, believed in seeking the intercessions of certain intermediary spiritual powers, apparently angels. Therefore, based on the witness of the Qur'an, we must conclude that Muhammad and his new religious community were formed within a context dominated not by polytheist belief, but rather pervaded by debates about the limits of monotheism.[206]

To this skeletal outline, we may add, as confirmed by the contemporary non-Islamic sources, that Muhammad's early followers regarded him not just as a prophet, but also as a political leader, since these witnesses regularly identify him as the "king" of the Arabs.[207] Given the fact that his new religious movement was also a polity that would soon conquer and occupy much of the known world, Muhammad's political leadership of this community during his lifetime seems quite certain. In this regard one should also note that incitement to armed conflict in furtherance of the expansion of Muhammad's new religious community and its dominion appear to have been a central focus of the historical Muhammad's teaching. Muhammad's military campaigns are a centerpiece of his traditional Islamic biographies, to the extent that, even if we are generally suspicious of these sources, their persistent memory of Muhammad as a late ancient Arabian warlord seems worthy of credence.[208] More importantly, however, not only does religiously motivated warfare, *jihad*, figure prominently within the Qur'an, but the first two sources mentioning Muhammad and his new religious movement, a Greek source written in north Africa in 634 and a homily by Sophronius of Jerusalem from 636, ascribe this teaching to him.[209] Likewise, the *Chronicle of Sebeos* mentioned above, perhaps our single best source for understanding the beginnings of Islam, describes Muhammad as preaching to his followers a duty to liberate the Abrahamic promised land by force.[210] No less importantly, the conquest of Mecca and the Hijaz under his leadership, and then of western Asia and north Africa soon thereafter by his followers offers seemingly irrefutable proof that this was a fundamental tenet of his teaching and the faith of his followers.

206. Hawting, *Idea of Idolatry*; Crone, "Religion of the Qur'ānic Pagans"; Crone, "Quranic Mushrikūn I"; Crone, "Quranic Mushrikūn II."

207. Brock, "Syriac Views," 14; Donner, *Muhammad and the Believers*, 111.

208. Ibrahim, *Muhammad's Military Expeditions*.

209. Dagron and Déroche, "Juifs et Chrétiens," 209–11; Papadopoulos-Kerameus, Ἀνάλεκτα Ἱεροσολυμιτικῆς 5, 167; Shoemaker, *Prophet Has Appeared*, 39–40, 51; Anthony, "Muhammad."

210. Abgarian, Պատմութիւն Սեբէոսի, 135; Shoemaker, *Prophet Has Appeared*, 64.

Closely related to this belief in the duty of religious conquest was undoubtedly an ardent conviction among Muhammad and his earliest followers that the world was about to end. Indeed, Muhammad and his followers lived in an age when imminent eschatological expectation was prevalent, as was a belief that the end of the world would be realized through the conquest and dominion of a divinely elected empire.[211] Therefore, if we may conclude that the political lives of Muhammad were largely correct in identifying him as a successful tribal chieftain with ambitions for conquest and the expansion of his polity that were shared by his followers, it is the eschatological lives that continue to best capture the nature of his religious message. (For the reasons outlined above, the economic lives seem to have missed the mark entirely.) If we look to the Qur'an, for instance, eschatology quickly leaps to the fore as one of its most prominent themes, and with some regularity it warns its audience that the end of history and the final judgment will soon come upon them. We may take confidence that this persistent proclamation of the world's impending end almost certainly goes back to Muhammad himself, for the very same reasons Schweitzer and other scholars of early Christianity after him have concluded that the historical Jesus too was an eschatological prophet.[212]

It is inherently unlikely that Muhammad's followers would invent such predictions and ascribe them to Muhammad if he had not actually taught as much, since soon after his death these forecasts became patently false, making him (and the Qur'an) appear to be, as it were, wrong on this point. Moreover, their preservation by the later community even though the end failed to come according to the anticipated schedule is also a sure sign that such imminent eschatological belief was elemental and ingrained in the faith of Muhammad and his earliest followers. Indeed, the impending apocalypse must have figured so prominently in Muhammad's preaching that such declarations of its proximate advent could not simply be erased and forgotten on account of their awkward and embarrassing inaccuracy but were instead preserved in abundance in the Qur'an. The same holds equally true of a number of eschatological hadith in which Muhammad forecasts the impending end of the world in the very near future. Most probably these traditions also arose within the same primitive layer as the

---

211. Shoemaker, "Reign of God"; Shoemaker, *Apocalypse of Empire*.

212. Schweitzer, *Von Reimarus zu Wrede*, 327–95; Schweitzer, *Quest of the Historical Jesus*, 328–95.

eschatological proclamations of the Qur'an, originating undoubtedly in the preaching of Muhammad himself.[213]

Therefore, in terms of what the historical Muhammad taught, his religious message, we can only identify some broad outlines at this stage. Given the fact that Muhammad's teachings were transmitted among his later followers orally from memory for decades, it is utterly implausible, if not impossible, that we would have in the Qur'an his very words. Nor may we regard the Qur'an as even a more or less accurate record of what Muhammad taught his followers in Mecca and Yathrib, perhaps with some minor changes to the wording along the way. It is in the very nature of oral tradition that its transmitters will regularly exercise immense freedom and creativity in their reproduction, giving little heed to exact wording or much at all beyond the basic outline of the gist and perhaps certain tropes and formulas, filling in huge gaps along the way each time a tradition is retold. We must also allow the possibility that many traditions of the Qur'an were added to after Muhammad's life, as his followers continued to encounter and interact with new religious content from their kindred People of the Book. Consequently, almost nothing in the Qur'an can be taken at face value as having originated with the historical Muhammad, absent further critical analysis and argument. At best, we may attribute the gist of the Qur'an's teachings and its major themes to Muhammad with some confidence.

This Muhammadan kernel would include, presumably, monotheism, eschatological fervor, divine revelation through prophecy, piety before God, personal morality within the community of the Believers, concern to prepare for the final judgment, expansion of the community through conquest, Abrahamic identity and a claim to the Abrahamic promised land, and embrace of the collective memory of the Abrahamic traditions (at least in parts). These themes are so persistent across the Qur'an and fundamental to its contents that one may assume them to in some sense be primitive and likely from Muhammad himself. It is, moreover, one should note, a religious worldview that is highly typical of western Asia in late antiquity, particularly among its Jewish and Christian inhabitants, which lends further credibility.[214] On the basis of the Constitution of Medina, which likely preserves early and authentic tradition about Muhammad's

---

213. Shoemaker, *Death of a Prophet*, 118–96; Shoemaker, "Muḥammad and the Qurʾān," 1090–99; Shoemaker, "Eschatological Reign"; Shoemaker, "Qurʾanic Eschatology," 464–73; the latter article is reproduced as the final chapter in this book.

214. Donner, *Narratives of Islamic Origins*, 70–75.

new religious community, we may also conclude with some probability that his community of the Believers was also open to Jews who nonetheless remained practicing and confessing Jews. Parts of the Qur'an seem to confirm this interconfessional nature of the early community, which also appears to have included Christian members on identical terms, even beyond Muhammad's death.[215] Indeed, the main points of this basic message are confirmed by the near contemporary witness of the Armenian *Chronicle of Sebeos*, who reports that under Muhammad a group of Arabs and Jews,

> all came together in unity of religion, and abandoning vain cults, they returned to the living God who had appeared to their father Abraham. Then Muhammad established laws for them: not to eat carrion, and not to drink wine, and not to speak falsely, and not to engage in fornication. And he said, "With an oath God promised this land to Abraham and his descendants after him forever. And he brought it about as he said in the time when he loved Israel. Truly, you are now the sons of Abraham, and God is fulfilling the promise to Abraham and his descendants on your behalf. Now love the God of Abraham with a single mind, and go and seize your land, which God gave to your father Abraham, and no one will be able to stand against you in battle, because God is with you."[216]

Thus, we may assume with some certainty that Muhammad's initial followers likely received something like this general religious framework from his teaching and were able to preserve an emphasis on these broad points, even as Muhammad's words and deeds became ever more faint, forgotten, and reimagined. Now the task remains to evaluate particular traditions and themes within the Qur'an critically and analytically on an individual basis to see if there may be some probability that they could be confidently assigned to the preaching of the historical Muhammad— much in the same manner that scholars have for generations now sought to do with the Gospels and the historical Jesus. The same holds true for Muhammad's traditional Islamic biographies, wherein we must warily and meticulously seek out what few kernels of reliable history may still be found among their great abundance of chaff. It is a vast labor, however, that has hardly begun in the face of widespread and misplaced scholarly conviction that all of the Qur'an's content can be reliably assigned to Muhammad's

---

215. So esp. Donner, *Muhammad and the Believers*.
216. Abgarian, Պատմութիւն Սեբէոսի, 135; Shoemaker, *Prophet Has Appeared*, 64.

preaching in Mecca and Yathrib, and that his traditional biographies provide a credible basic framework that may be adopted unreflectively. But this will be the arduous path forward for those who would set off on a truly critical quest for the historical Muhammad.

2

A New Arabic Apocryphon from Late Antiquity
The Qur'an

THE QUESTION OF THE Qur'an's literary genre has long vexed scholars, who have often struggled to find a category suitable for this frequently disjointed and disparate text. The Qur'an's distinctive literary qualities, not to mention its regular opacity, can make it challenging to identify a fitting precursor among the vast literary remains of Mediterranean and West Asian antiquity. The Islamic tradition, of course, is quite content to leave the matter of the qur'anic genre unresolved, eagerly pointing to its exceptionalism as important evidence of its uniqueness or inimitability (*i'jāz*). Not surprisingly, many modern scholars have willingly followed the Islamic tradition to this conclusion, an acquiescence to the Islamic tradition that is all too evident in much qur'anic scholarship from the previous century. Accordingly, one regularly finds pronouncements to the effect that "the Qur'an is an example of a genre of literature that has only one example."[1] Yet such a conclusion simply evades a difficult and important question: how should we conceive of the Qur'an as a work of literature in relation to its broader

---

1. Todd Lawson formulated the quotation above as being emblematic of this broader tendency within qur'anic studies: Lawson, *Quran: Epic and Apocalypse*, 78. As a specific example, see Gibb, *Arabic Literature*, 36: "As a literary monument the Koran thus stands by itself, a production unique to the Arabic literature, having neither forerunners nor successors in its own idiom."

literary environment? While this resolution is certainly adequate for the faithful Muslim, it should not be for the modern scholar.

Despite the inherent difficulties of attempting to classify a collection as peculiar as the Qur'an, scholars have proposed a wide range of alternatives for how we might understand the text as a whole. For instance, several scholars have looked to Jewish and Christian liturgical collections to identify possible models, concluding that the Qur'an should be understood as a hymnbook, or a lectionary, or a collection of psalms.[2] Not far off from these suggestions is the hypothesis that the Qur'an represents a sort of homiletic text, akin to the metrical homilies (*memre*) of the late ancient Syriac tradition.[3] Perhaps it is an extension of late ancient "question and answer" literature?[4] Or is it simply poetry, perhaps picking up and extending an earlier tradition of Arabic poetry in the pre-Islamic period?[5] Yet another proposal is that the Qur'an should be understood simultaneously according to the genres of an apocalypse and an epic.[6] None of these options, however, successfully encompasses the range of materials found in the Qur'an and their juxtaposition therein.

Such efforts to identify the Qur'an's genre are nevertheless thwarted and undermined at nearly every turn by the sheer diversity of the Qur'an's content. In actual fact, the Qur'an is a document not of a single literary genre, but instead a collection of traditions that themselves evidence a wide variety of genres. It is thus not a single composition, and also most likely is not the work of a single author, despite the confidence of the Islamic tradition and modern scholarship alike in this regard. Rather than an artfully composed work of literature, the Qur'an is, to the contrary, a late antique religious hodgepodge. Accordingly, its assemblage of textual materials holds enormous potential—still largely unrealized—for study of religious culture in the late ancient Near East, revealing a diversity and complexity of both belief and expression emerging at that time from Jewish and Christian monotheism that otherwise would be invisible from the sources of those two traditions alone. Thus, the Qur'an is not so much a *magnus opus* as

---

2. E.g., respectively: Lüling, *Über den Ur-Qur'an*, translated into English as Lüling, *A Challenge to Islam*; Luxenberg, *Die syro-aramäische Lesart*, translated into English as Luxenberg, *Syro-Aramaic Reading of the Koran*; Neuwirth, "Einige Bemerkungen"; and Neuwirth, "Die Psalmen."

3. Reynolds, *Qur'ān and its Biblical Subtext*, 230–58.

4. Bertaina, "Rethinking Genre."

5. Hoffmann, *Poetic Qur'ān*; Nicholson, *Literary History*, 159.

6. Lawson, *Quran: Epic and Apocalypse.*

religious miscellany, whose contents witness to a breadth of late ancient religious faith and practice that would otherwise be unknown.

There are, then, many genres within the Qur'an, as other scholars have occasionally noted, and the presence of these different genres or literary forms, seemingly drawn from different sources, invites us to analyze its contents using the methods of form criticism as developed in biblical studies. This type of criticism is particularly useful for analyzing a text composed of many smaller units of tradition, of various genres, and also for investigating their *Sitz im Leben*, that is, the circumstances that gave rise to a particular unit of tradition in the first place. Only from such a perspective can we see, as Guillaume Dye helpfully elucidates, that

> strictly speaking, the Qurʾān is not a book, but a *corpus*, namely the gathering of texts: 1) which were not originally intended to be put together in a codex, nor composed with this goal in mind, 2) which are heterogeneous (they belong to a variety of literary genres, and sometimes express divergent ideas), 3) which are, in some cases, independent, and in some others, are not (there are numerous parallel passages, some Qur'anic passages rewriting, correcting and responding to other passages). The Qurʾān, therefore, appears as a text which has several layers, and which contains many parallel stories—and this implies that there is, like in the Gospels, a 'synoptic problem' in the Qurʾān. In short, the Qurʾān is a text which is both *composite* and *composed*.[7]

Yet form critical analysis of the Qur'an that would analyze its contents according to such a perspective remains, unfortunately, almost completely unattempted. For the time being the best description of the various literary forms or genres that populate the Qur'an is the inventory of Alfred-Louis de Prémare. According to de Prémare the Qur'an includes primarily oracular proclamations, hymns, instructional discourses, narrative evocations, legislative and paraenetic texts, battle exhortations, and polemical discourses.[8] For obvious reasons, it is effectively impossible to encompass a collection of such diverse textual materials within a single literary genre, as others have noted. Thus, the Qur'an's resistance to being subsumed within a literary genre is not a consequence of its inimitability or uniqueness, but rather, it is an altogether expected result of its amalgamated nature.

7. Dye, "Le corpus coranique," 785–86.

8. de Prémare, *Aux origines du Coran*, 35–45. A good start toward a more thorough identification of the Qur'ans various literary forms as recently been published by Samji, *Qurʾān*.

The florilegia of late ancient Christianity could perhaps offer some kind of precedent for the Qur'an's gathering of various sorts of materials within a single volume. But the Qur'an's contents are quite different from these topical anthologies of quotations from writings of the church fathers. The Qur'an's traditions are not taken from known, named authorities, as in the case of florilegia, and their themes are likewise not theological and philosophical but rather legal, eschatological, kerygmatic, liturgical, and, especially, biblical, in the sense that the Qur'an frequently retells and alludes to traditions known otherwise in the Jewish and Christian Bible, as well as other related sources. For this reason, I would propose a different category for situating the Qur'an within the literary culture of late antiquity: the Qur'an is best understood as a biblical apocryphon with a powerful message of eschatological urgency, repentance, and restoration. Although admittedly not every single facet of the Qur'an is equally illuminated and explained by recognition of its apocryphal nature, the Qur'an's location within the broader phenomenon of Jewish and Christian production of biblical apocrypha in late antiquity seems unmistakable once we begin to look at it through this lens. Moreover, biblical apocrypha comprise a type of literature that is, as we will see, easily accommodated the Qur'an's assemblage of a wide range of materials and genres.

Until only rather recently, scholars tended to look upon apocryphal writings as failed Scriptures—one-time rivals to the now canonical texts that were either marginalized or discarded because their teachings were considered false or unreliable by the shadowy censors of early Christian and Jewish orthodoxies. Yet such a view of this sizeable and diverse corpus of Christian and Jewish literature neither does it justice, nor does it accurately comprehend the phenomenon in question. Over the last few decades, scholarship on apocryphal literature has become increasingly nuanced as it continues to distance itself from the *sola Scriptura* mentality that originally inspired this older "Scripture/rejected Scripture" binary. Instead, the apocryphal landscape is now found to be not only much more vast than once thought but also more varied in terms of form, content, and function. And it is within this more nuanced and expansive understanding of apocrypha that the Qur'an seems able to find a fitting home.

For much of the twentieth century, scholarship on apocrypha generally defined its subject as "writings which have not been received into the canon, but which by title and other statements lay claim to be of equal status (*gleichwertig*) to the writings of the canon, and which from the point of view of Form Criticism further develop and mold the literary genres (*Stilgattungen*) created and received in the NT, whilst foreign elements certainly intrude." Likewise, it was imagined that the production of apocrypha should be limited to the period before the closure of the New Testament canon, so that any "so-called" apocrypha produced after 300 CE should not be considered true apocryphal writings: only writings written with the original intent of their inclusion in the canon may be so named.[9] The result was a very narrow corpus, constricted by its delimitation according to the biblical norm. Such a framework effectively excludes acts of one of the apostles composed in the sixth century, or a gospel from the fourth, or life of the Virgin from the seventh: are these not equally apocrypha? Such a definition was obviously inadequate for the task of investigating the phenomenon of apocryphicity more broadly and separately from the question of the New Testament's canonization.

Fortunately, l'Association pour l'étude de la littérature apocryphe chrétienne (AELAC), and Éric Junod in particular, have advanced a more useful and inclusive definition of Christian apocrypha that has been widely adopted by scholars since the 1980s. According to Junod's improved definition, biblical apocrypha are "anonymous or pseudepigraphical texts ... that maintain a connection with the books of the New Testament as well as the Old Testament because they are devoted to events described or mentioned in these books, or because they are devoted to events that take place in the expansion of events described or mentioned in these books, because they focus on persons appearing in these books."[10] As a result, the canon of Christian apocryphal literature has been broadened considerably. Writings once dismissed as hagiographical or liturgical now must also be considered as apocryphal writings as well—the boundaries between these types of literature have become much blurrier than they were once imagined.[11] Likewise, this new perspective opens up the category of apocrypha to

---

9. Schneemelcher, *Neutestamentliche Apokryphen*, 1:6–7, 17–18, 32–35; ET: Schneemelcher, *New Testament Apocrypha*, 1:27–28, 40–41, 60–64.

10. Junod, "Apocryphes du Nouveau Testament," 409–14. Junod's definition is proposed particularly within the context of the history of Christianity, for particular reasons related to the mission of AELAC. I have adjusted it slightly above through omitting specific references to Christianity to create a more inclusive—but practically identical—definition of biblical apocrypha.

11. On the complex overlap between such genres and apocryphal literature, see esp. Shoemaker, "Early Christian Apocryphal Literature."

include more recent compositions, such as the *Book of Mormon* or the *Essene Gospel of Peace*—as well as the Qur'an, for that matter.[12]

Without question, I think, the Qur'an may be identified as a biblical apocryphon according to the terms defined by Junod: it is anonymous, it maintains a solid connection throughout to the writings of the Hebrew Bible and New Testament (as well as other related writings), focusing often on persons and events from these books while occasionally expanding on them. If such a writing is a biblical apocryphon, then certainly so also is the Qur'an. One should not make the mistake of identifying biblical apocrypha as a genre, since the vast corpus of apocryphal writings includes many examples of numerous genres (including, one might note, paraenesis, poetry, hymns and other liturgical texts, and apocalyptic and eschatological material). Moreover, like the Qur'an, many apocryphal writings themselves contain simultaneously materials reflecting a variety of different genres. Likewise, these diverse materials often derive from earlier, independent traditions that only come together in the compilation of the apocryphon. Finally, one should note, each of the different genres present in the Qur'an—oracular proclamations, hymns, instructional discourses, narrative evocations, legislative and paraenetic texts, and polemical discourses—are also common elements of biblical apocryphal literature. Only exhortations to battle seem to be missing from the biblical apocrypha, and these qur'anic materials seem to derive from the particularly militant character of the religious movement and community that Muhammad founded.

Some observations from Gabriel Reynolds are helpful in understanding the Qur'an's relation to the biblical traditions. In proposing that the Qur'an should be understood a sort of homily, similar to the rhymed homilies of the Syriac tradition, Reynolds makes the important point that we must not presume, as much previous scholarship has, "that the Qur'an was written to rival the Bible." Rather, he notes, "it would hardly be extraordinary if the Qur'an was instead written in harmony with Biblical literature." As much seems to be indicated, Reynolds rightly observes, by the manner in which the Qur'an presumes significant familiarity with the biblical writings on the part of its audience.[13] The Qur'an in fact depends on the biblical traditions, in regard to which it is, in effect, supplementary, like a

---

12. Regarding the production of apocrypha such as these and others up until the present moment, see esp. Piovanelli, "What Is a Christian Apocryphal Text"; Piovanelli, "Qu'est-ce qu'un 'écrit apocryphe chrétien.'"

13. Reynolds, *Qur'ān and its Biblical Subtext*, 232.

homily according to Reynolds, or, even more so, like a biblical apocryphon. Indeed, all of "homiletic" qualities that Reynolds identifies in the Qur'an find a much better explanation when recognized instead as part of a biblical apocryphon.

In a recent article addressing the broader question of the Qur'an's eschatology, Nicolai Sinai directly challenges the hypothesis that the Qur'an should be understood as a document in the mold of the Syriac homiletic tradition. In particular, Sinai identifies a crucial difference between the Qur'an and the Syriac homiletic tradition in the Qur'an's self-stylization as divine speech, which is certainly not the case for the Syriac homilies.[14] There is undeniably a significant difference in how these two textual traditions relate their contents to their readers. Yet at the same time, one must recognize that with disturbing frequency it is not at all clear just who it is that is "speaking" in the Qur'an's pronouncements and who is being addressed. Also in contrast to the Syriac homilies, the Qur'an does not defer directly to another textual authority, as the Syriac fathers to do the Bible. Instead, it speaks with its own authority without need to refer to an external repository of truth. Yet at the same time we must bear in mind that the Qur'an holds in the highest regard the Torah (*tawrāh*) and the Gospels (*ingīl*), as well as the Psalms (*zabūr*) and possibly even biblical apocalyptic literature (*ṣuḥuf*). Thus, as Reynolds and others have noted, we certainly may not presume that the Qur'an was understood from the beginning as a new revelation intended to supersede and displace these previous dispensations.[15] When and how the Qur'an attained this status among those who followed Muhammad is still not entirely clear. Accordingly, we should remain open to the possibility that until later in the seventh century, the Qur'an may have been understood as having a more supplementary, rather than supplanting, relation to the biblical traditions.

If we aim to bring categories and concepts from the Qur'an's late antique religious milieu in order to gain a better understanding of its genesis, it would be best to set aside entirely the early Christian homily as a possible analogue. The Qur'an simply does not possess the specific qualities that define a Christian homily and must instead be reckoned as something quite different. The truth of the matter is that there is very little in terms of form or content that defines the phenomenon of the early Christian homily.

---

14. Sinai, "Eschatological Kerygma," 236, 250.

15. Sinai, "Eschatological Kerygma," 248–50. See also Cook, "Qur'ān and Other Scriptures," 25–26; and Ben-Shammai, "*Ṣuḥuf* in the Qur'ān."

Indeed, the form of this type of literature is so diverse that, as Wendy Mayer observes, "all that we can claim is that a homily is something that conforms to a few essential conditions, but whose shape is elastic and changes with regional and cultural conditions and with time."[16] The emphasis on specific definitive "conditions" for a homily is paramount here. Homilies are defined by the conditions of their production for and their delivery in the context of Christian liturgical celebration. As such, their contents generally focus on moral instruction and exhortation for the congregation, particularly as related to the immediate liturgical context: the specific liturgical commemoration of the day, the biblical readings for the day, or "novel events (such as the arrival of new relics)."[17] I think it is safe to say that this is not, in fact, what the Qur'an is: I doubt sincerely that this text or even parts of it were composed as moral elaboration of the specific liturgical themes for Eucharistic celebrations, which is what classifying it as a homily effectively entails. One should additionally note a further problem of comparison with the Syriac *memra* tradition. As Mayer notes, the formal poetic structures of this homiletic tradition demanded texts that had been carefully composed prior to oral delivery and were not spontaneous oral deliveries.[18] If, then, the Qur'an were to be understood primarily as an extension of the *memra* tradition, we must also assume that it did not originate, at least in its present form, from spontaneous, oral teaching delivered without a script. If Muhammad's Qur'an were a *memra*, then it almost certainly must have been a written document from the very start. Perhaps this was indeed so, although in such case one must also consider the possibility that it was not necessarily Muhammad who wrote it.

If the Qur'an, then, is not a late ancient homily, it nevertheless remains that scholars have regularly described the text as possessing a strong homiletic character, or at least, having a great deal of homiletic content. These observations are not, it turns out, entirely incorrect: rather, they are the result of a category error and the imprecise usage of the terminology available for describing the religious literature of the late ancient Mediterranean world. The Qur'an is not a homily, nor do I find convincing evidence for identifying any part of its contents with the phenomenon of early Christian homiletics. Rather, the so-called "homiletic" elements of the Qur'an are simply misnamed, because while they do not share the homiletic form or

---

16. Mayer, "Homiletics," 570.
17. Mayer, "Homiletics," 568–69.
18. Mayer, "Homiletics," 571.

"occasion," they do share with the homiletic tradition its primary mode of discourse: paraenesis, or "moral exhortation." Paraenesis was a common style of literary discourse in antiquity with its roots in Greek philosophy and Hellenistic literature (including Hellenistic Judaism). Paraenetic discourse pervades the writings of the New Testament, and its importance within this corpus has been a major focus of biblical studies almost from the very beginning. Not surprisingly, early Christian discourse is replete with examples of paraenesis, and such moral exhortation is one of the most characteristic features of early Christian homiletic literature, where it is frequently joined to exegesis of the day's appointed readings or the theme of its commemoration.[19] The Christian homiletic tradition seems to have derived this paraenetic focus from the tradition of biblical paraenesis as well as contemporary Greco-Roman oratory.[20] Thus, while no part of the Qur'an seems to be homiletic in the proper sense of the term, there is a great deal that is paraenetic, a prominent feature that it shares not only with the Christian homiletic tradition, but with biblical apocrypha as well.

Sinai is clearly right, then, in my opinion, that the Qur'an does not stand in the tradition of Syriac homilies, for these and other reasons. At the same time, however, the alternative solution of elevating the Qur'an to the status of sacred scripture from the moment of its very origin also does not, it seems to me, provide the best means for understanding the complex relation between the Qur'an and the biblical tradition. In this respect, Reynolds's remarks regarding the Qur'an's relation to the writings of the Bible remain persuasive. Yet we need a category other than homily to understand the Qur'an's formation within the matrix of late ancient Judaism and Christianity and their Scriptures. Understanding the Qur'an as a biblical apocryphon, or in other parlance, particularly with respect to traditions from the Hebrew Bible, "rewritten bible," can take us very far toward this goal. Looking at the Qur'an from the perspective of late antiquity, the text becomes immediately recognizable a biblical apocryphon that participates in the broader phenomenon of Jewish and Christian production of apocryphal texts in this era.

To my knowledge previous scholarship has never fully recognized the apocryphal nature of the Qur'an and analyzed it accordingly, being content

---

19. See, e.g., Starr and Engberg-Pedersen, *Early Christian Paraenesis*. A helpful starting place, particularly for the importance of paraenesis in the biblical tradition, is Starr, "Paraenesis."

20. Regarding the latter, see esp. Maxwell, *Christianization and Communication*, chs. 1 and 2.

instead to identify the various traditions that it has borrowed from apocryphal literature. Nevertheless, this hunt for apocryphal parallels has always been done without full cognizance that this future sacred text should itself be seen from the vantage of the early seventh century as yet another effort to rewrite the traditions of the Bible comparable to so many earlier and contemporary Jewish and Christian apocrypha. The closest that we have seen to such an approach, in my estimation, is Sidney Griffith's study on *The Bible in Arabic*, where he persistently describes the Qur'an in relation to the biblical traditions in terms befitting an apocryphon. Griffith concludes, for instance, that "the Qur'ān's reprise of the Bible bespeaks the opening of a new book altogether in the growing library of books on the 'interpreted Bible'. Or perhaps it bespeaks not so much a new book, as a corrected, alternate scripture, one that recalls the Tanakh and the Bible."[21] Such a work is indeed best described, from the perspective of late ancient religious culture, as an apocryphon.

Many of the very qualities that Sinai identifies to distinguish the Qur'an from the Syriac homily tradition are in fact key characteristics of apocryphal writings.[22] Like the Qur'an, biblical apocrypha have their basis in the biblical tradition and depend heavily on these traditions for their content, yet they do not simply regurgitate biblical material. They are not passive recipients or mere echo chambers; instead, they creatively reformulate and reshape traditions taken from the biblical writings. Very often, they speak directly on their own authority and likewise present their audience with what is frequently purported to be divine speech, a quality most obvious in revelation dialogues and apocalypses, for instance. Apocryphal writings thus implicitly if not explicitly acknowledge the traditional authority of the biblical writings that came before them and inspired them. At the same time, however, they do not defer completely to the authority of the biblical texts, and their contents offer adaptations and expansions of the biblical traditions generally aimed at supplanting or correcting the very traditions that were their original inspiration. All of this sounds a great deal like the Qur'an, particularly in those sections that rewrite biblical traditions with authority. It is arguable, as Sinai notes, that the Qur'an "spurns the device

---

21. Griffith, *Bible in Arabic*, 84.

22. Regarding the category of apocrypha and the broad phenomenon of "apocryphicity" in relation to the biblical tradition see esp. Shoemaker, "Early Christian Apocryphal Literature"; Piovanelli, "What Is a Christian Apocryphal Text"; Piovanelli, "Qu'est-ce qu'un 'écrit apocryphe chrétien'"; and also the various essays in Mimouni, *Apocryphité*.

of pseudepigraphy." Yet so too do any number of apocrypha.[23] And, one should note, that while the Islamic tradition may attribute the Qur'an to Muhammad, it remains uncertain whether the authorship of its disparate contents is entirely his. From the historian's point of view, there is every reason to assume that the Qur'an's author remains anonymous.

Indeed, in order to fully appreciate the apocryphal status of the Qur'an, perhaps one must imagine how we might regard this text today if Muhammad's followers had been soundly defeated by the Romans at Yarmuk and their movement slowly dissolved in the years thereafter as the eschaton failed to arrive as anticipated. If we further suppose that somehow the Qur'an had come into being by this time, as the Islamic tradition effectively expects us to believe, and this text were the main remnant of Muhammad's religious movement, what would we make of it? Almost certainly, I suspect, on the basis of its content and its relation to the biblical tradition, we would identify it as a late ancient apocryphon. Ultimately, then, the main difference between the qur'anic apocryphon and so many other such compositions is that, like the Book of Mormon for example, a religious group eventually elevated it to a new scriptural authority. There is in fact much in common between these two apocrypha, the Qur'an and the Book of Mormon, so much so that in late nineteenth- and early twentieth-century America the comparison was frequently made in order to impugn the Book of Mormon. Yet in more recent years, scholars of religious studies have studied the similarities of these texts and their histories with more learned intent, enabling the two texts to illuminate one another through comparison.[24] Like the Qur'an, as well as the biblical writings themselves, the Book of Mormon contains "a variety of materials in different genres ranging from historical narratives, legal codes, and moral injunctions to revelations, prophecies, visions, and ecstatic poetry."[25] All three collections share the same generic diversity.

The Book of Mormon, for its part, is an "intensely American book" that has often been described as "the New World scripture," and "American

---

23. It is true that Junod includes "anonymous or pseudepigraphical" as qualities defining Christian apocryphal writings. Nevertheless, it is not at all clear to me why this should be a requirement. There are apocryphal texts with known authors.

24. In this regard, see especially Stark, "Theory of Revelations," which offers an extended comparison of Muhammad and Joseph Smith and the revelation ascribed to them. See also Underwood, "Prophetic Legacy"; Green, "Muhammad-Joseph Smith."

25. Hardy, "Book of Mormon," 136.

scripture," or an "American apocryphon."[26] As W. D. Davies notes, "Its substructure and its structures are in the Old Testament and the New Testament. But it also reinterprets and accommodates or transfers ancient forms, in a very remarkable way, to an American setting and mode," so that it presents "the Jewish-Christian tradition in an American key." "The territoriality of Judaism is reinterpreted by Americanizing it," and sacred sites from the biblical narrative are relocated onto American soil.[27] The Book of Mormon is, as Laurie Maffly-Kipp describes it, "a sacred drama of the Americas that correlated with biblical accounts of early human history."[28] If we were simply to substitute Arabian for American in the quotations above, the same statements would apply equally well to the Qur'an and early Islam. Thus, I would agree wholeheartedly with Sinai's characterization of the Qur'an "as a properly Arabic restatement of the Biblical heritage."[29] It is, then, a properly Arabic or Arabian apocryphon much as the Book of Mormon stands, as others have noted, as a properly American apocryphon that restates the biblical heritage in a distinctively American idiom. And just like the Book of Mormon, this Arabian apocryphon would eventually come to be an Arabian scripture.

The potential payoff from recognizing the Qur'an as a biblical apocryphon is twofold, as I see it. Firstly, understanding the Qur'an as an apocryphon is sure to bring new perspectives on the nature and significance of both this collection and many of its constituent parts. The category of apocrypha affords a new avenue for approaching the peculiar relationship between the Qur'an and the biblical traditions of Christianity and Judaism. As an apocryphon, we can understand now how the Qur'an recognizes and embraces the authority of these antecedent scriptural collections while simultaneously reconfiguring and supplementing their contents. Such adaptation and modification of biblical traditions is the vital essence of apocryphal writings. Likewise, an apocryphal Qur'an invites us to think newly about the conditions and motivations behind the production of both its individual elements and the collection itself.

---

26. Givens, *Book of Mormon*, 125; Givens, *By the Hand of Mormon*, 6; Vogel and Metcalfe, *American Apocrypha*.

27. Davies, "Israel, the Mormons and the Land," 89. See also Maffly-Kipp, *American Scriptures*, xvii.

28. Smith, *Book of Mormon*, xviii.

29. Sinai, "Eschatological Kerygma," 254.

No less significant, however, are the bonds that this perspective forges between the Qur'an and the religious literature of late antiquity. Viewing the Qur'an as a biblical apocryphon allows us to remove it from the subsequent history of the Islamic tradition and see it truly as a product of late ancient religious culture. Thus we can look at the Qur'an with new eyes in order to investigate and better comprehend its relations to the religious traditions of its historical matrix, including late ancient Christianity and Judaism in particular, without the distracting interference of the later Islamic tradition's interpretations of this compendium of late ancient religious culture. Recognizing the Qur'an as a biblical apocryphon anchors it to the religious landscape of late antiquity and invites us to read it in new ways within this context. Such a perspective offers us the possibility of approaching the Qur'an as if it were a text recently discovered in a cave somewhere, enabling us to interpret it completely afresh, without having so many questions already answered for us by the later Islamic tradition.[30] And given the well-known unreliability of the early Islamic historical tradition, such an approach does not seem unwarranted. Yet one thing is for sure: studying the Qur'an in this fashion will reveal it as the product of the religious cultures of the late ancient Near East, as well as affording new perspectives on this religious milieu at the same time. Among other things, this late ancient qur'anic apocryphon will certainly challenge us to rethink the boundaries of the scriptural canon in late antiquity, as well as conceptualizations of Scripture that were in circulation at this time. It could raise questions about the nature of boundaries between the various religious communities of the late ancient Near East, and the circulation of religious culture among them. Indeed, integrating the Qur'an more fully with the religious world of late antiquity in this way is certain to yield many new perspectives on both.

---

30. And idea also proposed in Lawson, *Quran: Epic and Apocalypse*, 53–54.

3

The Qur'an's Holy House
Mecca or Jerusalem?

ONE OF THE CLEAREST and most uncontestable facts to emerge from the contemporary Jewish and Christian witnesses to the rise of Islam is that Muhammad's earliest followers were well-nigh obsessed with restoring worship and dignity to the site of the destroyed Jewish temple in Jerusalem. These eyewitness accounts of various Jewish and Christian writers from the seventh century persistently signal that Jerusalem and the site of its then devastated temple were regarded with the highest sanctity by Muhammad's followers at the time when they entered the Holy Land. As soon as they captured Jerusalem, they hastened to return sanctity and prayer to the site of the temple, beginning work on erecting some sort of a shrine there almost immediately after they conquered Jerusalem. The convergence of this evidence from a wide range of independent sources not only is impressive but it is compelling.[1] There can be little question that Muhammad and his early followers regarded the then ruined Jerusalem temple and its location as a holy site of the highest order and quite likely a site of pilgrimage. Moreover, according to the recurrent testimony of our contemporary sources, Muhammad's followers understood themselves as in some sense reinstating the Jerusalem temple through their actions. Of course, they did not imagine themselves as actually restoring the temple itself—God alone would accomplish this at the climax of history. Instead, they were building

---

1. See most recently, Shoemaker, *Prophet Has Appeared*, esp. 11.

a structure that could serve a sort of ersatz temple, a placeholder for the real thing until the arrival of the impending eschaton, which they were expecting very soon, it would seem.

The culmination of the Believers' early building activities on the Temple Mount was the Dome of the Rock. And although this shrine was completed only at the very end of the seventh century, its planning and construction began decades before, probably as early as the 660s, if not even earlier. The sacred rock at the Dome's center was widely believed to have stood in the center of the temple's Holy of Holies, its most hallowed precinct. Moreover, the Dome, which is the earliest surviving Islamic monument, is not a mosque but something else entirely, indicating that it was constructed for some other purpose than daily prayer. Almost certainly, it would seem, the Dome was erected by the Believers to serve as a kind of temporary stand in for the temple as they awaited its final divine restoration. The Dome was built around a sacred stone which, according to contemporary Jewish tradition, was not only the "foundation stone" of God's creation but also the rock on which Abraham nearly sacrificed his son Isaac. This same rock, in Jewish and Christian memory, had in fact been housed within the temple's Holy of Holies when it still stood. In light of the considerable importance of Jerusalem's Holy House for Muhammad's earliest followers, then, one certainly is justified in wondering if perhaps the Jerusalem temple bears some direct historical relation to the Abrahamic Holy House of the Qur'an.[2]

What we find in the Qur'an, one must emphasize, is not a simple reflection of Mecca's pre-Islamic religious status or the role of its shrine in an annual pilgrimage. Already in the late nineteenth century, Julius Wellhausen demonstrated convincingly that in late antiquity Mecca simply was not a major pilgrimage center of any sort. There were pilgrimages and pilgrimage shrines in the Hijaz, it would seem, but Mecca itself was not the object of any such pilgrimage, nor did it possess a shrine of significance to anyone beyond its 500 or so inhabitants. Memories in the early Islamic tradition suggesting otherwise are simply projections of later Islamic practices back onto the blank canvas of pre-Islamic Mecca. So did Mecca even have some sort of a shrine in late antiquity? I think it is entirely reasonable to assume on general principles that the herdsmen of this small, remote village and their families would have had some sort of sacred shrine, as is customary in

---

2. See also Shoemaker, *Death of a Prophet*, 241–57; Shoemaker, *Apocalypse of Empire*, 154–68.

most cultures. Just what the nature of this shrine may have been, however, is a difficult question that is not easily answered based on the limited and much later information that we have from the Islamic tradition, as both Crone and Hawting have made clear. The existing structure of the Meccan Kaʻba does not help us much in this quest, since it is not only off limits to investigators, but this shrine was destroyed and rebuilt twice in close proximity at the end of the seventh century.[3] So what survives today is not the shrine of pre-Islamic Mecca but a product of competing religious interests during the second Islamic civil war, at a time when Mecca became newly incorporated into the older pilgrimage practices.

Therefore, as Gerald Hawting rightly discerns, the Qur'an already reflects the process of Islamicizing certain pre-Islamic pilgrimage practices, which originally were not focused on Mecca, by linking them directly with Mecca and establishing Muhammad's hometown as a distinctively Islamic holy place. It was a process that was still ongoing at the time when the Qur'an itself was being composed, which explains the messiness of the Qur'an's representations of the pre-Islamic pilgrimage and sanctuary.[4] Accordingly, it seems that we may safely conclude that prior to the rise of Islam, Mecca was not in fact some sort of renowned and important holy place, and likewise there is no reason to imagine that the Meccan economy was greatly enriched by the presence of any sort of major pilgrimage shrine. Rather, pre-Islamic Mecca remains little more than an obscure, sleepy, out of the way village deep within the deserts of Arabia, with no particular religious significance and a subsistence economy based in pastoralism.

Given, then, the absence of any evidence for a pilgrimage shrine or a major religious sanctuary in pre-Islamic Mecca, one is certainly justified in wondering whether the Kaʻba and "House" of the Qur'an should in fact be identified with a shrine in Mecca, as the Islamic tradition has come to interpret these references. After all, the Qur'an explicitly identifies the location of the House only once, placing it in "Bakka" rather than Mecca (3:96), continuing then in the following verse (97) to enjoin pilgrimage to this House in Bakka. One must emphasize in this case that, judging strictly on the basis of the Qur'an itself, and not the later Islamic tradition, Bakka clearly seems to be a different place from Mecca. The Islamic tradition is of course desperate to identify this Bakka and its sanctuary with the Meccan shrine still revered by Muslims today. Accordingly, in order to remedy the

3. E.g., Hawting, "House and the Book," 16.
4. Hawting, "Sanctuary and Text," 106, 109.

Qur'an's unambiguous and yet highly inconvenient location of its shrine in Bakka, many later Islamic scholars simply decided, without any actual historical basis, that either Bakka is an older name for Mecca or else Bakka refers specifically to the Ka'ba itself and its immediate surroundings within Mecca. There is, however, no justification for identifying Bakka with Mecca either in whole or in part other than a determined need to bring the Qur'an fully into agreement with the Islamic tradition.[5] Nothing allows us to assume that when the Qur'an says Bakka it means Mecca, particularly since it correctly names Mecca elsewhere (48:24).

So just where was Bakka then? Well, judging strictly on the basis of actual evidence from ancient sources, rather than wishful thinking, it would appear to indicate a location in Jerusalem, right next to the Jerusalem temple. If we look to the biblical tradition, which we know has deeply influenced the Qur'an's traditions, we find in Ps 84:6–7 a biblical passage identifying Jerusalem's Holy House with a barren place named *Bākā*, in the context of performing pilgrimage to this same Abrahamic House, the *ḥag* in Hebrew and *ḥaggā* in Aramaic (and as a loanword *ḥajj* in Arabic), a practice that the Hebrew Bible (Exod 23:14–17; Deut 16:16) enjoins three times during the year: for the feasts of Passover, Shavuot, and Sukkot. It is a truly remarkable parallel to Qur'an 3:96–97, one that is far too close to be simply ignored, as has long been the case.[6]

Scholars have of course scoured ancient literature searching for some toponym resembling Bakka that could possibly align the Qur'an's shrine with Mecca, yet always to no avail, excepting only the lone mention of Baka in this psalm, which draws us instead squarely into the orbit of the Jerusalem's holy house, the temple. As in the Qur'an, a place named Baka appears just once in the Hebrew Bible, in Ps 84:7, where the "valley of Baka" is closely linked with the Jerusalem temple, which the Psalm implies stood very near to this biblical valley. Even more importantly, however, there is complete agreement among scholars of the Hebrew Bible that this particular Psalm, 84, is a "pilgrim psalm," giving voice to the experience of pilgrims to Jerusalem as they drew near to the temple.[7] Scholars differ as to whether

---

5. E.g., Amir-Moezzi and Dye, *Le Coran des historiens*, 2:154; Hawting, *Idea of Idolatry*, 25; Crone and Cook, *Hagarism*, 21–22; Shoemaker, *Death of a Prophet*, 250.

6. But see Kerr, "Farüqter Heiland." I also thank Prof. Mark Durie for drawing my attention to this topic by sharing an early draft of an article that develops this topic further: Durie, "Note on al-Ṣafā and al-Marwah."

7. Alter, *Book of Psalms*, 371–72. See also Cohen, *Psalms*, 275; Kittel, *Die Psalmen*, 279; Gunkel, *Die Psalmen*, 368; Schmidt, *Die Psalmen*, 159–60; Kraus, *Psalmen II*, 748;

this psalm was actually sung as a part of the pilgrimage liturgy by or for the pilgrims, or is instead a kind of "(spiritual) 'pilgrimage song'" sung by those who longed for the temple but could not visit it. In any case, the pilgrimage context of this psalm is unanimously recognized, with the balance seemingly tipped in favor of viewing Psalm 84 as a hymn connected with the events of actual pilgrimage to the Jerusalem temple. Indeed, so vivid is the Psalm's allusion to a pilgrimage context that one scholar has even proposed that it should be understood as a liturgical text used by pilgrims at various stations along the way to the temple itself, with the valley of Baka being the staging area for their final ascent onto the Temple Mount.[8] One certainly has the sense that the more spiritualizing and interiorizing interpretations of the Psalm reflect the long shadow of German Pietism so clearly evident in much scholarship on the Hebrew Bible rather than an understanding of its cultic function in ancient Israel.[9] And regardless of what the psalmist's intent may have been, in Jewish tradition the valley of Baka soon became a location associated with ancient pilgrimage to the temple.

Whatever reading one may prefer for the Psalm as a whole, there can be little question that the verse naming the valley of Baka, which is the "Kernstück und Hohepunkt" of the Psalm, is itself directly associated with pilgrimage to the Holy House.[10] According to Jewish tradition, the valley of Baka lies somewhere in the vicinity of the temple, and various specific locations have been proposed. For instance, the haggadic midrashim on the Psalms suggest that the valley of Baka is the valley of Gehenna, to the east of the Temple Mount.[11] Nevertheless, Baka is most frequently identified with a valley to the west of the Temple Mount, so that to this day the Jerusalem neighborhood known as the "German Colony" also bears the name Baka, owing to its traditional association with this Psalm. In this

---

Böhl, *De Psalmen*, 2:151; Maillot and Lelièvre, *Les Psaumes*, 205; Hauge, *Between Sheol and Temple*, 38, 41.

8. So, e.g., Peters, "Jerusalem Processional"; Mowinckel, *Psalms*, 1:170–71, 2:107; and Ḥakham, *Psalms*, 2:265–75, esp. 273.

9. The best recent study of Psalm 84 is Hossfeld and Zenger, *Psalms 2*, 348–58, wherein various interpretations are considered but the apparent preference for a more "spiritual" interpretation seems to bear the influence of German Pietism more than an effort to locate this text in the context of Israelite/Jewish pilgrimage to the temple.

10. Culley, "Temple," 191; Loersch, "'Sie wandern,'" 15. Also Loretz, "Vorexilische und nachexilische Zion-Wallfahrten," 486; Wanke, *Die Zionstheologie*, 18; Mowinckel, *Psalms*, 1:6–7, 170–71, 2:107.

11. Braude, *Midrash on Psalms*, 2:65; for Talmudic references, see Kerr, "Farüqter Heiland."

place, according to the prevailing memory, ancient pilgrims to the temple would gather in preparation to make their ascent to the Temple Mount. Perhaps the most thorough and authoritative discussion of the valley of Baka as understood in the Jewish tradition is Amos Ḥakham's commentary on the Psalms published in the *Da'at Miqra* series. As Ḥakham explains, in this psalm the valley of Baka refers to "those who go up to the Temple and pass the parched waterless 'valley of Baca' on the way. This interpretation finds support in the Arabic." According to Jewish tradition, then, ancient pilgrims to Jerusalem's Holy House would assemble just to the southwest of the Temple Mount and pass through the nearby valley of Baka on their way up to the temple. And Psalm 84 is an ancient Jewish pilgrimage hymn representative of this practice.[12]

One should also note the strong scholarly consensus regarding the meaning of the name "valley of Baka" in this passage. It is true that in the Septuagint as well as the Vulgate the word *bk'* was rendered as "weeping" (*tou klauthmōnos / lacrimarum*), whence we derive the expression "vale of tears." Nevertheless, as experts on the Psalms are agreed, this stems from a misreading of *bk'* as *bkh*, which is not in fact supported by the text. In Hebrew, the word *bk'* (*bākā'*) refers instead to the balsam shrub, and since this shrub "grows only in dry waterless regions," its mention here designates this "valley of balsam shrubs" as a barren and waterless place.[13] Accordingly, the valley of Baka is clearly designated here as "a valley of drought" or "a desert valley." Thus, this valley lying just below God's Holy House, through which its pilgrims must process, is described by the Psalm as a dry and desert place. How interesting, then, that the Qur'an's Holy House is not only located in a place called Bakka, where it drew pilgrims, but the Qur'an also specifically indicates that its location near a "valley where no crops are sewn" (14:37). On the basis of these two passages, it would certainly appear that the Qur'an's Holy House was in the same place visited by the Jewish pilgrims of Psalm 84. Indeed, if we look more closely at Qur'an 3:96-97, the linkage between what the Qur'an names "the first House," the Islamic *Bayt al-Maqdis*, and Jerusalem's Holy House, the *Beit HaMikdash* only becomes more apparent. As much has been made fairly clear by the only study that, to my knowledge, directly compares this qur'anic passage with Psalm 84,

---

12. Ḥakham, *Psalms*, 2:268-69.

13. E.g., Hossfeld and Zenger, *Psalms 2*, 349; Robinson, "Three Suggested Interpretations," 378-79. See also Frants Buhl in Singer, *Jewish Encyclopedia*, 2:415; Loersch, "Sie wandern," 19.

Adolphe Regnier's posthumously published article "Quelques énigmes littéraires de l'inspiration coranique." As Regnier observes, in both the Qur'an and the Hebrew Bible, the place name *bakka/baka* is a hapax legomenon, but its occurrence in both writings in the context of pilgrimage to the Holy House is too remarkable to be mere coincidence. Regnier further observes, convincingly, that some additional shared vocabulary in the two passages seems to solidify the biblical intertextuality of the Qur'an's reference to a sacred house in *bakka*.[14]

Given the seemingly clear evidence of the Qur'an's intertextuality with Ps 84:6–7 in its descriptions of the Holy House, it is remarkable that this psalm's influence on the Qur'an has for so long remained almost entirely unrecognized. Indeed, one of Angelika Neuwirth's most enduring contributions to the study of the Qur'an is sure to be her careful identification and exposition of the manner in which the Qur'an frequently draws influence and inspiration from the Psalter.[15] Likewise, Neuwirth has often drawn our attention to the very complex relationship that exists between the Qur'an's House and the Jerusalem temple, pointing to a considerable amount of slippage between the two in both the Qur'an and the early Islamic tradition.[16] As Neuwirth has observed on numerous occasions, the Qur'an indicates great reverence for Jerusalem and the temple, whose traditions were only later transferred onto Mecca and its shrine, a point on which we find ourselves in full agreement with her.[17] It is only in respect to the timing of this transfer that we would disagree. For Neuwirth, and many others as well, any and all such developments in the Qur'an's traditions must be confined entirely within the lifetime of Muhammad, so that at his death both the Qur'an and the faith of Islam had been perfectly formed. Yet, as many scholars have rightly pointed out, there is no compelling historical reason whatsoever to impose such strictures, and it seems far more likely like that all of these things—the formation of the Qur'an and the faith of Islam as well as the transfer of the Believers' sacred geography from Jerusalem and its temple to the Hijaz and the Meccan shrine—took place over the course

---

14. Regnier, "Quelques énigmes," 148–50, and the English translation, Regnier, "Some Literary Enigmas," 250–52.

15. Neuwirth, "Die Psalmen," 157–91; Neuwirth, *Qur'an and Late Antiquity*, 241–54.

16. E.g., Neuwirth, "Locating the Qur'an," 175–81; also Neuwirth, "Face of God," 298–312, 305–12; Neuwirth, "Erste Qibla." See also Shoemaker, *Death of a Prophet*, 218–40.

17. See Neuwirth, *Qur'an and Late Antiquity*, 334–37, 400–402. See also similar ideas regarding Jerusalem and its temple in her articles cited in the previous footnote.

of decades after Muhammad's death. Accordingly, the different traditions in the Qur'an and the traditions regarding Jerusalem and the temple must be understood as reflecting the gradual process of this shift in the collective memory of Muhammad's earliest followers even as it was still taking place.

Undoubtedly fidelity to the Islamic tradition has prevented many other scholars from noticing the striking and seemingly obvious connection between Ps 84:6–7 and Qur'an 3:96–97. Indeed, according to Neuwirth's reading, this sura was composed quite late and only well after Muhammad and his followers had fully completed their switch from a Jerusalemite, temple-revering sacred geography to one grounded fully in Mecca and its shrine. Therefore, in this instance she follows the Islamic tradition in disregarding this biblical intertext and asserting instead that Bakka is simply Mecca, without offering further explanation.[18] Yet if one is truly interested in identifying instances of the Qur'an's intertextualities with the Psalms, then there no good reason to ignore such an obvious example as this direct echo of Psalm 84, one of the most well-known and beloved psalms, out of mere deference to the Islamic tradition.[19] If we are to take seriously the Qur'an's intertextuality with the Psalter, then we must acknowledge this instance as in fact a textbook example: it describes pilgrimage to the "first" Holy House dedicated to the God of Abraham, at a place named Bakka, which is an uncultivatable valley. It is a perfect match for the Psalm. Ironically, this close correspondence has certainly not been lost on many Muslim exegetes, who often assert that in Psalm 84 the Hebrew Bible directly refers to the ancient sanctuary founded by Abraham at Mecca (since for them Bakka is the same as Mecca), albeit presenting the Meccan shrine in deliberately obscured and disguised form as the Jerusalem temple.[20] Yet while such an interpretation obviously makes perfect sense to a devout Muslim, for the historian, let alone the historian of religion, such a reading of the Psalm's relation to the Qur'an is of course simply preposterous. At the same time however, this interpretation, apologetic though it may be, is undeniably correct in identifying the important connection between these two passages.

The clear alignment of the Qur'an's House with the Holy House in Jerusalem through the intertext with Psalm 84 certainly invites further consideration of the Qur'an's shrine, including both its nature and location.

---

18. Neuwirth, *Qur'an and Late Antiquity*, 401.

19. On the popularity of this particular psalm, see, e.g., Loersch, "Sie wandern," 13.

20. E.g., Lumbard, "Prophets and Messengers of God," 101–22, 112–13; Sardar, *Mecca*, 1–5.

We know, for instance, that the pilgrimage traditions and shrines of the Jerusalem area determined the shape of the Qur'an's traditions of the Nativity of Jesus, particularly in sura 19.[21] Since the Qur'an clearly shows reverence for the traditions of the church of the Kathisma, a major Marian shrine just three miles (5km) south of the Temple Mount, it is hardly a reach to suggest that the vanished Jerusalem temple was the Abrahamic Holy House initially revered by the Qur'an and its community. Moreover, in light of Neuwirth's careful delineation of the Qur'an's often blurry distinction between the two shrines, one wonders that there has not previously been much prior consideration of the possibility that the Qur'an's House is somehow directly connected with the Holy House of the biblical tradition, the place where Abraham offered sacrifice in the land promised to him and his descendants. The Qur'an says twice that the House is located at the "standing place of Abraham" (2:125; 3:97): what else is this if not the place where Abraham stood before God to offer his son as a sacrifice, only to be stopped at the last minute (Gen 22:1–14)? This legend of Abraham's near sacrifice of his son and their mutual sacrifice of a ram to God of course served to establish the temple's location on Mount Moriah in Jerusalem.

In sura 2:158 the location of the House is associated with two "symbols" or "signs" (*sha'āiri*) of God specified as al-Ṣafā and al-Marwa, further explaining that it is allowed for pilgrims to the House to walk around in them, presumably indicating that these are places. According to the later Islamic tradition, these "symbols" are to be identified with two small hills close to the Meccan Ka'ba. Of course, there is no evidence to support this interpretation from the Qur'an itself or from any other source from the seventh century or earlier. Indeed, judging from the Qur'an alone, one would have no idea that al-Ṣafā and al-Marwa were the names of two small rock outcroppings in Mecca. According to the later tradition, Abraham's mistress Hagar once ran between these two mounds frantically searching for water for her son Ishmael, an event that Islamic pilgrims commemorate by processing back and forth between the two locations at the beginning of the hajj. To my knowledge the first evidence locating either al-Ṣafā or al-Marwa anywhere near Mecca is an inscription in Mecca from 783 CE indicating the direction of al-Ṣafā—more than one hundred and fifty years after the traditional date of Muhammad's death.[22] Otherwise, the first sources to

---

21. Shoemaker, "Christmas in the Qur'ān"; Shoemaker, "Mary Between Bible and Qur'an"; Dye, "Lieux saints communs"; Dye, "Qur'anic Mary."

22. al-Anṣārī and al-Rāšid, *Silsilat Āṯār al-Mamlaka*, 2:111–13. I thank Prof. Harry

identify the Qur'an's al-Ṣafā and al-Marwa with locations in Mecca that I have found are the early ninth-century biographies of Muhammad by al-Wāqidī and Ibn Hishām and al-Azraqi's history of Mecca, all of which were written nearly two hundred years after the Muhammad's death.[23] Such late witnesses clearly offer no basis for concluding that in the early seventh century al-Ṣafā and al-Marwa would have been identified these Meccan crags.

At the same time, however, there are locations in Jerusalem that can readily be identified with these place names, as Robert Kerr has recently pointed out, namely, Mount Scopus and Mount Moriah, the latter being the site of the temple itself.[24] Mount Scopus, which lies just a little over one mile (just under 2 km) northwest of the Temple Mount, takes its name from the Greek word *skopos*, which means a "lookout" or "watchman." It is indeed an excellent location for a lookout, with one of the most commanding views of the Jerusalem area. As far back as the first-century Jewish historian Josephus, this high ridge was known as both "Skopos" and "Saphein," or "Lookout Mountain," if you will.[25] During the Jewish War of the late 60s CE, the Roman army used this strategic outlook as the main staging area for their operations in Jerusalem. In Hebrew the name of this mountain is Har HaṢofim, the "mountain of the lookouts," at least as far back as the beginning of the third century, as attested by the Mishnah (and seemingly Josephus before it), where it is mentioned in conjunction with the Passover pilgrimage and sacrifice (Moed, Pesahim 3:8). The singular form of *Ṣofim* is *Ṣofeh*, a term that is consistently translated in the Septuagint using the Greek singular *skopos*. Ṣafā is therefore easily understandable as an adaptation of the Hebrew *Ṣofeh* to the patterns of Arabic morphophonology. As for Marwa, one need look no farther than Mount Moriah itself, the location of the temple and of Abraham's near sacrifice of his son: the consonants *y* and *w* regularly alternate in early Arabic. Such close correspondence of these Jerusalem place names to the qur'anic al-Ṣafā and al-Marwa is surely more than mere coincidence, particularly when both pilgrimage and the Holy House are in view. Accordingly, here again, the data from the Qur'an

---

Munt for providing me with this reference and knowledge of this inscription.

23. al-Wāqidī, *Kitāb al-maghāzī*, 2:736–37; Ibn Hishām, *Kitāb sīrat Rasūl Allāh*, 1:71; Wüstenfeld, *Die Chroniken der Stadt Mekka*, 1:21–22, 33–34, 279–80.

24. Kerr, "Farüqter Heiland," 503–7.

25. Josephus, *J.W.*, 2.19.4; 5.2.3; *Ant.*, 11.8.5 (Thackeray, *Josephus*, 2:526–27; 3:220–21; 6:472–73).

itself seem to indicate that its House was in fact originally the demolished Holy House of Jerusalem's Temple Mount.

While Qur'an 3:96–97 and 14:37 align perfectly with the pilgrimage hymn of Ps 84:6–7, other qur'anic passages related to the Holy House are admittedly less straightforward and occasionally more problematic. The house as described in Qur'an 2:125–27 certainly would comport with the Jerusalem temple. Although circumambulation is perhaps signaled, the word in question (*li-l-ṭā'ifīna*) can also mean simply mean "those who go about" the House. Yet even if circumambulation of the house is in view, one should note that, on the one hand, it was customary in early Judaism to circumambulate the temple in times of pilgrimage, as the rabbis continued to remember. On the other hand, it remains entirely possible that the Islamic practice of circumambulation was only introduced at a later time, perhaps on the basis of the Qur'an, as others have suggested.[26] Qur'an 22:26–29 invites its audience to recall God's command to Abraham regarding the practices of pilgrimage and sacrifice at the House in a manner that is entirely compatible with having Jerusalem's Holy House in view here. So too the instructions that follow regarding other matters of the faith that remain valid for the faithful and are related to their devotion to the Holy House can be easily squared with the Jerusalem temple (2:30–33).

Sura 5:95, 97, which refers to a shrine named the Ka'ba, is admittedly a little tricker, since this is a term not known to have been applied to the Jerusalem temple. Nevertheless, one should note that in Jerusalem's sacred house, the sanctuary of its holy of holies was in fact in the shape of a cube (1 Kgs 6:20)—which is, of course, the meaning of the word *ka'ba*.[27] There is, moreover, no indication in this verse that the Ka'ba was in Mecca or anywhere else in the Hijaz, and likewise there is nothing that would preclude its identification with the Jerusalem temple. The house also appears in Qur'an 106, which enjoins its audience to "worship the Lord of this House," who has protected them. Yet there is no reason at all why this house of the

---

26. On Jewish circumambulation, see, e.g., Mishnah Sukkah 4.5 (Danby, *Mishnah*, 178); also Mowinckel, *Psalms*, 7, 10–11. On the possible late inclusion of circumambulation, see, e.g., Hawting, "Sanctuary and Text," 100, esp. n16. As Joseph Witztum notes, the mention of Ishmael in this context also could reflect a later addition, since in sura 37 the son is not named: Witztum, "Foundations," 39.

27. See, e.g., Hirsch in Singer, *Jewish Encyclopedia*, 6:446. Robert Kerr has, however, suggested that etymologizing this word from Greek κύβος, especially rendering κ with Arabic ك instead of ق, and the unexplained ع, a phoneme foreign to Greek, is unlikely. He suggests an etymology from, e.g., *ku'ba* "virginity," and that *ka'ba* formerly denoted a *Parthenon*. See Kerr, "Islamische Kabbala," 336–38.

Lord should be identified with Mecca rather than Jerusalem, all the more so given that the meaning of this brief sura is anything but clear. Certainly, the mere reference to Quraysh in this extremely obscure sura does not settle the matter in any way.[28] Indeed, so obscure is this passage that Daniel Beck has recently proposed, not at all implausibly, that sura 106 could be understood as a prayer regarding seasonal pilgrimage to Jerusalem rather than having anything at all too do with trade.[29]

The only remaining qur'anic passage to mention the Holy House is in sura 8:34–35, which reproves the unbelievers for preventing the righteous from worshipping at the inviolable place of prayer (*al-masjid al-ḥarām*), describing the prayers offered by the unrighteous at this House as amounting to nothing more than "whistling and hand-clapping." How this reference to the unbelievers' prayer at the House could be reconciled with the Jerusalem temple is admittedly not entirely clear, since at the time the temple lay in ruins and deliberate neglect. Of course, given the peculiar nature of the Qur'an, the persistent vagaries of its addressees, and its frequently extra-historical register, there is no guarantee that this particular passage addresses circumstances directly relevant to the experiences of Muhammad and his followers. At the same time, however, the reference here to people being kept away from this holy place is entirely consistent with the state of the temple in late antiquity, as well as the refusal of the Roman authorities to permit anyone to pray there. In this regard, it is noteworthy that, as Suliman Bashear discovered, the early Islamic commentators were often quite confused regarding the Qur'an's rebuke of those who prevented the worship of God in God's places of prayer in 2:114. A significant thread of the interpretive tradition of course identifies this divine admonishment as directed toward the Meccans who refused to allow the Believers to pray at Mecca's shrine. Yet at the same time, a number of commentators understood this passage instead as a reproof "concerning the barring of Muslims by the Byzantines from the Jerusalem sanctuary."[30] This alternative location of the Believers' sanctuary in Jerusalem in this instance surely preserves in its own right a compelling vestige of the considerable significance that Jerusalem and its ancient temple held in the sacred geography of Muhammad's earliest followers. And this alternative interpretation of Qur'an

---

28. The best discussion of the problems with understanding this sura is Crone, *Meccan Trade*, 204–14.

29. Beck, "Muḥammad's Night Journey."

30. Bashear, "Qur'ān 2:114," 215.

2:114 certainly invites us to bring a similar understanding to bear on the comparable prohibition of worship in the inviolable place of prayer in sura 84, along with the analogous repetitions of this charge in 2:217, 5:2, 22:25, 48:25–27.

If we look to the Qur'an's other mentions of the inviolable place of prayer, in each instance the phrase can intelligibly understood as referring in some sense to the Temple Mount, even in the case of the so-called "Night Journey" (17:1).[31] The identification of Jerusalem as the *masjid al-aqṣa* in this verse in contrast to the Meccan *ḥarām* of course did not develop until later on, and there is nothing at all in the verse itself indicating that either shrine was located in Mecca. Only the later interpretive tradition supplies this location and not the text itself.[32] Nevertheless, a few verses later in this same passage, in 17:7 the Qur'an says that "When the final promise has arrived, so that they will aggrieve your faces, and they will enter the *masjid* as they entered the first time and completely destroy what they conquered." Here once again, as is so often the case with the Qur'an, we meet yet another deeply cryptic passage, whose referents and meaning are utterly obscure from the text itself. Nevertheless, as others have noted, including most translators who simply translate *masjid* here as "temple," the language of destruction and reentry do indeed suggest that the *masjid* is not in Mecca but is Jerusalem's Holy House. So also do the references in this passage to the final promise and conquest, which further indicate a context of eschatological anticipation and military conquest. The phrase "the final promise" (*wa'du l-'ākhirati*), one should note, appears only one other time in the Qur'an, near the end of this same sura in verse 104. There "the final promise" unmistakably refers to an eschatological event, and the fulfillment of this last promise will bring about the restoration to the promised land: "And after that we said to the children of Israel, 'Dwell in the Land, and when the Final Promise has arrived, we will bring you a throng.'" Are we to understand Muhammad's followers as the anticipated throng? I think it is likely, but in any case, it would appear that the *masjid* of verse 7 is found in the land of the Abrahamic inheritance, and it will be restored to his descendants along with the Land at the eschaton, a meaning that should also presumably extend to *masjid*s of the sura's first verse as well.[33]

---

31. Once again, see the intriguing interpretation of this verse offered in Beck, "Muḥammad's Night Journey."

32. See, e.g., the discussion in Shoemaker, *Death of a Prophet*, 256–57.

33. This conclusion is seemingly unavoidable if one is determined, as Neuwirth, to

The Qur'an also, one must note, directs its audience on several occasions to face this inviolable place of prayer, the *masjid al-ḥarām*, whenever they pray. Yet since we know that Jerusalem was in fact the original direction of prayer for Muhammad and his earliest followers, there is then all the more reason to assume that the Qur'an's *masjid al-ḥarām* was originally identified with Jerusalem and its temple.[34] Moreover, in another article Bashear notes further disagreement within the early Islamic tradition as to whether Abraham's near sacrifice of his son involved either Isaac or Ishmael, as well as related rival memories concerning the location of this pivotal event: some of these later commentators of course identify a location somewhere in Mecca, but numerous others confidently name Jerusalem as the place. And as Bashear persuasively argues, the Ishmael/Mecca interpretive tradition does not seem to have achieved any prominence before the end of the first Islamic century.[35] Inasmuch as the binding of Isaac serves in the Jewish tradition to establish location of the Holy House on Jerusalem's Temple Mount, here again we seem to be confronting evidence that Muhammad and his early followers revered a House not in Mecca but rather the Jerusalem temple. In this case the tradition of Isaac's near sacrifice at the location of the Jerusalem temple is rendered credible early and perhaps even authentic by the criterion of embarrassment or dissimilarity. It is unlikely that such a tradition would have been fabricated much beyond the early history of Muhammad's new religious movement, since it directly contradicts the construction of a distinctively Islamic Abrahamic holy land in Mecca and Medina as an important marker of confessional distinction from Judaism and Christianity.

Likewise, one might add that the early inclusion of Jews within the community as Jews, as indicated by the so-called "Constitution of Medina," favors the temple's identity with the Qur'an's House. To be sure, the Qur'an's presentation of the House is highly complex, and its identification of the House with the temple is not always such a simple matter as it is in case of Bakka/Baka. But we must understand that the traditions of the Qur'an remained a work in progress seemingly for decades, and therefore it is no great surprise to find that in its presentation of the House the early identification of this qur'anic shrine with the Jerusalem temple has become increasingly blurry as other currents influenced the emerging collective

---

read sura 17 as a single literary unit: Neuwirth, "Erste Qibla," esp. 251–58.

34. See also Shoemaker, *Death of a Prophet*, 223–28; and Bashear, "Qibla Musharriqa."
35. Bashear, "Abraham's Sacrifice," 265, 277.

memories of Muhammad's followers. The facts that Muhammad and his followers likely lived at some distance from Jerusalem, at least at first, and also that at the time the temple lay in ruins do not present any hinderance to this interpretation. And to be clear, we are not proposing that Muhammad and his followers actually made pilgrimage to the temple during his lifetime, even as the Qur'an seems to express a longing and reverence for the Jerusalem temple and its pilgrimages as they existed in memory.

Nevertheless, in the 630s and 640s, who knows? Perhaps once the Temple Mount came under the control of Muhammad's followers, things may have changed, so that pilgrimages to the site of the vanished temple could resume. Such a possibility certainly invites new considerations of both the Dome of the Rock's significance and allegations of 'Abd al-Malik's attempt to "divert" the pilgrimage to Jerusalem. As Neuwirth rightly explains, even though the temple was "architecturally absent" in the early seventh century, its location and spiritual significance remained an extremely important "object of the Qur'anic memory."[36] The apocalyptic desires of Muhammad and his earliest followers were likewise focused squarely on the liberation and reclamation of the promised land as well as its Holy House. Thus, the "longing for Jerusalem," as Neuwirth describes it, that took hold of Muhammad and his earliest followers "reached far beyond the scope of the real world."[37] For them, Jerusalem's temple stood rather as the ultimate goal of their "eschatological exodus," as Erich Zenger interprets the pilgrimage hymn in Psalm 84, an intertextual element that also undoubtedly spills over into the Qur'an's reference to the House in sura 3:96–97.[38]

---

36. Neuwirth, *Qur'an and Late Antiquity*, 288.
37. Neuwirth, *Qur'an and Late Antiquity*, 334.
38. Hossfeld and Zenger, *Psalms 2*, 354.

4

The Eschatological Reign of God in the Qur'an: The *Amr Allāh*

THE QUR'AN'S VOCABULARY FOR identifying the eschaton is quite varied and diverse, which is not at all surprising given that eschatology is its second most prominent theme, after its persistent call to monotheism. Among the most frequent names for this ultimate event is "the Hour" (*al-sā'a*; e.g., 16:77, 54:1), which occurs roughly some fifty times. Also common is "the Day" (*al-yawm*; e.g., 21:104, 22:2), which appears dozens of times throughout the Qur'an, often further qualified as "the Day of Judgment" (*al-yawm al-dīn*; e.g., 1:4, 56:56), "the Last Day" (*al-yawm al-ākhir*; e.g., 60:6), "the Day of Decision" (*al-yawm al-furqān* or *al-yawm al-faṢl*; e.g., 8:41, 77:38),[1] or simply "that Day" (*wa-yawm a'din*), among many other possible combinations. Nevertheless, one of the Qur'an's frequent terms for naming the eschaton is also one of the least understood, namely, *amr*, a word appearing a little over one-hundred and fifty times throughout the Qur'an. Of course, the word *amr* can mean several different things, and its use in the Qur'an certainly is not always eschatological.[2] Yet at the same time one should note that the eschatological usage of *amr* is prevalent, occurring some twenty times in reference to the eschaton, as well as to the related concept of God's reign, often with the more specific designation of

---

1. Or possibly "the Day of Salvation" if one follows Donner's reading of *furqān* from the Syriac *purqānā*: Donner, "Quranic *Furqān*."
2. Baljon, "Amr of God," 8.

the *amr allāh*, the "*amr* of God." Yet despite such frequent eschatological usage, *amr* remains, as David Cook notes, "probably the most difficult of all the apocalyptic vocabulary to translate."[3]

Most frequently, *amr* is translated in these eschatological contexts as "the command" or occasionally as the even more ungainly as "the affair," neither of which captures the meaning of the word satisfactorily. Indeed, in most such cases the resulting translation is quite awkward and only makes sense when, by the very awkwardness itself, one recognizes that "command" or "affair" effectively represents a qur'anic technical term for the eschaton for which interpreters have not found an adequate translation. This approach yields such translations as "God's command comes; so seek not to hasten it" (16:1 Arberry), or "The affair of Allah has come, seek not to hasten it" (Bell).[4] Although these translations are technically correct, they certainly do not make much sense in English. Cook proposes understanding the term as indicating "the direct rule or regime of God," often with reference to a dispensation or period of revelation. With this interpretation, we come very close, I think, to the meaning of God's eschatological *amr* as appears in the Qur'an.[5]

Obviously, our best source for seeking to understand this perplexing and yet pivotal eschatological term from the Qur'an lies in the matrix of apocalyptic traditions from the late ancient Near East that have likely influenced the Qur'an. And as we will explain further in a moment, parallel expressions from the apocalyptic discourse of the Qur'an's late ancient religious milieu bring much clarity to a term that is otherwise opaque when read within the qur'anic text alone. Despite its significance in qur'anic eschatology, scholarly discussion of this apocalyptic *amr* remains strangely absent from most previous investigations of Qur'an and its eschatology.[6] For instance, the *amr* is largely overlooked in the relevant articles of the *Encyclopedia of the Qur'an*, where the only meaningful discussion of this eschatological term, it would seem, appears in a few pages of Tilman Nagel's article on "Theology and the Qur'an," where he maintains that the Qur'an

---

3. Cook, *Studies in Muslim Apocalyptic*, 271–72, where the frequency of these terms is also noted. See also Hasson, "Last Judgment," which oddly fails to mention the term *amr* at all.

4. For *amr* as "affair," see also Rubin, "Prophets and Prophethood," 292–93.

5. Cook, *Studies in Muslim Apocalyptic*, 272.

6. Such is the case, e.g., in Rüling, *Beiträge zur Eschatologie*, Smith, "Eschatology," and Hasson, "Last Judgment."

understands *amr* as meaning effectively the same thing as "revelation."[7] The articles in the *Encyclopaedia of Islam*, in both of its two most recent editions, focus primarily on the use of this term in Islamic philosophy and theology, rather than its eschatological significance in the Qur'an, a matter that receives no consideration at all.[8] Even Paul Casanova, in his path-breaking work, *Mohammed et la fin du monde*, refers only once to the eschatological *amr* of God, a term which he identifies, rightly I would argue, as effectively equivalent to the kingdom of God proclaimed by Jesus in the New Testament Gospels.[9]

One of the most troubling omissions occurs in the recent *Concise Dictionary of Koranic Arabic* compiled by Arne Ambros. At the end of this volume, Ambros includes an appendix of qur'anic "designations of the Omega event," i.e., the eschaton, and astonishingly, his list of more than two dozen terms fails to include any mention of *amr*. This absence is reinforced even more glaringly by the dictionary itself, for when one consults the entry for '-M-R, the entry is utterly devoid of any indication that *amr* is in fact one of the most common qur'anic terms for the eschaton. It is a significant oversight in a work that purports to encompass and represent "the state of the art of Koranic philology" at the beginning of the twenty-first century.[10] One can only understand this failure an important symptom of the fact that the "state of the art" in qur'anic studies still has yet to reckon sufficiently with the reality that the Qur'an is a thoroughly eschatological text that repeatedly warns with great urgency against the impending arrival of the final judgment and the eschaton. Perhaps for this reason the Qur'an's frequent reference to the eschaton as the *amr* has become a major blind spot for a broad swath of contemporary scholarship on the Qur'an.

Indeed, it would appear that the only significant study on the meaning of the *amr* of God in the Qur'an for the better part of the last century is a brief article by Johannes M. S. Baljon on "The 'Amr of God' in the Koran."[11] In his article, Baljon responds to what was long an orthodoxy of qur'anic interpretation reaching back to Hubert Grimme,[12] that the word *amr* in the Qur'an designates a concept effectively equivalent to the "Word

---

7. Nagel, "Theology and the Qur'ān," 266, 270–71.
8. Pines, "Amr"; Schwarb, "Amr (theology)."
9. Casanova, *Mohammed*, 22.
10. Ambros and Procházka, *Concise Dictionary*, 27–28, 366–67, back cover.
11. Baljon, "Amr of God."
12. Grimme, *Mohammed*, 2:51.

of God," the divine *Logos*, in the sense that Jews and Christians had adopted such a concept from Greek philosophy. God's *amr* refers, according to this interpretation, to some sort of divine hypostasis that mediates between God and the world.[13] One finds such an understanding of *amr* in the Qur'an as recently as Rudi Paret's much praised translation, where he translates Q 16:2, for instance, "Er läßt die Engel mit dem Geist von seinem Logos (*amr*) herabkommen" ("He causes the angels to descend with the spirit of his Logos [*amr*]").[14] Yet Baljon argues, persuasively, that such an understanding of *amr*, particularly in relation to the *amr allāh*, generally does not suit its usage in the Qur'an very well. When *amr* is used with reference to human beings, he observes, its meanings are generally among the following: "command, affair, intentions, deeds/conduct, or religion." When used with respect to God, he notes that *amr* is commonly rendered as "command," as mentioned above. But Baljon concludes that such translation frequently fails to capture the full force of this term and that "generally *amr Ullāh* has a more pregnant sense."[15] Instead, this word regularly indicates a broader set of divine attributes, and it would appear, then, that Baljon's article has more or less settled this question. Indeed, equations of the qur'anic *amr* with the Hellenistic Logos have since become relatively rare.[16] For instance, Ambros in his previously mentioned *Dictionary of Koranic Arabic* notes that in certain instances *amr* has been "understood sometimes as 'Logos,'" yet he immediately proclaims this interpretation as "highly debatable"—even as he overlooks entirely its relatively frequent eschatological usage.[17]

To summarize Baljon's argument briefly, then, he notes that God's *amr* in the Qur'an sometimes refers to God's arrangement and maintenance of the order of the universe, while in other instances it indicates God's divine guidance or favor for individuals or nations, often in the form of a divine

13. Baljon, "Amr of God," 7–8.

14. Paret, *Der Koran*, 216. Paret frequently translates *amr* as "Logos" elsewhere in his translation. See also Paret, *Koran: Kommentar*, 25.

15. Baljon, "Amr of God," 8–9.

16. See, however, Reynolds and Qarā'ī, *Qurʾān and the Bible*, e.g., 732 as well as the other passages referenced there, which introduces the interpretive tradition of identifying the *amr* with the Logos. More significantly, however, Sean Anthony's contribution on "The Creation" at the recent conference on "Biblical Traditions in the Qur'an" hosted by the British Academy (October 11–12, 2018) made some persuasive arguments for understanding the term *amr* as referring to something like the Logos in the context of the Qur'an's creation traditions. The paper should eventually appear in published form in *Biblical Traditions in the Qur'an*, forthcoming with Princeton University Press.

17. Ambros and Procházka, *Concise Dictionary*, 28.

"command." Most frequently, however, God's *amr* in the Qur'an indicates the impending eschaton and the ensuing divine judgment, and this is the usage that interests us the most. Likewise, Baljon observes that *amr* is often used to indicate God's "government" and "providential rule," which God often manifests directly in the form of various dispensations, thus connecting with Cook's suggested meaning.[18] This final meaning of *amr* as referring to God's "reign" or "rule" has been largely overlooked, unfortunately, and yet, it is a translation that effectively encompasses the range of meanings identified by Baljon. God's divine reign of course includes the maintenance and direction of the order of the universe as well the lives of individuals and nations, while also referring the restoration of divine rule at the end of time in the eschaton. By understanding *amr allāh* thus, as designating "God's reign," "God's dominion," "God's sovereignty," or, if we follow Kazimirski, even "God's empire," we can better comprehend the meaning of this term as it would have resonated within the context of late ancient eschatological discourse.[19] Indeed, contrary to Baljon, who sought to find the meaning of this phrase through comparison with the Hebrew Bible and Arabic poetry, without much success it bears noting, as we will see, the religious discourse of the Qur'an's broader cultural context offers the best hermeneutic resource for refining our understanding of the *amr allāh*.

In passages where *amr* is used with a clear eschatological valence, generally a translation designating "reign" or "dominion" is quite fitting, marking a reference to God's coming eschatological rule. Yet at the same time, even these English terms cannot fully convey the meaning of *amr*. Ultimately, we must understand something more akin to the biblical terms *basileia* or *malkūt* and their semantic ranges. This is particularly so with regard to the common qur'anic expression *amr allāh*, which in most instances is best rendered as the "reign" or "rule of God." Such a translation certainly suits the passages in question more sensibly than either "God's command" or "God's affair," which are at best both vague and awkward. For instance, in the Qur'an's first eschatological usage of *amr*, in sura 2:109, this reading yields, "Forgive and grant pardon until God brings his reign": this is much preferable, and more meaningful I believe, than the alternatives "until God brings his command" or "until God brings his affair." Sura 4:47 similarly

18. Baljon, "Amr of God," 9–11.
19. See Shoemaker, *Death of a Prophet*, 77; Shoemaker, "Reign of God"; Shoemaker, *Apocalypse of Empire*. See also Biberstein-Kazimirski, *Dictionnaire arabe-français*, 1:54; Steingass, *Arabic-English Dictionary*, 77; Lane and Lane-Poole, *Arabic-English Lexicon*, 1:96c.

invokes the coming reign of God as it warns its readers concerning the coming judgment. "O you who have been given the Scripture, believe in what We have sent down, confirming what is with you, before We obliterate faces and turn them on their backs or curse them as we cursed the men of the sabbath, and the reign of God will be fulfilled." In the next sura, the Qur'an warns the Believers against having any association with the Jews and Christians, noting that perhaps when "God brings his triumph and his reign, then they will come to regret what they have kept secret among themselves" (5:52). The eschatological *amr* of God appears three times in sura 9, firstly in a caution against associating with unbelieving family members, forewarning those who do to "wait until God brings his reign" (9:24), when they will bear the consequences. In similar vein, verse forty-eight rebukes those who failed to struggle on God's behalf, because they did not believe in God and the Last Day. These unbelievers, the Qur'an notes, had been stirring up discord in the community, "until the truth came and the reign of God was victorious." Finally, sura 9 later notes in regard to the final judgment that "there are others who are deferred to the reign of God, whether He punishes or relents toward them" (106).

In sura 10 the eschatological *amr* appears in a parable about rain. The resulting abundance of the earth convinces humankind that they are themselves in control of their circumstances, Nevertheless, this delusion will come to an end suddenly when "our reign comes on it by night or in the day-time; and we make it stumble as if it had not flourished yesterday. Thus we make the signs distinct for a people who reflect" (10:24). A similar yet peculiar usage occurs in 13:31, where the Qur'an seems to allude cryptically to some of the signs of the eschaton that it describes in other passages. "Perhaps a recitation by which the mountains were set in motion or the earth sundered or the dead caused to speak—No. God's reign is fulfilled." Sura 16 uses the term *amr* four times, perhaps most notably with its opening proclamation of the eschaton's arrival: "The reign of God has come; so do not seek to hasten it." The following verse then continues to describe the eschaton, as God "sends down the angels with the spirit from his dominion, upon those of his servants that he wishes." According to verse twelve, "he has subjected night and day and the sun and moon to your service, and the stars too are held subject to his sovereignty." A little later in the same sura, the Qur'an responds to those who have doubts about the eschaton's arrival: "Do they expect anything other than that the angels will come to them, or that the reign of your Lord is coming?" (16:33). Finally this sura warns again of the eschaton's proximity, declaring that "the reign of the hour is like the twinkling of an eye or nearer" (16:77).

God's eschatological *amr* also appears in the opening verses of sūra 30, *Sūrat al-Rūm*, the only predictive passage of the Qur'an and likewise a passage whose apocalyptic qualities have been long overlooked until quite recently.[20] According to canonical vocalization of this passage, the Qur'an here remarks that "the Greeks [Romans] been defeated in the nearest (part) of the land [the Holy Land]. But after their defeat, they will triumph in a few years. The reign [*amr*] of God is before and after, and on that Day [*wa-yawm a 'din*] the Believers will rejoice in the victory of God. The Promise of God!" The Qur'ān's concern here with Rome's imperial fortunes is rather interesting, particularly since the Believers are said to rejoice at Rome's victory. The historical circumstances, according to this vocalization, are seemingly Iran's invasion and occupation of the eastern Roman Empire, followed by Rome's triumph in 628. The traditional explanation for the Believers' apparent sympathy toward the Romans in this passage understands the conflict described here as a war between Iranian paganism and Byzantine monotheism. Since the Christians were, after all, a monotheistic "people of the book," the Qur'an here sympathizes with their triumph over paganism. Yet these same events were apocalyptically electric for both the Christians and Jews of Byzantium, and, one imagines, for the Iranians as well, particularly in light of the millennium's fast approaching end on the Zoroastrian calendar. Surely it is significant, then, that in its sole reference to contemporary world affairs, the Qur'an addresses the most eschatologically charged political events of the era, which it here aligns with the eschatological reign of God, the last day, and the promise of God. In such case, it would seem that, as Tommaso Tesei persuasively argues, here the Qur'an has absorbed some of the rhetoric of Roman imperial eschatology that had become prominent in the religious discourse of the late ancient Near East. Nor does the alternative vocalization of this passage pose any sort of hindrance to this interpretation.[21] The variant instead reads that "the Romans have conquered in the near part of the Land. But they, after their victory, will be conquered in a few years." Following this reading, we must conclude that Muhammad's followers adopted the imperial eschatological scripts of

20. My understanding of this passage owes much to the excellent recent article by Tommaso Tesei: "Romans Will Win."

21. As witnessed, for instance, by al-Tirmidhī, *al-Jāmiʿ al-Ṣaḥīḥ*, 5:no. 3192. See also the discussion of the vocalization and interpretation of this verse in El-Cheikh, "Sūrat al-Rūm."

late ancient Judaism, Christianity, and Zoroastrianism and applied them to their own conquests, so that their victory, rather than that of the Romans, would usher in the reign of God and the last day.

Other examples of the Qur'an's eschatological *amr* as the coming reign of God could be multiplied,[22] but we should also consider other uses of *amr* to see how well this interpretation of God's *amr* as "reign" or "dominion" holds in these contexts. Often the Qur'an identifies God's *amr* in conjunction with God's role as creator. Taking as our sample the relevant passages adduced by Baljon, one can see that in these instances such an understanding of the term seems quite appropriate. According to 10:3, "Your Lord is God, who created the heavens and the earth in six days, then set Himself on the Throne, governing [his] dominion," a phrase echoed in 10:31, where God is the one "who governs [his] dominion." In 7:54, the Lord similarly is named the creator of heaven and earth, so that "the sun and the moon and the stars are subject to his rule. His indeed is the creation and dominion." Likewise, according to 30:25, "the sky and earth stand fast because of His rule," and in 65:12, "God, who created seven heavens and of the earth their like, [his] reign descends among them." According to 32:5, "He governs [his] dominion from heaven to earth; then it ascends to him in a day, the measure of which is a thousand years." One suspects here that this "day" should evoke the last day.

Several qur'anic verses closely associate God's *amr* with "the spirit," as Baljon also notes, a point emphasized more recently by Gabriel Reynolds. Yet in these instances too, the understanding of God's *amr* as indicating "reign" or "dominion" again brings clarity. We have already considered the first of these, 16:2, where "God sends down the angels with the spirit from his dominion." According to 17:85, "They will ask you about the Spirit. Say, 'The spirit is from the dominion of the Lord.'" In 40:15, God "sends forth the Spirit from his dominion upon those of his servants whom he wishes, to warn of the Day of Meeting." Similarly, in 42:52, the Qur'an says "And thus we revealed to you [the] Spirit from our dominion." It was passages such as these, it would seem, that originally inspired the reading of *amr* as "Logos," imagined here as a requisite counterpart to the Spirit, to make, as it were, as a kind of qur'anic Trinity. Nevertheless, in each instance "dominion" or "realm" affords a much better and consistent—and less Christianizing—translation. Even in recounting the stories of the biblical Patriarchs, such as Noah and Abraham, the Qur'an's mention of God's *amr* suits the meaning

22. E.g., 40:78; 45:17–18; 47:21; 57:14; 82:19.

of "reign" or "dominion," For instance, Noah warns his son of the coming flood, telling him that "today there is no protector from the reign of God" (11:43). As for Abraham, the Angels ask him, "Do you wonder at God's reign? . . . Your Lord's reign has come" (11:73, 76). Moses, for his part, rebukes the Israelites when they built the golden calf, worrying that by their actions they may "have hastened the reign of [the] Lord" (7:150). Even the wicked Iblis "committed ungodliness against the rule of the Lord" (18:51).

It bears noting that the Qur'an also speaks regularly of God's eschatological kingdom, in a manner corresponding to similar language in early Judaism and Christianity. Fred Donner, in his recent study *Muhammad and the Believers*, concludes that much of the Qur'an's eschatology points toward "a program aimed at establishing 'God's kingdom on Earth,' that is, a political order (or at least a society) informed by the pious precepts enjoined by the Qur'an and one that should supplant the sinful political order of the Byzantines and Sasanians."[23] As Donner rightly notes, however, the Qur'an never uses the *exact* phrase "kingdom of God." I more than suspect that this is in large part because it uses instead the near equivalent term "reign of God." Yet at the same time, Donner's remark is not entirely accurate. On at least five occasions, the Qur'an refers to God's kingdom (*al-malakūt*), and in each instance the context is unmistakably eschatological. These passages certainly must be read alongside of the references to God's *amr* as indicators of his coming eschatological dominion. For instance, 6:73 describes God as "He who created the heavens and the earth in truth. On the day he says 'Be,' it is. His word is the truth. And his is the kingdom on the Day when the trumpet is blown." Likewise, 22:56 remarks that "The kingdom on that Day is God's. He will judge between them. Those who believe and do righteous deeds will be in the Gardens of Bliss." According to 25:25–26, "On the Day when the heaven is split asunder by clouds and the angels are sent down—on that Day the kingdom will be the Merciful one's, and it will be a hard day for the unbelievers." 40:16 warns readers concerning "the Day when they come forth, with nothing about them being concealed from God. 'Whose is the kingdom today?' It is God's the One, the Mighty." Finally, 54:50–55 seems to combine the two notions of God's reign and kingship. Here God's eschatological reign coincides with the dwelling of the righteous in God's kingdom: "Our reign is singular, like a flash to the eye. . .Everything they did is in the scrolls. Everything little and great

---

23. Donner, *Muhammad and the Believers*, 85.

is recorded. Those who are god-fearing [will dwell] among gardens and a river in a sure abode in the presence of the Mighty King."

Finally, one must consider the prominence that imperial eschatology, that is, the eschaton's arrival through the triumph of a divinely favored empire, held in the religious cultures of the late ancient Near East that gave birth to the Qur'an. The Jews, Christians, and Zoroastrians of late antiquity alike were expecting the eschaton's imminent advent, which they imagined would be fulfilled through their own imperial triumph. In Byzantium, the sixth century opened to widespread expectations that the world was nearing an end, since the year 500, according to contemporary calculations, marked the beginning of the seventh millennium since the creation of the world. The end of course did not arrive, but its delay did little to deflate eschatological anticipations, which remained strong, it would seem, throughout the sixth century and into the seventh. Numerous sources of various genres and from various places indicate that Christians of the sixth century were expecting to witness the end very soon. These eschatological expectations reached their peak, however, in the early seventh century, just at the moment that Muhammad's new religious movement was coming into its own. The tumult of the last Roman-Persian war stoked eschatological hopes across the Near East, and for the Christians, Heraclius's crushing defeat of the Persians and his restoration of the True Cross to Jerusalem intensified convictions that the end of the world was at hand. The literature of this era speaks with newfound urgency about the eschaton's near approach, and one of the most significant such texts, the *Syriac Alexander Legend*, was the source of the Qur'ān's traditions about Alexander the Great. From this borrowing we may conclude that Muhammad and his followers had direct contact with this vibrant and contemporary Byzantine eschatological tradition.[24]

The Jews and Zoroastrians of late antiquity, for their part, shared in the eschatological enthusiasm of the age. Messianic expectations rose sharply among the Jews of Palestine during the early seventh century, largely in reaction to Persia's "liberation" of Jerusalem and the holy land from the Romans and perhaps even a temporary revival of Jewish autonomy. As with the Christians of Byzantium, imminent eschatological expectations were both prominent and powerful within contemporary Judaism. Eschatological expectations were also running high in the Sasanian Empire during the late sixth and early seventh centuries: according to the Zoroastrian

---

24. See Shoemaker, *Apocalypse of Empire*, 64–89.

calendar, the millennium of Zoroaster would come to an apocalyptic end at the middle of the seventh century. Moreover, Jews, Christians, and Zoroastrians of this age all shared the belief that the ultimate triumph of an earthly empire would play an essential role in bringing about the consummation of the ages. For over a century before the rise of Islam the Byzantine Christians had been expecting the impending end of the world, and they believed that this would be achieved through the triumph and expansion of the Christian Roman Empire. During the years in which Muhammad was active in founding his new religious movement, these beliefs had only intensified, reaching their peak, it would seem, during the reign of Heraclius. The same is equally true of Judaism in this age, which saw in the dramatic victories of the Iranian, Roman, and, finally, Arab empires evidence that the Messiah would soon appear to restore the kingdom of Israel. In Iran, with the date of the millennium's close just decades away, it was certain that the Sasanian empire's revival and global hegemony would commence at any moment. And Bahrām VI Čōbīn's brief messianic reign at the end of the sixth century and Iran's conquest and occupation of the Roman Near East under Khosrow II in the early seventh undoubtedly fueled expectations that the Iranian Empire was in the process of fulfilling its eschatological destiny. Thus, the urgent eschatology of the Qur'an clearly shares in this broader trajectory of religious culture in the late ancient Near East.[25]

The political or imperial qualities of these contemporary eschatological expectations are vital for understanding the eschatology of the Qur'an and its early community, and especially, I would argue, for understanding the meaning of God's eschatological *amr*. Among the Jews, Christians, and Zoroastrians of the age there were widespread expectations that through the political triumph of their respective tradition, God's sovereignty would soon be restored in the world at the eschaton. In Christian parlance, this would be the fulfillment of the "reign of God," while Jewish eschatological hopes eagerly awaited the arrival of God's eschatological sovereignty in the messiah's reestablishment of the divinely chosen kingdom of Israel. This cultural-linguistic context should certainly guide our understanding of the Qur'an's proclamation of the arrival of God's *amr*. And unquestionably, regardless of what its author(s) may have originally meant by the term, once the Qur'an entered into the sectarian milieu of the late ancient Near East, the eschatological *amr allāh* could hardly have avoided identification with the coming reign of God, particularly in conversations with Jews and

---

25. See Shoemaker, *Apocalypse of Empire*, 90–115.

Christians. To this we should add the fact that after the death of Muhammad, the Qur'an's community was led by a ruler with the title *amir al-mu'minin*, the "commander" or "ruler of the believers." Such usage clearly signals that for the early Believers, the root *'-m-r* was associated with political power, and accordingly, God's *amr* was being fulfilled in the success of their divine chosen polity, under the leadership of their *amir*. The Qur'an, then, and the empire that it inspired afford what amounts to a remarkable instantiation of the political eschatology that we find expressed elsewhere in Jewish, Christian, and Zoroastrian writings of this era.

5

Qur'anic Eschatology in Its Biblical and Late Ancient Matrix

THERE CAN BE LITTLE doubt, as I have now argued on numerous occasions, that Muhammad was, like Jesus before him, an eschatological prophet.[1] Although we know almost nothing with any certainty about the historical Muhammad—even less than we know about the historical Jesus, the one thing that we may conclude about Muhammad with a high degree of confidence is that, like Jesus, he preached the impending arrival of the eschaton to his followers, an event which Muhammad seems to have expected even in his own lifetime. We of course do not have any writings by Muhammad, and accordingly the only basis that we have for reconstructing his religious teaching is the Qur'an, a text whose relationship with the historical Muhammad is much more complicated than many scholars, including most specialists on the Qur'an, have been ready to admit.[2] Nevertheless, the Qur'an remains the only literary document to survive from the first century of Islam's history, and even if it is by no means a verbatim transcript of what Muhammad taught, as many scholars astonishingly insist, it seems safe to assume that it represents Muhammad's teaching as it was remembered by

---

1. In addition to the first chapter in this volume, see also Shoemaker, *Death of a Prophet*, 118–96; Shoemaker, "Muḥammad and the Qur'ān"; Shoemaker, "Reign of God has Come."

2. Again, see chapter one and also Shoemaker, *Death of a Prophet*, e.g., 2, 73–74, 118–19, 125–26, 139–43; Shoemaker, "Muḥammad and the Qur'ān," 1084–87; Shoemaker, *Creating the Qur'an*, 167–68.

his earliest followers over the course of the second half of the seventh century. And judging from the Qur'an, it is abundantly clear that Muhammad and his earliest followers held an eschatological worldview whose contours ultimately derive almost entirely from the Jewish and Christian biblical traditions.

According to the Islamic tradition, Muhammad did not write down the Qur'an, but its traditions circulated orally for decades after his death. At some point during the seventh century, these traditions were collected into a single volume and given a standard text that would henceforth be a new scripture for Muhammad's followers. Although most scholars of Islamic studies have accepted with confidence the Islamic tradition's account of the Qur'an's canonization under the Caliph Uthman (644–56), for the most part this simply reflects an uncritical acceptance of the received tradition. The Sunni tradition itself, for instance, transmits no fewer than a dozen alternative traditions regarding the Qur'an's canonization, while the Shi'i tradition remembers these events quite differently. Despite the all too comfortable scholarly consensus in accepting the traditional Sunni narrative of the Qur'an's canonization, careful historical-critical analysis of the data favors instead a date for its canonization under the Caliph Abd al-Malik (685–705).[3] An interval of six decades or even only two between the end of Muhammad's life and the final redaction of the Qur'an certainly invites the possibility that a number of its traditions may have been altered or even introduced during the course of transmission, a question that remains insufficiently explored in the current state of scholarship on the Qur'an's formation. Most specialists on early Islam and the Qur'an are unyielding in their insistence that the words of the Qur'an should be identified with Muhammad's preaching in Mecca and Medina, as if the text were simply a transcript of what Muhammad said. Whenever any sort of defense for this implausible assumption is offered, these scholars almost always appeal to the remarkable capacity of preliterate peoples and the Arabs especially to remember and transmit oral teaching with incredible accuracy. Nevertheless, studies of memory over the last century and a half have demonstrated again and again that this is not true. Our memories are surprisingly inaccurate, particularly in the absence of any written record. Generally oral cultures are effective at preserving the bare bones "gist" of a memory over

---

3. See Shoemaker, *Creating the Qur'an*. Also de Prémare, *Aux origenes du Coran*; Robinson, *'Abd al-Malik*.

time, but in the context of oral transmission the content begins to be radically altered from the very start.[4]

Since we remember the past solely for the sake of understanding the present, as these memories are transmitted, they are quickly reshaped according to the present concerns of those transmitting them. Thus, as specialists on orality and memory have demonstrated time and again, oral transmission is not the rote transmission of a literary artifact from the past but is instead a constant process of recomposition of earlier traditions that usually is successful in preserving the gist. This is no less true of preliterate cultures than literate ones. Accordingly, we must radically reorient our understanding of the Qur'an and its formation. No longer can we naively imagine the text as a record of words directly from Muhammad's lips faithfully and perfectly remembered by his followers over decades. Instead, we must understand the Qur'an as a text that was composed and recomposed in the process of its transmission alongside the various other religious cultures of western Asia in the seventh century. The Qur'an, then, is not a transcript of Muhammad's teachings in Mecca and Medina, but rather a sacred text preserving the gist of his message, which formed in dialogue with the traditions of Judaism and Christianity and other religious groups in the "sectarian milieu" of the late ancient Near East.

Still less explored, but certainly no less important, is the possibility that certain parts, indeed possibly a significant amount, of the qur'anic text may predate Muhammad. Such incorporation of older written material is suggested by a number of qualities about the Qur'an itself, including its frequent near unintelligibility. The earliest Islamic interpretive tradition is often completely out to sea in trying to determine the meaning of certain passages, and in many cases these early scholars are uncertain about how to vocalize the text. Needless to say, this is not compatible with the Islamic tradition's account of a purely oral transmission from the start and the codification of this tradition within mere decades of Muhammad's death. The easiest explanation is that at least parts of the Qur'an were transmitted initially in purely written form, with the text's vocalization unknown. Quite possibly, these sections of the Qur'an derive from older, written documents whose contents were revered by Muhammad and his earliest followers, but whose vocalization and meaning were not entirely clear to members of the

---

4. Shoemaker, *Creating the Qur'an*, 171–203.

early community after his passing, and perhaps may have been unclear even to Muhammad himself.[5]

Nevertheless, if we proceed from the previously stated assumption that the Qur'an is our best witness to Muhammad's religious beliefs and reflects his teachings as they were remembered and transmitted by his followers over the course of the seventh century, we may take some confidence that Muhammad and his earliest followers had an apocalyptic worldview and were expecting the eschaton's arrival within their own lifetime. The logic that leads us to this conclusion is essentially identical to the basic arguments laid forth by Albert Schweitzer with respect to Jesus. Indeed, if we apply the same questions and methods to the beginnings of Islam that we have to Christian origins, we find then that Muhammad too was an apocalyptic prophet who believed himself to have been living in the last days. Like the Christian Gospels, the earliest narratives of Islamic origins have been heavily influenced by the theological interests of the later community, inviting the conclusion, as John Wansbrough proposed, that all "historical" knowledge of Muhammad and the origins of Islam has been lost, obscured by the imagination of medieval Islam. Alternatively, however, one may adopt a position, following Schweitzer, of "thoroughgoing eschatology" in regard to Muhammad and the Qur'an, which reveals a historically probable Muhammad, who, like Jesus, was an eschatological prophet of the end times.[6]

The Eschaton's Arrival in the Qur'an

The Qur'ān is simply rife with eschatology and urgent eschatology in particular. As scholars have largely come to agree with regard to similar traditions attributed to Jesus, it is unlikely that the Qur'an's confident forecasts that end of the world as imminent were invented and attributed to Muhammad by his later followers, since soon after his death they would have become patently false, making him appear to be, as it were, wrong. Thus, it would only make sense for Muhammad's followers to transmit such traditions if in fact he had actually taught the eschaton's near approach. The later fabrication of such traditions seems by comparison highly improbable, while the

---

5. See Shoemaker, *Creating the Qur'an*, 234–38; Shoemaker, "You Pass by Them."

6. See, again, the first chapter in this volume, see also Shoemaker, *Death of a Prophet*, 118–96; Shoemaker, "Muḥammad and the Qur'ān"; Shoemaker, "Reign of God has Come."

preservation of such material against the interests of the later tradition suggests that it preserves a credible approximation of the *ipsissima vox Machometi*. While such an image of Muhammad will perhaps be of little relevance for modern believers, much like Schweitzer's Jesus, it nevertheless presents an historically plausible reconstruction worthy of standing alongside of the historical Jesus, having been recovered using comparable methods.

Turning then to the Qur'an's apocalyptic worldview and its biblical sources, we should note firstly that the Qur'an knows many names for the eschaton. Among the most frequent is "the Hour" (*al-sāʿa*; e.g., 16:77; 54:1), which occurs some fifty times. Also common is "the Day" (*al-yawm*; e.g., 21:104; 22:2), which appears dozens of times throughout the Qur'an, often further qualified as "the Day of Judgment" (*al-yawm al-dīn*; e.g., 1:4; 56:56), "the Last Day" (*al-yawm al-ākhir*; e.g., 60:6), "the Day of Decision" (*al-yawm al-furqān* or *al-yawm al-faṣl*; e.g., 8:41; 77:38),[7] or simply "that Day" (*wa-yawm aʾḍin*), among many other possible combinations. Nevertheless, one of the most frequent, and also least understood, terms that the Qur'an uses for the eschaton is *amr*, a word appearing a little over one hundred and fifty times throughout the Qur'an. Of course, the word *amr* can mean several different things, and its use in the Qur'an certainly is not always eschatological.[8] At the same time one should note that the eschatological usage of *amr* is prevalent, occurring some twenty times in reference to the eschaton, as well as to the related concept of God's reign, often with the more specific designation of the *amr allāh*, the "*amr* of God." Yet despite such frequent eschatological usage, *amr* remains, as David Cook notes, "probably the most difficult of all the apocalyptic vocabulary to translate."[9]

Most frequently, *amr* is translated in these eschatological contexts as "the command" or occasionally even more ungainly as "the affair," neither of which captures the meaning of the word satisfactorily. Indeed, in most such cases the resulting translation is quite awkward and only makes sense when, by the very awkwardness itself, one recognizes that "command" or "affair" effectively represents a qur'anic technical term for the eschaton for which interpreters have not found an adequate translation. This approach yields such translations as "God's command comes; so seek not to hasten

7. Or possibly "the Day of Salvation" if one follows Donner's reading of *furqān* from the Syriac *purqānā*: Donner, "Quranic *Furqān*."

8. Baljon, "Amr of God," 8.

9. Cook, *Studies in Muslim Apocalyptic*, 271–72, where the frequency of these terms is also noted. See also Hasson, "Last Judgment," which oddly fails to mention the term *amr* at all.

it" (16:1 Arberry), or "The affair of Allah has come, seek not to hasten it" (Bell).[10] Although these translations are technically correct, they certainly do not make much sense in English. Cook proposes understanding the term as indicating "the direct rule or regime of God," often with reference to a dispensation or period of revelation. Indeed, the translation of 16:1 as "The reign of God has come, do not seek to hasten it" communicates the eschatological urgency of this pronouncement in English much more clearly. With this interpretation, we come very close, I think, to the meaning of God's eschatological *amr* as appears in the Qur'an.[11] In passages where *amr* is used with a clear eschatological valence, generally a translation designating "reign" or "dominion" is quite fitting, marking a reference to God's coming eschatological rule. Yet at the same time, even these English terms cannot fully convey the meaning of *amr*. Ultimately, we must understand something more akin to the biblical terms *basileia* or *malkūt* and their semantic ranges.

In this regard, one should also note that the Qur'an regularly speaks of God's eschatological kingdom, in a manner corresponding to similar language in early Judaism and Christianity, a point that has been occasionally overlooked. Fred Donner, in his recent study *Muhammad and the Believers*, concludes that much of the Qur'an's eschatology points toward "a program aimed at establishing 'God's kingdom on Earth,' that is, a political order (or at least a society) informed by the pious precepts enjoined by the Qur'an and one that should supplant the sinful political order of the Byzantines and Sasanians."[12] As Donner rightly notes, however, the Qur'an never uses the precise phrase "kingdom of God." I more than suspect that this is in large part because it uses instead the near equivalent term "reign of God." Yet at the same time, Donner's remark is not entirely accurate. On at least five occasions, the Qur'an refers to God's kingdom (*al-malakūt*), and in each instance the context is unmistakably eschatological. These passages certainly must be read alongside of the references to God's *amr* as indicators of his coming eschatological dominion. For instance, 6:73 describes God as "He who created the heavens and the earth in truth. On the day he says 'Be,' it is. His word is the truth. And his is the kingdom on the Day when the trumpet is blown." Likewise, 22:56 remarks that "The kingdom on that Day is God's. He will judge between them. Those who believe and do righteous deeds

---

10. For *amr* as affair, see also Rubin, "Prophets and Prophethood," 292–93.
11. Cook, *Studies in Muslim Apocalyptic*, 272; see also the preceding chapter.
12. Donner, *Muhammad and the Believers*, 85.

will be in the Gardens of Bliss." According to 25:25–26, "On the Day when the heaven is split asunder by clouds and the angels are sent down—on that Day the kingdom will be the Merciful one's, and it will be a hard day for the unbelievers." 40:16 warns readers concerning "the Day when they come forth, with nothing about them being concealed from God. 'Whose is the kingdom today?' It is God's the One, the Mighty." Finally, 54:50–55 seems to combine the two notions of God reign and kingship. Here God's eschatological reign coincides with the dwelling of the righteous in God's kingdom: "Our reign is singular, like a flash to the eye. . .Everything they did is in the scrolls. Everything little and great is recorded. Those who are god-fearing [will dwell] among gardens and a river in a sure abode in the presence of the Mighty King."

The arrival of the reign of God—or the Hour or the last day—is announced by the appearance of a number of signs, according to the Qur'an. Indeed, the Qur'an asks whether the unbelievers are "waiting for everything except the Hour, so that it will come upon them suddenly," boldly warning its audience that "Its portents have already come!" (47:18). According to the Qur'an, then, the signs of the eschaton had already begun to appear among its audience, a sure sign that we are dealing with a text and a community that were expecting the imminent end of history and the arrival of the divine judgment. Among the Hour's signs are celestial events: the sun will be darkened, as will the moon and stars; the stars will be thrown down and the sky stripped away (75:8; 77:8; 81:1–2, 11; 82:1–2). The sky will be "split asunder by clouds" and will be "rolled up" like a scroll; it will "turn crimson like red leather" and "be like molten copper" (21:104; 39:67; 25:25; 55:37; 70:8; 73:18). The sky also "will bring a visible smoke which will envelop the people" (44:10–11; 55:35?) Likewise, the moon will be split at the Hour's arrival, an event that, according to the Qur'an, had in fact already taken place: "The Hour has drawn near—the moon has been split" (54:1). Quite possibly, this passage refers to the recent experience of a lunar eclipse by members of the Qur'an's community.[13] On earth, the Hour's tokens include earthquakes, in which mountains will be moved—they will

---

13. Cook, "Messianism and Astronomical Events"; Rubin, "Muḥammad's Message," 43–44. See also Cook, *Studies in Muslim Apocalyptic*, 273, esp. n7; Cook, "Muslim Materials on Comets and Meteorites," 134–35; Aḥmad, "Did Muḥammad Observe the Canterbury Meteor Swarm?"; Aḥmad, "Dawn Sky on Laylat al-Qadr"; Rada and Stephenson, "Catalogue of Meteor Showers in Medieval Arab Chronicles," 9–10. Nevertheless, as Cook rightly observes, many of these studies place a little too much confidence in the traditional Islamic accounts of the beginnings of Muhammad's revelations.

be "flattened and become scattered dust," "like tufts of wool," leaving the earth "an empty plain" (20:106; 52:10; 56:4–6; 70:9; 79:7; 81:3; 99:1). The "earthquake of the Hour" will cause "every nursing mother to neglect the child she is suckling, and every pregnant woman will deliver her burden" (22:2). The seas will be made to boil and will pour forth (81:6; 82:3). Camels ten-months pregnant will be unattended, and the wild beasts will be driven together (81:4–5) As Jane Smith notes, in many regards this scheme reflects "a reverse process of creation."[14]

In addition to describing these signs, some of which have already appeared, the Qur'an maintains that the day of judgment is "the Imminent" (40:18), or, as stated elsewhere even more forcefully, "the Imminent is imminent" (53:57). The chastisement is near (78:40), and the Qur'an promises that the punishments of hell and the bliss of paradise will be known soon "with the eye of certainty," that is, at first hand (102:7). Thus, Qur'an rebukes those who disregard its warning, threatening that they will soon behold the Hour and its punishments with their own eyes (19:75). A number of other qur'ānic passages respond to disbelief concerning the Hour and its imminent appearance among its opponents, which seems to indicate that the Qur'an's message was indeed perceived by others in its religious milieu as a proclamation of the coming eschaton. When some question the Hour's impending arrival, the Qur'an warns, "soon they shall know. Our Word has already gone before to Our servants . . . So withdraw from them for a time, and watch them; soon they shall see! Is it to Our punishment that they seek to hasten?" (37:170–79). Others wanting to persist in their sinful ways ask, "When will the day of Resurrection be?" (75:6), to which the Qur'ān responds, the day of judgment is "nearer to you and nearer. Then nearer to you and nearer!" (75:34–35), warning elsewhere, "No indeed; soon they will know! Again, no indeed; soon will know!" (78:4–5). When the Hour comes, "on the day they see it, it will be as if they have tarried only for an evening or its forenoon" (79:46): "let them eat and enjoy themselves and be diverted by hope. Soon they will know." (15:3). In the face of such disbelief, the Qur'ān counsels the faithful regarding the Hour, "be thou patient with a fair patience. They think it is far away; but we see it near" (70:5–7). And so the Hour will come suddenly upon the unbelievers and "take them whilst they are disputing" (36:49). Several other passages suggest that the eschaton will arrive before the qur'anic messenger's death (10:46; 13:40; 23:93–95; 40:77; 43:41), and as I have argued elsewhere, it appears that Muhammad's

---

14. Smith, "Eschatology," 47.

earliest followers in fact believed that he would not die before the Hour's arrival.[15]

Of course, according to the Qur'an, the Hour had still not arrived, even if its portents have and the eschaton itself appears to be looming just over the horizon. The precise moment of its advent remains unknown, as the Qur'an notes on several occasions: while God has already determined the time of its arrival (11:106), God alone knows when this will occur (7:187; 31:34; 41:47; 43:85). Yet despite these moments of agnosticism, the Qur'an expresses confidence that the Hour has drawn quite near even in these very same passages. Although "the knowledge is only with God," says the Qur'an, "you will soon know who is in manifest error" (67:26–29; 79:44–46). Although the Hour is imminent, the Qur'an reminds its readers that a day for God is one thousand years (22:47; cf. 32:5), or fifty thousand years according to an alternative calculus (70:4). With the acknowledgement of this chronometric difference, these very same passages nonetheless underscore the Hour's impending arrival as something threateningly close: "they think that it is far away; we think it near" (70:6–7; cf. 22:55). There are, however, handful of qur'anic passages that express slight hesitance concerning Hour's proximity, softening its immediacy by introducing a note of uncertainty even as they maintain a strong sense of the Hour's imminence. One such verse says, "Perhaps it is near," although when it comes "you will think you have tarried but little" (17:51–52). "Perhaps some of that which you seek to hasten is already close behind you" (27:72). Elsewhere the Qur'an warns that while God alone knows when the Hour will descend, "Perhaps the Hour is nigh" (33:63; cf. 42:17). Finally, while these passages could seem to encourage continued conviction in the face of the eschaton's unanticipated delay (e.g., 11:8; 40:77), only twice does the Qur'an suggest the possibility that the Hour's arrival may not be imminent. Despite various warnings of the Hour's proximity throughout the Qur'an, only two passages prevaricate, remarking almost identically, "I do not know whether what you are promised is near or far" (21:109), and "I do not know whether what you are promised is near, or whether my Lord is setting a term for it" (72:25).

The Qur'an thus witnesses to a variety of ideas concerning the arrival of the eschaton, a quality that it shares, not insignificantly, with the Christian New Testament. According to the Qur'an, the eschatological reign of God has already arrived, while the Hour remains "Imminent." Nevertheless, the Hour's chronological distance is "the twinkling of an eye or nearer,"

---

15. Shoemaker, *Death of a Prophet*, esp. 178–88, 195–98.

and "its portents have already come." And even though the moment of its arrival is known to God alone, and a day for God is a thousand years, the Qur'an maintains that the Hour is very near. At the same time, we have noted, there are a few passages that express some hesitance with respect to the hour's immediacy, while a single repeated verse is equivocal. How can one make sense of these tensions within the Qur'an? Quite possibly this diversity of perspectives reflects the fact that the Qur'an is a composite document, and its contents reflect the work of multiple "authors" who were working in different contexts. At the same time, how are we to imagine that these eschatological traditions may have made sense to those who had aligned themselves with Muhammad's new religious movement in the seventh century?[16]

If we take seriously the proclamation in 16:1 that the reign of God has already arrived, then we must understand that the eschatological process has already been set in motion. Nevertheless, it is not yet complete, as the warnings of the Hour's imminent advent indicate. As I have explained elsewhere, I suspect that Muhammad and his followers understood the formation of their community of righteous Believers as itself having inaugurated the course of the eschaton and its arrival. The community of the Believers was beginning to realize the reign of God through the miraculous expansion of their divinely favored polity. Their successes would soon culminate in the Hour's arrival, and with it, the final judgment and the complete subjection of the universe to God's sovereignty or rule (*amr*). As for those

---

16. One recent interpretation of this dissonance has been offered by Mark Durie, in which he postulates Muhammad's initial conviction that the *eschaton* was imminent, followed by a crisis of personal faith when it did not arrive, which Muhammad resolved by deciding that the judgment of the Hour that he was proclaiming should be expected much later. Thus, the differences in the Qur'an reflect stages in the progression of Muhammad's faith. With this Durie proposes to have identified a chronology that does not depend on Muhammad's traditional biographies, and to be sure what he proposes is not unreasonable—indeed, it seems very much like the sort of narrative that Bell, Watt, Paret, and others have proposed before him (Shoemaker, *Death of a Prophet*, 127–33). Nevertheless, Durie's explanation remains nevertheless a biographical one: it finds coherence in the Qur'an's divergences by reading them through the biography of their supposed author, Muhammad. The only difference is that, in this instance, the biography of Muhammad is one invented by Durie and the read onto the text. I do not find such a reading persuasive: it reflects yet another version of Foucault's "author function," according to which a hermeneutic metanarrative is introduced via the biography of the imagined author to bring interpretive concord and closure to an otherwise disparate set of literary traditions (Shoemaker, *Death of a Prophet*, 163–64). Likewise, Durie's interpretation does not do justice, in my opinion, to the persistent and potent conviction that the Hour is threateningly near across the Qur'an. See Durie, *Qur'an*, 47–73.

passages signaling some note of uncertainty regarding the Hour's proximity, as I have argued before, I suspect that many these verses have been altered with very minor interpolations that partially qualify an original sense of eschatological urgency, a solution previously proposed also by Bell. By simply introducing a word or two near the beginning of the verse, once bold warnings of the Hour's immediacy could have easily been recast into more ambiguous statements to suit the reality of the Hour's abeyance.[17] As for the two truly equivocal passages, which are nearly identical, I strongly suspect that these are later interpolations, since they are so out of step with what the Qur'an has to say elsewhere about the Hour, intended to address the awkward circumstance of the Hour's unexpected delay.

It is worth noting, I would add, that with the exception of 33:63, all of these hesitating passages are from so-called Meccan suras. While I reject this chronological schema for the Qur'an's contents as an unproven set of assumptions drawn predominantly from the Islamic tradition, for those scholars who would embrace it, this point is worth considering. There has often been more willingness to accept a message of eschatological urgency during the supposed Meccan period, even among scholars who are reluctant to identify this as a defining element of earliest Islam.[18] Yet if these verses as they stand belong to the earliest period of Islam, then one should perhaps consider that those passages professing the eschaton's imminent arrival would possibly reflect a later intensification of imminent eschatological belief, rather than an artifact.

If we understand the Qur'an's view of the eschaton, then, as a process that had begun to unfold for its audience, we are also in a better position to understand the signs that will precede the final Hour. Clearly some of the Hour's portents had already been made manifest and had been witnessed by at least some of the Qur'an's audience, even as the Hour itself remained imminent. Yet according to the Qur'an there were additional signs of the Hour that had not yet revealed themselves. For instance, at the last day Gog and Magog will break forth from their confinement behind the Gates of Alexander (18:98–99; 21:96–97), an event that seemingly had not yet transpired. Likewise, as the final judgment descends, God will "bring forth from the earth a beast that will address them, 'Mankind was not convinced

---

17. Shoemaker, *Death of a Prophet*, 168. See also Bell, *Qurʾān*, 2:604.

18. E.g., Bell, *Origin of Islam*, 107; Buhl, *Das Leben Muhammeds*, 196–97; Buhl, *Muhammeds liv* (1998), 138–39; Bell and Watt, *Introduction to the Qurʾān*, 54, 158; Rodinson, *Mohammed*, 123.

by our signs'" (27:82). The ultimate sign, however, will be the blast of a great trumpet, which, as we have seen already above, will herald the arrival of the kingdom of God (6:73) and somehow coincide with the ravages of Gog and Magog (18:99). With it the earth and mountains will be lifted up and shattered (69:13–14), and the dead will be resurrected and assembled for the final judgment (20:102–4, 28:87, 74:8, 78:18). Indeed, one passage, but only one, indicates that there will in fact be two successive blasts of the eschatological trumpet before the hour: at the first blast, "all who are in the heavens and all who are on the earth will swoon, except for those whom God wishes. Then there will be a second blast, and behold, they will be standing, looking and waiting" (39:68). Closely related to the trumpet's blast, one imagines, is the Qur'an's mention of a loud "cry" or a "shout" that will similarly herald the eschaton's arrival (36:29; 38:15; 49:53; 50:42; 79:13).

Finally, the Qur'an expects Jesus to return just before the Hour, as one of its signs. Jesus is regularly named the Messiah in the Qur'an (e.g., 3:45; 4:157, 171–72; 5:17, 72, 75; 9:30–31), but the key passage for associating his return with the Hour's arrival is 43:57–61. According to the canonical vocalization, the final verse of this passage proclaims that the subject of the Qur'an's revelation is nothing less than "knowledge of the Hour; doubt not concerning it" (43:61), a reading that, in its own right, seems to indicate the imminent eschatology that prevailed among Muhammad's earliest followers. Yet according to an early alternative vocalization, the canonical form "knowledge (*'ilm*) of the Hour" should instead be read as "a sign (*'alam*) of the Hour." Since Jesus is the subject of the immediately preceding verses, by this reading he remains the subject of verse 61, so that he is identified as "a sign of the Hour; doubt not concerning it, and follow me." As Sean Anthony and Muhammad Ali Amir-Moezzi have both noted (among others), there is good reason to suspect that this alternative vocalization was in fact the primitive one.[19] This reading not only makes better sense of the passage, but it also comports with our understanding of the early development of the Islamic apocalyptic tradition. Indeed, elsewhere the Qur'an notes that Jesus will be present for the Final Judgment, when he will serve as a witness against the people of the Book (4:159).

This noncanonical reading's dissonance with the later Islamic tradition and its agreement with major tendencies identified by David Cook in

---

19. Anthony, "Muhammad," 248n13; Amir-Moezzi, "Muḥammad the Paraclete," 46–48. Cf. al-Khaṭīb, *Muʿjam al-qirāʾāt*, 8:392–93.

the early apocalyptic tradition also vouch for its antiquity. As Cook notes, the earliest Islamic apocalyptic traditions indicate that Jesus was indeed the first messianic figure in Islam. Otherwise it is difficult to explain, as he argues, why his return maintains such a prominent role in Islamic eschatology to this day, and likewise the great concern taken in the later tradition to diminish Jesus's eschatological role also seems to signal its antiquity.[20] Furthermore, certain reports about the faith of Muhammad's earliest followers from Jewish sources relate that the messiah's immediate advent was a central element of Muhammad's message.[21] Christ's return at the eschaton is also attested in a number of early *ḥadīth*, whose antiquity is highly probable, since it is unlikely that later Muslims would have successfully forged traditions so discordant with other orthodoxies of what eventually became "classical" Islam.[22] One would imagine, then, that the substitution of "knowledge" (*'ilm*) here for "a sign" (*'alam*) reflects a broader tendency in the later Islamic apocalyptic tradition that seeks to minimize the eschatological role of Jesus, whose return at the eschaton was expected by the Qur'an and the earliest community.

The Biblical Matrix of the Qur'an's Eschatology

The Qur'an's varied terminology for the eschaton is well attested in both the biblical and early Jewish and Christian traditions, and undoubtedly these were its sources. Variations on the use "Day" are very common in both prior Jewish and Christian tradition. "The Day of the Lord" is one of the most common expressions in the Hebrew Bible[23] for the eschaton (e.g., Isa 2:12; Amos 5:18; Joel 2:1), and not surprisingly, the expression also appears regularly in the New Testament (e.g., 1 Thess 5:2; 2 Cor 1:14; Acts 2:20; 2 Pet 3:10). Likewise, "the Last Day" or "Last Days" are frequent stand-ins for the eschaton, both in the Hebrew Bible (e.g., Isa 2:2; Hos 3:5; Mic 4:1;

---

20. Cook, *Studies in Muslim Apocalyptic*, 79, 170–73, 178, 202, 212–13, 323–24.

21. *Doctrina Iacobi* V.16 (Dagron and Déroche. "Juifs et chrétiens," 209–11); *Secrets of Rabbi Shimʿōn b. Yoḥai* (Jellinek, *Bet ha-midrash*, 3:78). See also Bashear, "Riding Beasts," and Crone and Cook, *Hagarism*, 3–6; and Shoemaker, *Prophet Has Appeared*, 22, 40–44, 141–43, 147–48, 179.

22. Amir-Moezzi, "Muḥammad the Paraclete," 31.

23. I would note that I use the term Hebrew Bible merely to avoid using the Christian terminology of Old Testament. In using this term I mean to include not only the collection of Jewish scripture, the Tanakh, but also the Christian collections of the Septuagint, Vulgate, and other Christian biblical canons.

Dan 8:19; 2 Esd 7:73, 84) and the New Testament (John 6:39-44; 12:48; Acts 2:17; 1 Tim 3:1; 1 Pet 1:5). "That day" also is frequent in the Hebrew Bible (Isa 2:11, 17; Jer 25:33; Ezek 38:14; Amos 8:9; Zech 12:3-4) and the New Testament (e.g., Matt 7:22; Mark 13:32; John 14:20; 1 Thess 5:4; 2 Tim 4:8). "Day of Judgment" also is very common in both collections (e.g., Prov 11:4; Amos 6:3; Esth 18:8; Hos 10:15; Isa 3:18; 2 Esd 7:43; Matt 12:36; John 12:48; 2 Tim 4:8; 2 Pet 2:9). "Day of Decision" seems to be limited to the Hebrew Bible (2 Esd 7:104; Esth 10:11; Wis 3:18), while "Hour," a common New Testament term (e.g., Matt 24:44; Mark 13:32; John 4:21, 23; 1 John 2:18; Rev 3:3; 14:7) also occurs in the Hebrew Bible, but less frequently (Esth 10:11; Sir 18:20).

Finally, the idea of God's eschatological "reign" or "dominion" or "the kingdom of God" is ubiquitous in the biblical tradition. Admittedly, such precise wording is not found in the Hebrew Bible, but the notion of God's eternal sovereignty certainly is (e.g., 1 Chr 29:11), while the book of Daniel, without using the exact phrase, has the eschatological reign of God as a constant theme (e.g., Dan 4:3). Moreover, the anticipated "messiah" of early Jewish apocalypticism was expected to be a divinely appointed king, whose function will be to restore God's sovereignty to the universe and whose appearance will coincide with the complete and final establishment of God's eternal reign. The term "messiah," which means anointed, reflects a distinctive Israelite practice of anointing kings, and the messiah is so called because as king he will be anointed.[24] Therefore, the messiah's appearance will coincide with the complete and final establishment of God's eternal reign. For this reason, the idea of God's eschatological reign becomes quite prominent in post-biblical Jewish apocalypticism, as seen, for example, in the importance of this eschatological concept in the literature from Qumran.[25] Likewise, Christian Judaism is defined from other sorts of Judaism by its identification of Jesus of Nazareth as the awaited messiah who has indeed come to establish the kingdom or reign of God.[26] Although subsequent Christian interpretation of this reign of God has varied significantly,

---

24. One of the best discussions of this topic remains Schürer et al., *History of the Jewish People*, 488-590.

25. E.g., Collins, *Apocalypticism in the Dead Sea Scrolls*, 71-109; Collins, *Scepter and the Star*.

26. In Greek, the relevant word is *basileia*, which means not only "kingdom," as it is usually translated from the New Testament, but equally "reign" or "dominion" or "sovereignty," and one will find these terms often used interchangeably with—or even instead of—kingdom in biblical scholarship.

in its earliest sense it was an eschatological term, and its realization in the life and ministry of Jesus was understood as inaugurating the end of the universe. Indeed, the imminent arrival of the eschatological reign of God seems to have been at the core of Jesus of Nazareth's teaching, as it was for John the Baptist before him.[27] The term accordingly appears dozens of times in the New Testament, and both the gospel writers and Paul regularly use it in reference to the impending eschaton (e.g., Mark 1:14–15; Acts 1:3; John 3:3–5; 1 Cor 15:50; Gal 5:21; 2 Thess 1:5).

Given the Qur'an's lexical debt to the biblical tradition with regard to its terminology for the eschaton, it is certainly no surprise to discover that its expected portents of the eschaton also derive from this same source.[28] In the Bible as in the Qur'an, signs in the heavens will herald the eschaton's arrival: the sun and moon will be darkened (Isa 13:10; Amos 8:9; Joel 2:31; Mark 13:24; Rev 6:12), and the stars will fall from the sky (Isa 13:10; Mark 13:25; Rev 6:13, 13:12). The heavens will be split open and rolled up (Isa 34:4, Heb 1:12, Rev 6:14), and they will melt (Ps 46:6, 2 Pet 3:10) and smoke (Joel 2:30, Acts 2:19). Likewise, there will be tremendous earthquakes (Isa 13:13, Ezek 38:19, Hag 2:20, 2 Esd 9:3, Mark 13:8, Rev 6:12, 11:13, 16:18) in which mountains will be leveled (Ezek 38:20, Mic 1:4, Nah 1:5, Rev 6:14, 16:20) and the oceans will dry up (Nah 1:4, Rev 16:12, 21:1). Likewise, Gog and Magog will break forth from the north and come against God's people (Ezek 38–39; Rev 20:7–10) and two beasts will come forth and speak to humankind, one from the sea (Rev 11:7; 13:1–10) and one from the earth (Rev 13:11–18). The eschaton's arrival will also be heralded by the sound of a trumpet (Isa 27:13; Joel 2:1; Zeph 1:16; Zech 9:14; 2 Esd 6:23; Matt 24:31; 1 Cor 15:52; 1 Thess 4:16; Rev 8:2) and also a great eschatological shout (Ps 46:6; Jer 25:30; Joel 3:16; Amos 1:2; Esth 11:5; 1 Thess 4:16; Rev 10:3; 14:18), sounds which are occasionally linked in the biblical tradition (1 Thes 4:16; Heb 12:19; Rev 1:10; 4:1). Finally, according to the Christian tradition, Christ will return to earth at the eschaton (Mark 8:38; Acts 1:11; 1 Thess 4:16). As one can see, then, all aspects of the Qur'an's conceptualization of the eschaton and the portents of its arrival have very strong precedents in the biblical tradition, from which they no doubt ultimately derive.

---

27. See, e.g., Weiss, *Die Predigt Jesu vom Reiche Gottes*; Kümmel, *Promise and Fulfilment*.

28. The biblical parallels to many of these signs as described in sura 81 are briefly noted in Cuypers, *Une apocalypse coranique*, 40–42.

The biblical traditions also provide precedent for the eschatological urgency of the Qur'an, as if that were somehow needed. As already noted, the eschaton's imminence is clearly evident in the New Testament, in the gospels as well as Paul. One need only compare, for instance, "the reign of God has come near" (Mark 1:15) or "the reign of God has come upon you" (Matt 12:28) with "the reign of God has come" (Q 16:1). On this basis, Michel Cuypers notes Muhammad's strong similarity to Jesus as prophet of the end times whose mission inaugurates the events of the eschaton.[29] There also examples from the Hebrew Bible as well: for instance, Haggai, which expects Zerubbabel to assume to the throne of David as Israel's messianic king, Joel, which understands a contemporary plague of locusts as a sign that the end would soon arrive, and Daniel, which envisions an eschatological triumph of the righteous just over the horizon. The New Testament also offers clear parallels to the Qur'an's occasional agnosticism regarding the eschaton's proximity. In fact, the gospel traditions show comparatively more vacillation regarding the eschaton's imminence than the Qur'an. In a number of passages the Gospels refer to the kingdom as something to be expected in the more distant future. Yet our understanding of the diversity of eschatological perspectives in the gospel traditions presents a well-honed and tested model for interpreting similar material in the Qur'an. In the Qur'an as in the Jesus traditions, one outlook clearly predominates: the preponderance of this evidence overwhelmingly speaks to belief in a cataclysmic eschatological event looming just on the horizon, presumably expected within the lifetime of Muhammad and his audience.[30] The lone qur'anic tradition that equivocates should be understood, as similar doubts in the Gospels, as an addition by the early Islamic community as it struggled to make sense of the eschaton's continued deferral.

Likewise, in the New Testament as in the Qur'an, the precise moment of the eschaton's arrival is something known to God alone. For instance, Jesus himself says "But about that day or hour no one knows, neither the angels in heaven, nor the Son, but only the Father" (Mark 13:32), and "It is not for you to know the times or periods that the Father has set by his own authority" (Acts 1:7). Similarly, the New Testament notes the vast difference between divine and human calculations of time, echoing the psalmist's remark that "that with the Lord one day is like a thousand years, and a thousand years are like one day" (2 Pet 3:8; cf. Ps 90:4). Yet

---

29. Cuypers, *Une apocalypse coranique*, 47–48.
30. Cf. Sanders, *Jesus and Judaism*, 152–53; Sanders, *Historical Figure of Jesus*, 176–77.

as with the comparable passages from the Qur'an, in the New Testament such sentiments are consistently joined with statements of the proximity of the eschaton, which "will come like a thief" (2 Pet 3:10).[31] In both cases, one imagines, that these uncertainties about the eschaton's precise timing have been introduced to explain why it did not arrive with the immediacy that was originally expected by members of the respective communities. Indeed, it is hard to comprehend why these musings about knowledge of the eschaton's timing would have been pertinent at all unless there were in fact some need to apologize for its unanticipated delay.

Finally, as in the Qur'an, the New Testament Gospels also witness to a tradition that the eschaton has already arrived. There is a minority tradition in which Jesus relates that the kingdom of God had already come upon his audience and was manifest particularly in his miraculous works (esp. Matt 12:28; Matt 11:2–6). Scholars agree that these sayings are almost certainly authentic, since it is difficult to identify a motive for their later invention, logic which applies in the case of the Qur'an as well. The only question is how to understand such proclamations that the eschaton had already arrived alongside a much stronger tradition expecting its advent in the near future. In the case of the New Testament, it seems that while Jesus preached that the eschaton was to be expected in the immediate future, at the same time he and his followers also seem to have believed that the beginning of the kingdom was already present in his teachings and miracles.[32] Something analogous is clearly at work in the Qur'an as well, which seems to understand the mission of its messenger and the formation of his community as events coterminous with and inaugurating the eschaton. In fact, one suspects that this sort of logic must be typical of most eschatological movements. If the eschaton is believed to be near, then certainly it must already be set on the course of its ultimate advent, so that its signs have begun to appear and the process of its birthing had begun, like a dawn that had broken with the sun still yet to rise.

31. On this point, see also Sinai, "Eschatological Kerygma," 237.

32. The first to propose this seems to have been Kümmel, *Promise and Fulfilment*, first published in 1945. More recently, see, e.g., Meier, *Marginal Jew*, 2:237–506, esp. 451–54, 1042–46; Dunn, *Jesus Remembered*, 466–67; Theissen and Merz, *Historical Jesus*, 252–78. Sanders allows that it is certainly possible that Jesus believed this about himself and his ministry, but he maintains that the evidence cannot establish it as probable: Sanders, *Jesus and Judaism*, 131–41; and Sanders, *Historical Figure of Jesus*, 175–78. Regarding the status of this view as reflecting the current consensus, see Theissen and Merz, *Historical Jesus*, 244; and Dunn, *Jesus Remembered*, 467.

One imagines, however, that it was not from the Bible directly that the Qur'an drew these on these biblical traditions; rather, it undoubtedly knew them instead through their espousal by contemporary Jews and Christians. These fundamental elements of the biblical eschatological tradition provided the subsequent foundation and the building materials for the structure of eschatological expectations in late ancient Judaism and Christianity. The Jewish and Christian apocalyptic scripts of this era persisted in anticipation of the "last day" or "hour" or the "reign of God," an event whose advent would be heralded by the various sorts of signs identified in the biblical writings: earthquakes, celestial wonders, the appearance of Gog and Magog, the blast of a trumpet, and an eschatological shout. At that time, according to Judaism, the Messiah would take command of God's eschatological kingdom, while in Christianity, the Messiah, Jesus, will return and establish the reign of God. Thus, it was primarily through Jewish and Christian reworking and transmission of these biblical traditions in apocryphal, theological, and other texts from late antiquity that Qur'an and its community would have encountered and assimilated biblical eschatology.

Qur'anic Eschatology in its Late Antique Matrix

In a recent article addressing the broader question of the Qur'an's eschatology, Nicolai Sinai has provided a number of examples from the Syriac tradition, more specifically from the writings of Ephrem and Jacob, demonstrating the persistence of these ideas into the fourth, fifth, and sixth centuries. There he notes similarly that "the Qur'anic texts are simply appropriating ideas that had much wider, and much more fluid, circulation in oral Christian sermons for which the Syriac homiletic corpus would have served as a blueprint."[33] Yet of course, these ideas were not limited to Syriac Christian culture in late antiquity, and accordingly we must avoid the pitfall of limiting our analysis of the Qur'an in relation to its broader religious milieu to Syriac sources. While there are obvious reasons for supposing that Syriac Christian culture would have been especially accessible to members of the Qur'an's early community, we should not look to Syriac alone in our effort to contextualize the Qur'an. Christian culture in the late ancient Near East was linguistically complex, and its various language traditions must not be treated as silos, as if one could study only one in isolation. Syriac Christianity in this era was not at all segregated from other cultural-linguistic

---

33. Sinai, "Eschatological Kerygma," 241.

traditions, and to comprehend fully the Qur'an's religious milieu, one must also simultaneously engage writings in Coptic, Armenian, Georgian, Ethiopic, Latin, and, above all, Greek. Indeed, in this time and place, the late ancient Near East, Greek held a position of privilege and esteem in relation to these other language traditions, and in the seventh century in particular, the Syriac tradition has been characterized as governed by "Hellenolatry."[34] Thus, when we compare the Qur'an's traditions with Syriac Christian culture, we have in fact only begun to situate its content in relation to late ancient Christianity, particularly given the fact that formative Islam took shape largely within the deeply Hellenized, multicultural context of late ancient Syro-Palestine.

Unfortunately, the present article does not afford an occasion to explore in detail the persistence of these eschatological memes in late ancient Judaism and Christianity, and likewise the study of apocalypticism in late antiquity remains relatively underdeveloped. Nevertheless, as one would only expect, these biblical foundations of eschatology continued to govern the discussion of these topics in Jewish and Christian literature, even if we are not able to demonstrate the extent here. Sinai's excellent study provides a sufficient sample to demonstrate that these ideas were not simply forgotten between the Bible and the Qur'an, but they remained active in directing Jewish and Christian eschatological expectations and their expression.[35] Nevertheless, in this same article, Sinai argues against understanding the Qur'an as the passive recipient of these biblical eschatological traditions, as a mere "echo chamber," maintaining that the Qur'an instead takes a "corrective stance" in its appropriation of the biblical traditions. In contrast to the Syriac homiletic literature, he notes, the Qur'an shows "the consistent elimination of the soteriological and eschatological function of Christ," no attachment of "any salvific significance to orthodoxy," and a failure to prescribe the observance of "Christian rituals such as baptism and the Eucharist."[36] It is true that the Qur'an lacks these elements, but at the same time, these are not eschatological matters but rather soteriological ones. Admittedly, then, these points evidence a clear difference between the soteriologies of the Qur'an and late ancient Christianity, but these topics

---

34. See, e.g., Johnson, *Languages and Cultures*, 1–8.

35. In this regard one can also consult, e.g., Shoemaker, *Apocalypse of Empire*; Daley, *Hope of the Early Church*; Olster, "Byzantine Apocalypses,"; Himmelfarb, *Jewish Messiahs*; Himmelfarb, "*Sefer Eliyyahu*,"; Sivertsev, *Judaism and Imperial Ideology*; Reeves, *Trajectories*.

36. Sinai, "Eschatological Kerygma," 221, 246–47.

are simply not relevant for gauging Qur'an's appropriation of eschatological traditions from the biblical tradition. There are many significant points where the Qur'an diverges from the orthodoxies of late ancient Christianity and may show more direct influence from Judaism, but these do not include its eschatology, which, as Sinai himself finally notes is, in fact, greatly if not wholly indebted to the biblical traditions.[37]

While Christ's soteriological role in Christianity is not exactly pertinent to an evaluation of qur'anic eschatology, the eschatological role of the Christ, or the messiah, is certainly worth considering. In a recent article, Mohammad-Ali Amir-Moezzi raises precisely this issue: if, as seems to be the case, the Qur'an has its roots in the traditions of Jewish and Christian monotheism, and it bears a message of the eschaton's impending arrival, why, then, does it not also proclaim the imminent coming of the messiah?[38] I would suggest that, in fact, it does, as discussed above, according to what was likely the original reading of Qur'an 43:61, which identifies the Son of Mary as "a sign of the Hour," presumably indicating his return at the eschaton's arrival. The Qur'an's identification of Jesus the son of Mary as the messiah or Christ is itself quite clear (3:45; 4:157, 171–72; 5:17, 72, 75; 9:30–31). Likewise, as already noted, certain reports about the faith of Muhammad's earliest followers from Jewish sources relate that the messiah's immediate advent was a central element of Muhammad's message.[39] Christ's return at the eschaton is also attested in a number of early *ḥadīth*, whose antiquity is highly probable, since it is unlikely that later Muslims would have successfully forged traditions so discordant with other orthodoxies of what eventually became "classical" Islam.[40] Indeed, as David Cook observes, Jesus was in all likelihood the first messianic figure in Islam, again, as we noted above. Otherwise, it is once again difficult to understand why his return occupies such a prominent role in Islamic eschatology to this day. The fact that the later tradition shows significant concern to diminish his eschatological role also seems signal the antiquity of this tradition.[41] Accordingly, it appears

---

37. Sinai, "Eschatological Kerygma," 247.

38. Amir-Moezzi, "Muḥammad the Paraclete," 44.

39. *Doctrina Iacobi* V.16 (Dagron and Déroche, "Juifs et chrétiens," 209–11); *Secrets of Rabbi Shimʿōn b. Yoḥai* (Jellinek, *Bet ha-midrash*, 3: 78). See also Bashear, "Riding Beasts," and Crone and Cook, *Hagarism*, 3–6.

40. Amir-Moezzi, "Muḥammad the Paraclete," 31.

41. Cook, *Studies in Muslim Apocalyptic*, 79, 170–73, 178, 202, 212–13, 323–24.

that expectation of Christ's return at the eschaton was likely proclaimed in the Qur'an and was a part of the primitive kerygma of its community's faith.

According to Sinai, who is one of the only scholars to have written recently on qur'anic eschatology and its antecedents, the Qur'an's eschatology is "moralistic rather than apocalyptic: the Qur'an exhibits no interest in speculating about the future course of history leading up until the end of the world or in reassuring a group of people who seem to be on the losing side of history that they are, in fact, on the winning side."[42] Apocalyptic is not, I think, the correct term here to modify eschatology, but one can distinguish in theory between historical eschatology or apocalypses and other eschatological pronouncements where the context is instead immediate and thus focused on warning the audience of the impending judgment and its consequences. The latter type is most common in the Qur'an, but the former is certainly not absent. Again as noted above, the Qur'an frequently signals the occurrence of various signs, some of which have already appeared, indicating the eschaton's steady approach. Moreover, the beginning of sura 30, as I understand it, looks to the recent conflicts between Rome and Iran as signs that the End has drawn near. To be sure, there is no grand historical narrative of the rise and fall of empires along the way to the eschaton, as in Daniel, for instance. But in this respect, the eschatology of the Qur'an resembles even more so that of the New Testament (excepting perhaps the Apocalypse), where the eschaton is expected imminently, and thus there is little point to lay out a lengthy course of future history to proceed the eschaton because, very little future history in fact remains. The Qurʾān relates eschatology in action, not in the future; the Hour was already arriving even as the community was forming. Furthermore, it is no surprise at all that the Qur'an does not offer reassurance to "a group of people who seem to be on the losing side of history," since this style of apocalyptic appears to have been characteristic of Judaism primarily during Hellenistic and Roman eras. In late antiquity and the medieval period, the apocalyptic tradition had significantly transformed to favor not the downtrodden but instead those who were victorious in earthly conflicts, as I have recently explained in another context.[43]

---

42. Sinai, "Eschatological Kerygma," 236. In this regard, Sinai's arguments are very beholden to those of Andræ, "Der Ursprung des Islams," and indeed, his article is built around extensive interaction with this important monograph from a century ago.

43. Shoemaker, *Apocalypse of Empire*.

The religious culture of the late ancient Near East in the sixth and early seventh centuries was in fact permeated by intense, imminent eschatological expectation. Not only, then, should we expect that this prominent feature of the Qur'an's larger cultural context would have had a significant influence on its content, but without question it would have determined how many hearers or readers understood the Qur'an's eschatological pronouncements. In Byzantium, the sixth century opened to widespread expectations that the world was nearing an end, since the year 500, according to contemporary calculations, marked the beginning of the seventh millennium since the creation of the world. The end of course did not arrive, but its delay did little to deflate eschatological anticipations, which remained strong, it would seem, throughout the sixth century and into the seventh. Numerous sources of various genres and from various places indicate that Christians of the sixth century were expecting to witness the End very soon. These eschatological expectations reached their peak, however, in the early seventh century, just at the moment that Muhammad's new religious movement was coming into its own. The tumult of the last Roman-Persian war stoked eschatological hopes across the Near East, and for the Christians, Heraclius's crushing defeat of the Persians and his restoration of the True Cross to Jerusalem intensified convictions that the end of the world was at hand. The literature of this era speaks with newfound urgency about the eschaton's near approach, and one of the most significant such texts, the *Syriac Alexander Legend*, was the source of the Qur'ān's traditions about Alexander the Great. From this borrowing we may conclude that Muhammad and his followers had direct contact with this vibrant and contemporary Byzantine eschatological tradition.[44]

The Jews and Zoroastrians of late antiquity, for their part, shared in the eschatological enthusiasm of the age. Messianic expectations rose sharply among the Jews of Palestine during the early seventh century, largely in reaction to Persia's "liberation" of Jerusalem and the holy land from the Romans and perhaps even a temporary revival of Jewish autonomy. As with the Christians of Byzantium, imminent eschatological expectations were both prominent and powerful within contemporary Judaism. Eschatological expectations were also running high in the Sasanian Empire during the late sixth and early seventh centuries: according to the Zoroastrian calendar, the millennium of Zoroaster would come to an apocalyptic end at the middle of the seventh century. Moreover, Jews, Christians, and

---

44. See Shoemaker, *Apocalypse of Empire*, 64–89.

Zoroastrians of this age all shared the belief that the ultimate triumph of an earthly empire would play an essential role in bringing about the consummation of the ages. For over a century before the rise of Islam the Byzantine Christians had been expecting the impending end of the world, and they believed that this would be achieved through the triumph and expansion of the Christian Roman Empire. During the years in which Muhammad was active in founding his new religious movement, these beliefs had only intensified, reaching their peak, it would seem, during the reign of Heraclius. The same is equally true of Judaism in this age, which saw in the dramatic victories of the Iranian, Roman, and, finally, Arab empires evidence that the Messiah would soon appear to restore the kingdom of Israel. In Iran, with the date of the millennium's close just decades away, it was certain that the Sasanian empire's revival and global hegemony would commence at any moment. And Bahrām VI Čōbīn's brief messianic reign at the end of the sixth century and Iran's conquest and occupation of the Roman Near East under Khosrow II in the early seventh undoubtedly fueled expectations that the Iranian Empire was in the process of fulfilling its eschatological destiny. Thus, the urgent eschatology of the Qur'an clearly shares in this broader trajectory of religious culture in the late ancient Near East.[45]

The political or imperial qualities of these contemporary eschatological expectations are vital for understanding the eschatology of the Qur'an and its early community, and especially, I would argue, for understanding the meaning of God's eschatological *amr*. Among the Jews, Christians, and Zoroastrians of the age there were widespread expectations that through the political triumph of their respective tradition, God's sovereignty would soon be restored in the world at the eschaton. In Christian parlance, this would be the fulfillment of the "reign of God," while Jewish eschatological hopes eagerly awaited the arrival of God's eschatological sovereignty in the messiah's reestablishment of the divinely chosen kingdom of Israel. This cultural-linguistic context should certainly guide our understanding of the Qur'an's proclamation of the arrival of God's *amr*. And unquestionably, regardless of what its author(s) may have originally meant by the term, once the Qur'an entered into the sectarian milieu of the late ancient Near East, the eschatological *amr allāh* could hardly have avoided identification with the coming reign of God, particularly in conversations with Jews and Christians. To this we should add the fact that after the death of Muhammad, the Qur'an's community was lead by a ruler with the title *amir al-muʾminin*,

---

45. See Shoemaker, *Apocalypse of Empire*, 90–115.

the "commander" or "ruler of the believers." Such usage clearly signals that for the early Believers, the root '-m-r was associated with political power, and accordingly, God's *amr* was being fulfilled in the success of their divine chosen polity, under the leadership of their *amir*. The Qur'an, then, and the empire that it inspired afford what amounts to a remarkable instantiation of the political eschatology that we find expressed elsewhere in Jewish, Christian, and Zoroastrian writings of this era.

In summary, then, the Qur'an's eschatology is highly derivative of the eschatological traditions of the Hebrew Bible and the New Testament, which it has undoubtedly inherited from late ancient Judaism and Christianity.[46] There is in fact almost nothing in qur'anic eschatology that does not find strong parallels in these antecedent traditions, and, accordingly, one must conclude that they were its sources for this material, again, as they were transmitted by the Christians and Jews of late antiquity. Only two minor points stand out as important exceptions. Firstly, in the Qur'an the Messiah does not serve as judge in the final judgment, as in the Christian tradition, but instead Christ's role according to the Qur'an will be to serve as a witness against (some of?) the people of the Book. Likewise, the qur'anic beast is significantly different from the beast of the Apocalypse of John. In contrast to this biblical beast, the Qur'an's beast not only speaks, but he also appears to serve God and works to persuade humankind to obey God, rather than to lead them into perdition.[47] Otherwise, the Qur'an's understanding of the eschaton's arrival appears to derive almost entirely from the biblical tradition.

---

46. So also concludes David Cook: Cook, "Qur'ān and Other Scriptures."

47. I thank Nicolai Sinai and Sean Anthony for drawing these two points to my attention.

Bibliography

Abgarian, Gevorg V., ed. Պատմութիւն Սեբէոսի *[Patmutʻiwn Sebeosi]*. Erevan: Haykakan SSH Gitutʻyunneri Akademiayi Hratarakchʻutʻyun, 1979.
Afsaruddin, Asma. *The First Muslims: History and Memory*. Oxford: Oneworld, 2008.
Aḥmad, ʻImad. "The Dawn Sky on Laylat al-Qadr." *Archaeoastronomy* 11 (1989–1993) 97–100.
———. "Did Muhammad Observe the Canterbury Meteor Swarm?" *Archaeoastronomy* 11 (1989–1993) 95–96.
Ali, Kecia. *The Lives of Muḥammad*. Cambridge: Harvard University Press, 2014.
Alter, Robert. *The Book of Psalms: A Translation with Commentary*. New York: Norton, 2007.
Ambros, Arne A., and Stephan Procházka. *A Concise Dictionary of Koranic Arabic*. Wiesbaden: Reichert, 2004.
Amir-Moezzi, Mohammad Ali. "Muḥammad the Paraclete and ʻAlī the Messiah: New Remarks on the Origins of Islam and of Shiʻite Imamology." *Der Islam* 95 (2018) 30–64.
Amir-Moezzi, Mohammad Ali, and Guillaume Dye, eds. *Le Coran des historiens*. 2 vols. Paris: Cerf, 2019.
Andræ, Tor. "Der Ursprung des Islams und das Christentum." *Kyrkohistorisk Årsskrift* 23 (1923) 149–206; 24 (1924) 213–92; 25 (1925) 45–112.
———. *Les origines de l'Islam et le Christianisme*. Translated by Jules Roche. Paris: Adrien-Maisonneuve, 1955.
———. *Mohammed, sein Leben und sein Glaube*. Göttingen: Vandenhoeck & Ruprecht, 1932.
———. *Mohammed: The Man and His Faith*. Translated by Theophil William Menzel. New York: Barnes & Noble, 1935.
al-Anṣārī, ʻAbd-ar-Raḥmān aṭ-Ṭaiyib, and Saʻd ʻAbd-al-ʻAzīz ar al-Rāshid. *Silsilat Āṯār al-Mamlaka al-ʻArabīya as-Saʻūdīya*. 13 vols. Riyad: Al-Mamlaka al-ʻArabīya as-Saʻūdīya, Wizārat al-Maʻārif, Wakālat al-Āṯār wa-ʼl-Matāḥif, 2003.
Anthony, Sean W. *Maʻmar ibn Rāshid: The Expeditions: An Early Biography of Muhammad*. Library of Arabic Literature. New York: New York University Press, 2014.
———. *Muhammad and the Empires of Faith*. Berkeley: University of California Press, 2020.
———. "Muhammad, the Keys to Paradise, and the Doctrina Iacobi: A Late Antique Puzzle." *Der Islam* 91 (2014) 243–65.

Bibliography

Armstrong, Karen. *Muhammad: A Biography of the Prophet.* New York: HarperSanFrancisco, 1993.

———. *Muhammad: A Prophet for Our Time.* Eminent Lives. London: Harper, 2006.

Aslan, Reza. *No God but God: The Origins, Evolution, and Future of Islam.* New York: Random House, 2005.

Ayoub, Mahmoud. *The Crisis of Muslim History: Religion and Politics in Early Islam.* Oxford: Oneworld, 2003.

Al-Azmeh, Aziz. "Islamic Origins for Neo-Conservatives." Self-published, 2020. https://www.academia.edu/43195797/ISLAMIC_ORIGINS_FOR_NEO_CONSERVATIVES.

Baird, William. *History of New Testament Research.* 3 vols. Minneapolis: Fortress, 1992, 2003, 2013.

Baljon, Johannes M. S. "The 'Amr of God' in the Koran." *Acta Orientalia* 23 (1959) 7–18.

Bashear, Suliman. "Abraham's Sacrifice of his Son and Related Issues." *Der Islam* 67 (1990) 243–77.

———. "Apocalyptic and other Materials on early Muslim-Byzantine Wars: A Review of Arabic Sources." *Journal of the Royal Asiatic Society* 1 (1991) 173–207.

———. Muslim Apocalypses and the Hour: A Case-Study in Traditional Reinterpretation." *Israel Oriental Studies* 13 (1993) 75–100.

———. "Qibla Musharriqa and Early Muslim Prayer in Churches." *Muslim World* 81 (1991) 267–82.

———. "Qur'ān 2:114 and Jerusalem." *Bulletin of the School of Oriental and African Studies* 52 (1989) 215–38.

———. "Riding Beasts on Divine Missions: An Examination of the Ass and Camel Traditions." *Journal of Semitic Studies* 37 (1991) 37–75.

———. "The Title 'Fārūq' and Its Association with 'Umar I." *Studia Islamica* 72 (1990) 47–70.

Beaucamp, Joëlle, and Christian Julien Robin. "Le christianisme dans la péninsule Arabique d'après l'épigraphie et l'archéologie." *Travaux et mémoires* 8 (1981) 45–61.

Beck, Daniel A. "Muḥammad's Night Journey in its Palestinian Context—a Perfect Solution to a Forgotten Problem (Q 17:1)." 2021. https://www.academia.edu/17318352/Mu%E1%B8%A5ammad_s_Night_Journey_in_its_Palestinian_Context_a_Perfect_Solution_to_a_Forgotten_Problem_Q_17_1_.

Becker, C. H. *Christianity and Islam.* New York: Harper, 1909.

———. "Der Islam als Problem." *Der Islam* 1 (1910) 1–21.

Bell, Richard. *The Origin of Islam in its Christian Environment.* London: Macmillan, 1926.

———. *The Qur'ān.* 2 vols. Edinburgh: T. & T. Clark, 1937–1939.

Bell, Richard, and W. Montgomery Watt. *Bell's Introduction to the Qur'ān.* Edinburgh: Edinburgh University Press, 1970.

Ben-Shammai, Haggai. "*Ṣuḥuf* in the Qur'ān—A Loan Translation for 'Apocalypses.'" In *Exchange and Transmission across Cultural Boundaries: Philosophy, Mysticism and Science in The Mediterranean World*, edited by Haggai Ben-Shammai et al., 1–15. Jerusalem: Israel Academy of Sciences and Humanities, 2013.

Benedict XVI. *Jesus of Nazareth: From the Baptism in the Jordan to the Transfiguration.* Translated by Adrian J. Walker. New York: Doubleday, 2007.

———. *Jesus of Nazareth: Holy Week: From the Entrance into Jerusalem to the Resurrection.* Translated by Philip J. Whitmore. San Francisco: Ignatius, 2011.

———. *Jesus of Nazareth: The Infancy Narratives*. Translated by Philip Whitmore. New York: Image, 2012.

Bergsträsser, Gotthelf, and Otto Pretzl. *Geschichte des Qorāns III: Geschichte des Qorāntexts*. 2nd ed. Leipzig: Dieterich, 1938.

Bertaina, David. "Rethinking Genre and the Qur'an: Question-and-Answer Literature." In *International Qur'ānic Studies Association Blog*, 2014.

Biberstein-Kazimirski, Albert de. *Dictionnaire arabe-français*. 2 vols. Paris: Maisonneuve, 1860.

Blachère, Régis. *Le problème de Mahomet: Essai de biographie critique du fondateur de l'Islam*. Paris: Presses universitaires de France, 1952.

Böhl, Franz Marius Theodor. *De Psalmen*. 3 vols. Tekst en uitleg. Groningen: Wolters, 1946.

Braude, William G. *The Midrash on Psalms*. 2 vols. Yale Judaica Series 13. New Haven: Yale University Press, 1959.

Brock, Sebastian P. "Syriac Views of Emergent Islam." In *Studies on the First Century of Islam*, edited by G. H. A. Juynboll, 9–21, 199–203. Carbondale: Southern Illinois University Press, 1982.

Brodtkorb, E., and K. O. Nakken. "The Relationship between Epilepsy and Religiosity Illustrated by the Story of the Visionary Mystic Wise-Knut." *Epilepsy and Behavior* 46 (2015) 99–102.

Brooks, E. W., et al., eds. *Chronica minora III*. 2 vols. Corpus Scriptorum Christianorum Orientalium 5–6, Scriptores Syri 5–6. Paris: Reipublicae, 1905.

Brown, Jonathan A. C. *Misquoting Muhammad: The Challenge and Choices of Interpreting the Prophet's Legacy*. London: Oneworld, 2014.

———. *Muhammad: A Very Short Introduction*. Oxford: Oxford University Press, 2011.

Buhl, Frants. *Das Leben Muhammeds*. Translated by Hans Heinrich Schaeder. Leipzig: Quelle & Meyer, 1930.

———. "Muḥammad." In *The Encyclopaedia of Islām*, edited by M. Th. Houtsma et al., 641–57. Leiden: Brill, 1936.

———. *Muhammeds liv*. 3rd ed. Herning: Kristensen, 1998.

———. *Muhammeds liv: med en indledning om forholdene i Arabien før Muhammeds optraeden*. Copenhagen: Gyldendalske, 1903.

Buhl, Frants, [and A. T. Welch]. "Muḥammad." In *The Encyclopaedia of Islam*, edited by P. J. Bearman et al., 360–76. Leiden: Brill, 1960–2005.

Bulliet, Richard W. *The Camel and the Wheel*. Cambridge: Harvard University Press, 1975.

Caetani, Leone. *Annali dell'Islām*. 10 vols. Milan: Hoepli, 1905–1926.

———. "The Art of War of the Arabs, and the Supposed Religious Fervour of the Arab Conquerors." In *The Expansion of the Early Islamic State*, edited by Fred M. Donner, 1–14. Aldershot, UK: Ashgate, 2008.

———. *Studi di storia orientale*. Vol. 1. *Islam e cristianesimo. L'Arabia preislamica. Gli Arabi antichi*. Milan: Hoepli, 1911.

Calder, Norman. *Studies in Early Muslim Jurisprudence*. Oxford: Clarendon, 1993.

Casanova, Paul. *Mohammed et la fin du monde: étude critique sur l'Islam primitif*. Paris: Gauthier, 1911–1924.

Casson, Lionel. *The Periplus Maris Erythraei: Text with Introduction, Translation, and Commentary*. Princeton: Princeton University Press, 1989.

Bibliography

Caussin de Perceval, A. P. *Essai sur l'histoire des Arabes avant l'islamisme: pendant l'époque de Mahomet, et jusqu'à la réduction de toutes les tribus sous la loi musulmane.* Paris: Didot, 1847.

Cohen, A. *Psalms: Hebrew Text and English Translation.* 5th impression ed. London: Soncino, 1962.

Cole, Juan. *Muhammad: Prophet of Peace amid the Clash of Empires.* New York: Nation, 2018.

Collins, John J. *Apocalypticism in the Dead Sea Scrolls.* Literature of the Dead Sea Scrolls. London: Routledge, 1997.

———. *The Scepter and the Star: Messianism in Light of the Dead Sea Scrolls.* 2nd ed. Grand Rapids: Eerdmans, 2010.

Conrad, Lawrence I. "Abraha and Muḥammad: Some Observations Apropos of Chronology and Literary *Topoi* in the Early Arabic Historical Tradition." *Bulletin of the School of Oriental and African Studies* 50 (1987) 225–40.

———. "Theophanes and the Arabic Historical Tradition: Some Indications of Intercultural Transmission." *Byzantinische Forschungen* 15 (1990) 1–44.

Cook, David. "The Beginnings of Islam as an Apocalyptic Movement." *Journal of Millennial Studies* 1 (2001). http://www.bu.edu/mille/publications/winter2001/cook.html.

———. "Messianism and Astronomical Events during the First Four Centuries of Islam." In *Mahdisme et millénarisme en Islam*, edited by Mercedes García-Arenal, 29–52. Aix-en-Provence: Édisud, 2001.

———. "Muslim Apocalyptic and *Jihād*." *Jerusalem Studies in Arabic and Islam* 20 (1996) 66–105.

———. "Muslim Materials on Comets and Meteorites." *Journal for the History of Astronomy* 30 (1999) 131–60.

———. "The Qurʾān and Other Scriptures." In *The Routledge Handbook on Early Islam*, edited by Herbert Berg, 25–36. Routledge Handbooks. London: Routledge, 2018.

———. *Studies in Muslim Apocalyptic*, Studies in Late Antiquity and Early Islam 21. Princeton: Darwin, 2002.

Cook, Michael. *Early Muslim Dogma: A Source-Critical Study.* Cambridge: Cambridge University Press, 1981.

———. *Muhammad.* Oxford: Oxford University Press, 1983.

Crone, Patricia. *God's Rule: Government and Islam.* New York: Columbia University Press, 2004.

———. "How Did the Quranic Pagans Make a Living?" *Bulletin of the School of Oriental and African Studies* 68 (2005) 387–99.

———. *Meccan Trade and the Rise of Islam.* Princeton: Princeton University Press, 1987.

———. "The Quranic Mushrikūn and the Resurrection, Part I." *Bulletin of the School of Oriental and African Studies* 75 (2012) 445–72.

———. "The Quranic Mushrikūn and the Resurrection, Part II." *Bulletin of the School of Oriental and African Studies* 76 (2013) 1–20.

———. "Quraysh and the Roman Army: Making Sense of the Meccan Leather Trade." *Bulletin of the School of Oriental and African Studies* 70 (2007) 63–88.

———. "The Religion of the Qurʾānic Pagans: God and the Lesser Deities." *Arabica* 57 (2010) 151–200.

———. *Roman, Provincial and Islamic Law.* Cambridge Studies in Islamic Civilization. Cambridge: Cambridge University Press, 1987.

———. *Slaves on Horses: The Evolution of the Islamic Polity*. Cambridge: Cambridge University Press, 1980.

———. "What Do We Actually Know about Mohammad?" 2008. https://www.opendemocracy.net/en/mohammed_3866jsp/.

Crone, Patricia, and M. A. Cook. *Hagarism: The Making of the Islamic World*. Cambridge: Cambridge University Press, 1977.

Culley, Robert C. "The Temple in Psalms 84, 63, and 42–43." In *"Où demeures-tu?" (Jn 1,38) la maison depuis le monde biblique: en hommage au professeur Guy Couturier à l'occasion de ses soixante-cinq ans*, 187–97. Montreal: Fides, 1994.

Cuypers, Michel. *Une apocalypse coranique: une lecture des trente-trois dernières sourates du Coran*. Rhétorique sémitique 15. Pendé: Gabalda, 2014.

Dagron, Gilbert, and Vincent Déroche. "Juifs et chrétiens dans l'Orient du VIIe siècle." *Travaux et mémoires* 11 (1991) 17–273.

Daley, Brian E. *The Hope of the Early Church: A Handbook of Patristic Eschatology*. Cambridge: Cambridge University Press, 1991.

Danby, Herbert, trans. and ed. *The Mishnah*. Oxford: Oxford University Press, 1967.

Davies, W. D. "Israel, the Mormons and the Land." In *Reflections on Mormonism: Judaeo-Christian Parallels*, edited by Truman G. Madsen, 79–97. Provo: Religious Studies Center, Brigham Young University, 1978.

de Prémare, Alfred-Louis. *Aux origines du Coran: questions d'hier, approches d'aujourd'hui*, L'Islam en débats. Paris: Téraèdre, 2004.

Decharneux, Julien. *Creation and Contemplation: The Cosmology of the Qur'ān and Its Late Antique Background*. Berlin: de Gruyter, 2023.

Donner, Fred M. "From Believers to Muslims: Confessional Self-Identity in the Early Islamic Community." *al-Abḥāth* 50–51 (2002) 9–53.

———. *Muhammad and the Believers: At the Origins of Islam*. Cambridge: Harvard University Press, 2010.

———. *Narratives of Islamic Origins: The Beginnings of Islamic Historical Writing*. Studies in Late Antiquity and Early Islam, 14. Princeton: Darwin, 1998.

———. "Quranic *Furqān* " *Journal of Semitic Studies* 52 (2007) 279–300.

Dost, Suleyman. "Pilgrimage in Pre-Islamic Arabia: Continuity and Rupture from Epigraphic Texts to the Qur'an." *Millennium* 20 (2023) 15–32.

Dunn, James D. G. *Jesus Remembered*. Grand Rapids: Eerdmans, 2003.

Durie, Mark. "A Note on al-Ṣafā and al-Marwah." Unpublished manuscript, 2021.

———. *The Qur'an and Its Biblical Reflexes: Investigations into the Genesis of a Religion*. Lanham, MD: Lexington, 2018.

Dye, Guillaume. "Le corpus coranique: contexte, chronologie, composition, canonisation." In *Le Coran des historiens*, edited by Mohammad Ali Amir-Moezzi and Guillaume Dye, forthcoming. Paris: Cerf, 2019.

———. "Lieux saints communs, partagés ou confisqués: aux sources de quelques péricopes coraniques (Q 19: 16–33)." In *Partage du sacré: transferts, dévotions mixtes, rivalités interconfessionnelles*, edited by Isabelle Dépret and Guillaume Dye, 55–121. Brussels: E.M.E. & InterCommunications, 2012.

———. "The Qur'anic Mary and the Chronology of the Qur'ān." In *Early Islam: The Sectarian Milieu of Late Antiquity?*, edited by Guillaume Dye, 159–201. Brussels: University of Brussels Press, 2023.

Ehrman, Bart D. *Jesus: Apocalyptic Prophet of the New Millennium*. New York: Oxford University Press, 1999.

El-Badawi, Emran Iqbal. *The Qurʾān and the Aramaic Gospel Traditions*. London: Routledge, 2014.
El-Cheikh, Nadia Maria. "Sūrat al-Rūm: A Study of the Exegetical Literature." *Journal of the American Oriental Society* 118 (1998) 356–64.
Engberts, Christiann, and Herman Paul. "Scholarly Vices: Boundary Work in Nineteenth-Century Orientalism." In *Epistemic Virtues in the Sciences and the Humanities*, edited by Jeroen van Dongen and Herman Paul, 79–90. Cham: Springer, 2017.
Ewald, Heinrich. "Aus Muhammeds Leben von Abdalmalik ibn-Hischam." *Zeitschrift für die Kunde des Morgenlandes* 1 (1837) 87–102; 191–204.
Garipzanov, Ildar H. *Graphic Signs of Authority in Late Antiquity and the Early Middle Ages, 300–900*. Oxford: Oxford University Press, 2018.
Geiger, Abraham. *Judaism and Islam*. New York: Ktav, 1898.
———. *Was Hat Mohammed aus dem Judenthume aufgenommen*. Bonn: Baaden, 1833.
Gibb, H. A. R. *Arabic Literature—An Introduction*. 2nd rev. ed. Oxford: Clarendon, 1963.
Givens, Terryl L. *The Book of Mormon: A Very Short Introduction*. Oxford: Oxford University Press, 2009.
———. *By the Hand of Mormon: The American Scripture That Launched a New World Religion*. Oxford: Oxford University Press, 2002.
Goldziher, Ignác. *Muhammedanische Studien*. 2 vols. Halle: M. Niemeyer, 1889–90.
———. *Muslim Studies*. Translated by C. R. Barber and S. M. Stern. Edited by S. M. Stern. 2 vols. London: Allen & Unwin, 1967–1971.
Görke, Andreas. "The Historical Tradition about al-Hudaybiya. A Study of ʿUrwa b. al-Zubayr's Account." In *The Biography of Muhammad: The Issue of the Sources*, edited by Harald Motzki, 240–75. Islamic History and Civilization 32. Leiden: Brill, 2000.
Görke, Andreas, and Gregor Schoeler. *Die ältesten Berichte über das Leben Muhammads. Das Korpus ʿUrwa ibn Az-Zubair*. Studies in Late Antiquity and Early Islam 24. Princeton: Darwin, 2008.
———. "Reconstructing the Earliest *Sīra* Texts: The Hiǧra in the Corpus of ʿUrwa b. al-Zubayr." *Der Islam* 82 (2005) 209–20.
Green, Arnold H. "The Muhammad-Joseph Smith Comparison: Subjective Metaphor or a Sociology of Prophethood." In *Mormons and Muslims: Spiritual Foundations and Modern Manifestations*, edited by Spencer J. Palmer, 63–84. Provo: Religious Studies Center, Brigham Young University, 1983.
Griffith, Sidney H. *The Bible in Arabic: The Scriptures of the 'People of the Book' in the Language of Islam*. Princeton: Princeton University Press, 2013.
Grimme, Hubert. *Mohammed*. Volume 1, *Das Leben nach den Quellen*. Darstellungen aus dem Gebiete der nichtchristlichen Religionsgeschichte 7. Münster: Aschendorff, 1892.
———. *Mohammed*. Volume 2, *Einleitung in den Koran, System der koranischen Theologie*. Darstellungen aus dem Gebiete der nichtchristlichen Religionsgeschichte 11. Münster: Aschendorff, 1895.
Gunkel, Hermann. *Die Psalmen*, Göttinger Handkommentar zum Alten Testament 2. Göttingen: Vandenhoeck & Ruprecht, 1926.
Hainthaler, Theresia. "Christian Arabs before Islam. A Short Overview." In *People from the Desert: Pre-Islamic Arabs in History and Culture*, edited by Nader Al Jallad, 29–44. Wiesbaden: Reichert, 2012.
———. *Christliche Araber vor dem Islam: Verbreitung und konfessionelle Zugehörigkeit: Eine Hinführung*. Eastern Christian Studies 7. Leuven: Peeters, 2007.

Bibliography

Ḥakham, ʿAmos. *Psalms with the Jerusalem Commentary*. Translated by Israel V. Berman. 3 vols. Jerusalem: Mosad Harav Kook, 2003.

Hardy, Grant. "The Book of Mormon." In *The Oxford Handbook of Mormonism*, edited by Terryl Givens and Philip L. Barlow, 134–48. New York: Oxford University Press, 2015.

Harris, Horton. *The Tübingen School*. Oxford: Clarendon, 1975.

Hasson, Isaac. "Last Judgment." In *Encyclopaedia of the Qurʾān*, edited by Jane Dammen McAuliffe, 3:136–45. 6 vols. Leiden: Brill, 2001–6.

Hauge, Martin Ravndal. *Between Sheol and Temple: Motif Structure and Function in the I-Psalms*. Journal for the Study of the Old Testament Supplement series 178. Sheffield: Sheffield Academic, 1995.

Hawting, Gerald R. "The House and the Book: Sanctuary and Scripture in Islam (2017 IQSA Presidential Address)." *Journal of the International Qurʾanic Studies Association* 3 (2018) 3–23.

———. *The Idea of Idolatry and the Emergence of Islam: From Polemic to History*, Cambridge Studies in Islamic Civilization. Cambridge: Cambridge University Press, 1999.

———. "The Origins of the Muslim Sanctuary at Mecca." In *Studies on the First Century of Islamic Society*, edited by G. H. A. Juynboll, 23–47. Carbondale: Southern Illinois University Press, 1982.

———. "Sanctuary and Text: How Far Can the Qurʾān Throw Light on the History of the Muslim Sanctuary?" In *Die Koranhermeneutik von Günter Lüling*, edited by Tamer Georges, 93–110. Berlin: de Gruyter, 2018.

Haykal, Muhammad Husayn. *Ḥayāt Muḥammad*. Cairo: Maṭbaʿat Dār al-Kitāb al-Miṣrī, 1935.

———. *The Life of Muhammad*. Translated by Ismaʾil R. Al-Faruqi. Indianapolis: North American Trust Publications, 1976.

Hazleton, Lesley. *The First Muslim: The Story of Muhammad*. New York: Riverhead, 2013.

Heschel, Susannah. *Abraham Geiger and the Jewish Jesus*. Chicago: University of Chicago Press, 1998.

———. *The Aryan Jesus: Christian Theologians and the Bible in Nazi Germany*. Princeton: Princeton University Press, 2008.

Himmelfarb, Martha. *Jewish Messiahs in a Christian Empire: A History of the Book of Zerubbabel*. Cambridge: Harvard University Press, 2017.

———. "*Sefer Eliyyahu:* Jewish Eschatology and Christian Jerusalem." In *Shaping the Middle East: Jews, Christians, and Muslims in an Age of Transition, 400–800 C.E.*, edited by Kenneth G. Holum and Hayim Lapin, 223–38. Bethesda: University Press of Maryland, 2011.

Hirschfeld, Hartwig. *New Researches into the Composition and Exegesis of the Qoran*. Asiatic Monographs 3. London: Royal Asiatic Society, 1902.

Hodgson, Marshall G. S. *The Venture of Islam: Conscience and History in a World Civilization*. 3 vols. Chicago: University of Chicago Press, 1974.

Hoffmann, Thomas. *The Poetic Qurʾān: Studies on Qurʾānic Poeticity*. Wiesbaden: Harrassowitz, 2007.

Horovitz, Josef. *The Earliest Biographies of the Prophet and their Authors*. Edited by Lawrence I. Conrad, Studies in Late Antiquity and Early Islam 11. Princeton: Darwin, 2002.

———. "Jewish Proper Names and Derivatives in the Koran." *Hebrew Union College Annual* 2 (1925) 145–227.

———. *Koranische Untersuchungen*. Berlin: Koranische Untersuchungen, 1926.

Hossfeld, Frank-Lothar, and Erich Zenger. *Psalms 2: A Commentary on Psalms 51–100*. Translated by Linda M. Maloney. Hermeneia. Minneapolis: Fortress, 2005.

Howard-Johnston, James. *Witnesses to a World Crisis: Historians and Histories of the Middle East in the Seventh Century*. Oxford: Oxford University Press, 2010.

Hoyland, Robert G. *Arabia and the Arabs: From the Bronze Age to the Coming of Islam*. London: Routledge, 2001.

———. "The Earliest Christian Writings on Muhammad: An Appraisal." In *The Biography of Muhammad: The Issue of the Sources*, edited by Harald Motzki, 276–97. Leiden: Brill, 2000.

———. "Early Islam as a Late Antique Religion." In *The Oxford Handbook of Late Antiquity*, edited by Scott F. Johnson, 1053–77. New York: Oxford University Press, 2012.

———. *In God's Path: The Arab Conquests and the Creation of an Islamic Empire*: Oxford University Press, 2015.

———. *Seeing Islam as Others Saw It: A Survey and Evaluation of Christian, Jewish and Zoroastrian Writings on Early Islam*. Studies in Late Antiquity and Early Islam 13. Princeton: Darwin, 1997.

———. "Writing the Biography of the Prophet Muhammad: Problems and Solutions." *History Compass* 5 (2007) 581–602.

Humphreys, R. Stephen. *Islamic History: A Framework for Inquiry*. Princeton: Princeton University Press, 1991.

Hurgronje, C. Snouck. "Der Mahdi." *Revue coloniale internationale* 1 (1886) 25–59.

———. *Mohammedanism; Lectures on Its Origin, Its Religious and Political Growth, and Its Present State*. New York, London: Putnam, 1916.

———. "Une nouvelle biographie de Mohammed." *Revue de l'histoire des religions* 30 (1894) 48–70, 149–78.

Ibn Hishām, 'Abd al-Malik. *Kitāb sīrat Rasūl Allāh [Das leben Muhammed's nach Muhammed ibn Ishâk bearbeitet von Abd el-Malik ibn Hischâm]*. Edited by Ferdinand Wüstenfeld. 2 vols. Göttingen: Dieterichsche Universitäts-Buchhandlung, 1858–60.

Ibrahim, Ayman S. *Muhammad's Military Expeditions: A Critical Reading in Original Muslim Sources*. New York: Oxford University Press, 2024.

———. "Review of Juan Cole, *Muhammad: Prophet of Peace Amid the Clash of Empires*." *Review of Qur'anic Research* 5 (2019).

Irving, Washington. *Lives of Mahomet and His Successors*. London: Murray, 1850.

Al-Jallad, Ahmad, and Hythem Sidky. "A Paleo-Arabic Inscription on a Route North of Ṭā'if." *Arabian Archaeology and Epigraphy* 33 (2022) 202–15.

Jebara, Mohamad. *Muhammad, the World-Changer: An Intimate Portrait*. New York: St. Martin's, 2021.

Jeffery, Arthur. "The Quest of the Historical Muhammad." *The Moslem World* 6 (1926) 327–48.

Jellinek, Adolph, ed. *Bet ha-midrash: Sammlung kleiner Midraschim und vermischter Abhandlungen aus der ältern jüdischen Literatur*. 6 vols. Leipzig: Nies, 1853–1877.

Johnson, Scott Fitzgerald, ed. *Languages and Cultures of Eastern Christianity: Greek*. The Worlds of Eastern Christianity, 300–1500. Surrey, UK: Ashgate, 2015.

Junod, Éric. "Apocryphes du Nouveau Testament ou apocryphes chrétiens anciens? Remarques sur la désignation d'un corpus et indications bibliographiques sur instruments de travail récents." Études théologiques et religieuses 59 (1983) 409–21.

Juynboll, G. H. A. *Muslim Tradition: Studies in Chronology, Provenance, and Authorship of Early Ḥadīth*. Cambridge Studies in Islamic Civilization. Cambridge: Cambridge University Press, 1983.

Kerr, Robert M. "Die islamische Kabbala: eine Neuorientierung." In *Die Entstehung einer Weltreligion V*, edited by M. Groß and K.-H. Ohlig, 319–42. Berlin-Tübingen: Schiler, 2019.

———. "«Farüqter Heiland» et le Ḥağğ original à Jérusalem: Quelques remarques sur le messianisme de l'islam naissant." In *Die Entstehung einer Weltreligion VI: Vom umayyadischen Christentum zum abbasidischen Islam*, edited by Markus Gross and Robert M. Kerr, 458–507. Berlin: Schiller & Mücke, 2021.

al-Khaṭīb, ʿAbd al-Laṭīf Muḥammad, ed. *Muʿjam al-qirāāt*. Damascus: Dār Saʿd al-Dīn, 2010.

Kister, M. J. "'A Booth like the Booth of Moses . . . ': A Study of an Early Ḥadīth." *Bulletin of the School of Oriental and African Studies* 25 (1962) 150–55.

Kittel, Rudolf. *Die Psalmen*. Kommentar zum Alten Testament 13. Leipzig: Scholl, 1929.

Kraus, Hans-Joachim. *Psalmen II, Psalmen 60–150*. 6th ed. Biblischer Kommentar Altes Testament, Bd. 15, 2. Neukirchen-Vluyn: Neukirchener, 1989.

Kümmel, Werner Georg. *Promise and Fulfilment: The Eschatological Message of Jesus*. Translated by D. M. Barton. London: SCM, 1957.

Lammens, Henri. "The Age of Muhammad and the Chronology of the Sira." In *The Quest for the Historical Muhammad*, edited by Ibn Warraq, 188–217. Amherst, NY: Prometheus, 2000.

———. "Fatima and the Daughters of Muhammad." In *The Quest for the Historical Muhammad*, edited by Ibn Warraq, 218–329. Amherst, NY: Prometheus, 2000.

———. *Fatima et les filles de Mahomet*. Rome: Sumptibus Pontificii Instituti Biblici, 1912.

———. "The Koran and Tradition: How the Life of Muhammad Was Composed." In *The Quest for the Historical Muhammad*, edited by Ibn Warraq, 169–87. Amherst, NY: Prometheus, 2000.

———. "L'âge de Mahomet et la chronologie de la Sîra." *Journal Asiatique*, series 10, 17 (1911) 209–50.

———. *La Mecque à la veille de l'Hégire*. Mélanges de l'Université Saint-Joseph 9.3. Beirut: Imprimerie Catholique, 1924.

———. *Le berceau de l'Islam: l'Arabie occidentale à la veille de l'hégire. Ier volume: Le clima—Les Bédouins*. Rome: Pontifical Biblical Institute Press, 1914.

———. "Qoran et tradition: Comment fut composée la vie de Mohamet?" *Recherches de Science Religieuse* 1 (1910) 25–61.

Lane, Edward William, and Stanley Lane-Poole. *Arabic-English Lexicon*. New York: Ungar, 1955.

Lawson, Todd. *The Quran: Epic and Apocalypse*. London: Oneworld Academics, 2017.

Lewis, Bernard. "An Apocalyptic Vision of Islamic History." *Bulletin of the School of Oriental and African Studies* 13 (1950) 308–38.

———. *The Arabs in History*. 6th ed. New York: Oxford University Press, 2002.

Lindstedt, Ilkka. *Muḥammad and His Followers in Context: The Religious Map of Late Antique Arabia*. Leiden: Brill, 2023.

———. "Surah 5 of the Qurʾān: The Parting of the Ways?" *Journal of Late Antique, Islamic and Byzantine Studies* 3 (2024) forthcoming.

———. "Who Is In, Who Is Out? Early Muslim Identity through Epigraphy and Theory." *Jerusalem Studies in Arabic and Islam* 46 (2019) 147–246.

Loersch, Sigrid. "'Sie wandern von Kraft zu Kraft': Glück und Segnung auf dem Pilgerweg nach Ps 84,6-8." In *Sie wandern von Kraft zu Kraft: Aufbrüche, Wege, Begegnungen: Festgabe für Bischof Reinhard Lettmann*, 13–27. Kevelaer: Butzon & Bercker, 1993.

Loretz, Oswald. "Vorexilische und nachexilische Zion-Wallfahrten mit kultischem 'Gott-Schauen' nach Psalm 84." *Ugarit-Forschungen* 40 (2008) 477–87.

Lüling, Günter. *A Challenge to Islam for Reformation: The Rediscovery and Reliable Reconstruction of a Comprehensive Pre-Islamic Christian Hymnal Hidden in the Koran under Earliest Islamic Reinterpretations*. Rev. ed. Delhi: Motilal Banarsidass Publishers, 2003.

———. *Über den Ur-Qurʾan: Ansätze z. Rekonstruktion vorislam, christl. Strophenlieder Qurʾan*. Erlangen: Lüling, 1974.

Lumbard, Joseph. "Prophets and Messangers of God." In *Voices of Islam*, edited by Vincent J. Cornell, 1:101–22. 5 vols. Praeger Perspectives. London: Praeger, 2006.

Luxenberg, Christoph. *Die syro-aramäische Lesart des Koran: ein Beitrag zur Entschlüsselung der Koransprache*. Berlin: Das Arabische Buch, 2000.

———. *The Syro-Aramaic Reading of the Koran: A Contribution to the Decoding of the Language of the Koran*. Rev. ed. Berlin: Schiler, 2007.

Macdonald, M. C. A. "Ancient Arabia and the Written Word." In *The Development of Arabic as a Written Language*, edited by M. C. A. Macdonald, 5–28. Proceedings of the Seminar for Arabian Studies 40 Supplement. Oxford: Archaeopress, 2010.

———. "On the Uses of Writing in Ancient Arabia and the Role of Palaeography in Studying Them." *Arabian Epigraphic Notes* 1 (2015) 1–50.

Maffly-Kipp, Laurie F. *American Scriptures: An Anthology of Sacred Writings*. New York: Penguin Classics, 2010.

Maillot, Alphonse, and André Lelièvre. *Les Psaumes: commentaire*, Volume 2, *Psaumes 51 à 100*. Genève: Labor et Fides, 1966.

Makki, M. S. *Medina, Saudi Arabi: A Geographic Analysis of the City and Region*. Amersham, Bucks: Avebury, 1982.

Margoliouth, D. S. *Mohammed and the Rise of Islam*. Heroes of the Nations. New York: Putnam, 1905.

———. "Muhammad." In *Encyclopaedia of Religion and Ethics*, edited by John A. Selbie et al., 878. New York: Scribner, 1908.

Maxwell, Jaclyn LaRae. *Christianization and Communication in Late Antiquity: John Chrysostom and His Congregation in Antioch*. Cambridge: Cambridge University Press, 2006.

Mayer, Wendy. "Homiletics." In *The Oxford Handbook of Early Christian Studies*, edited by Susan Ashbrook Harvey and David G. Hunter, 565–83. Oxford Handbooks in Religion and Theology. Oxford: Oxford University Press, 2008.

Meier, John P. *A Marginal Jew: Rethinking the Historical Jesus*. 3 vols. New York: Doubleday, 1994.

Mimouni, Simon Claude, ed. *Apocryphité: histoire d'un concept transversal aux religions du Livre: en hommage à Pierre Geoltrain*, Bibliothèque de l'Ecole des hautes études, Sciences religieuses 113. Turnhout: Brepols, 2002.

Bibliography

Mingana, Alphonse. "Syriac Influence on the Style of the Kur'ān." *Bulletin of the John Rylands Library* 11 (1927) 77–98.

Mirza, Mahan. "Muḥammad." In *The Oxford Encyclopedia of Politics and Islam*, edited by Emad El-Din Shahin, 2:86–92. Oxford: Oxford University Press, 2014.

Mowinckel, Sigmund. *The Psalms in Israel's Worship*. Translated by D. R. Ap-Thomas. 2 vols. New York: Abingdon, 1962.

Morris, Ian. "Mecca and Macoraba." *Al-ʿUṣūr al-Wusṭā* 26 (2018) 1–60.

Motzki, Harald. "The Murder of Ibn Abī l-Ḥuqayq: On the Origin and Reliability of Some *Maghāzī* Reports." In *The Biography of Muhammad: The Issue of the Sources*, edited by Harald Motzki, 170–239. Leiden: Brill, 2000.

Muir, William. *The Life of Mahomet*. 4 vols. London: Smith, Elder, 1858–1861.

Munt, Harry. *The Holy City of Medina: Sacred Space in Early Islamic Arabia*. Cambridge Studies in Islamic Civilization. Cambridge: Cambridge University Press, 2014.

Nagel, Tilman. *Mohammed: Leben und Legende*. Munich: Oldenbourg, 2008.

———. *Mohammed: Zwanzig Kapitel über den Propheten der Muslime*. Berlin: Oldenbourg, 2014.

———. *Muhammad's Mission: Religion, Politics, and Power at the Birth of Islam*. Translated by Joseph S. Spoerl. Berlin: de Gruyter Oldenbourg, 2020.

———. "Theology and the Qur'ān." In *Encyclopaedia of the Qur'ān*, edited by Jane Dammen McAuliffe, 5:256–75. 6 vols. Leiden: Brill, 2001–6.

Nehmé, Laïla, ed. *The Darb al-Bakrah: A Caravan Route in North-West Arabia Discovered by Ali I. al-Ghabban: Catalogue of the Inscriptions*. Riyad: Saudi Commission for Tourism & National Heritage, 2018.

———. *Guide to Hegra: Archaeology in the Land of the Nabataeans of Arabia*. Paris: Skira, 2021.

———. "New Dated Inscriptions (Nabataean and pre-Islamic Arabic) from a Site Near al-Jawf, ancient Dūmah, Saudi Arabia." *Arabian Epigraphic Notes* 3 (2017) 121–64.

Neuenkirchen, Paul. "Late Antique Syriac Homilies and the Quran." *Mélanges de l'Institut dominicain d'études orientales* 37 (2022) 3–28.

Neuwirth, Angelika. "Die Psalmen—im Koran neu gelesen (Ps 104 und 136)." In *Im vollen Licht der Geschichte. Die Wissenschaft des Judentums und die Anfänge der kritischen Koranforschung*, edited by Angelika Neuwirth et al., 157–91. Wurzburg: Ergon, 2008.

———. "Einige Bemerkungen zum besonderen sprachlichen und literarischen Charakter des Koran." In *19. Deutscher Orientalistentag in Freiburg 1975*, edited by Wolfgang Voigt, 736–39. Wiesbaden: Steiner, 1977.

———. "Erste Qibla—Fernstes Masǧid?: Jerusalem im Horizont des historischen Muḥammad." In *Zion, Ort der Begegnung: Festschrift für Laurentius Klein zur Vollendung des 65. Lebensjahres*, edited by Ferdinand Hahn et al., 227–70. Bodenheim: Athenäum, Hahn, Hanstein, 1993.

———. "Face of God—Face of Man: The Significance of the Direction of Prayer in Islam." In *Self, Soul and Body in Religious Experience*, edited by Albert I. Baumgarten et al., 298–312. Studies in the History of Religions 78. Leiden: Brill, 1998.

———. "Locating the Qur'an in the Epistemic Space of Late Antiquity." *Ankara Üniversitesi İlâhiyat Fakültesi dergisi* 54 (2013) 189–203.

———. *The Qur'an and Late Antiquity: A Shared Heritage*. Translated by Samuel Wilder. New York: Oxford University Press, 2019.

———. "Structural, Linguistic and Literary Features." In *The Cambridge Companion to the Qurʾān*, edited by Jane Dammen McAuliffe, 97–113. Cambridge Companions to Religion. Cambridge: Cambridge University Press, 2006.

Nicholson, Reynold Alleyne. *A Literary History of the Arabs*. 2nd ed. Cambridge: Cambridge University Press, 1930.

Nöldeke, Theodor. *Geschichte des Qorâns*. Göttingen: Dieterich, 1860.

———. Review of Leone Caetani, *Annali dell'Islam*. *Wiener Zeitschrift für die Kunde des Morgenlandes* 21 (1907) 297–312.

———. "Zur tendenziözen Gestaltung der Urgeschichte des Islam's." *Zeitschrift der Deutschen Morgenländischen Gesellschaft* 52 (1898) 16–33.

Olster, David. "Byzantine Apocalypses." In *The Encyclopedia of Apocalypticism*, edited by John J. Collins et al., 2:48–73. New York: Continuum, 1999.

Palmer, Andrew. *The Seventh Century in West-Syrian Chronicles*. Translated Texts for Historians 15. Liverpool: Liverpool University Press, 1993.

Papadopoulos-Kerameus, Athanasios. Ἀνάλεκτα Ἱεροσολυμιτικῆς σταχυολογίας *(Analekta hierosolymitikēs stachyologias)* 5. St. Petersburg: Kirsbaum, 1898.

Paret, Rudi. *Der Koran*. Stuttgart: Kohlhammer, 1966.

———. *Der Koran: Kommentar und Konkordanz: mit einem Nachtrag zur Tachenbuchausgabe*. 7th ed. Stuttgart: Kohlhammer, 2005.

———. *Mohammed und der Koran; Geschichte und Verkündigung des arabischen Propheten*. Stuttgart: Kohlhammer, 1957.

Penn, Michael Philip. *When Christians First Met Muslims: A Sourcebook of the Earliest Syriac Writings on Islam*. Oakland: University of California Press, 2015.

Peters, F. E. *Jesus and Muhammad: Parallel Tracks, Parallel Lives*. New York: Oxford University Press, 2011.

———. *Mecca: A Literary History of the Muslim Holy Land*. Princeton: Princeton University Press, 1994.

———. *Muhammad and the Origins of Islam*. Albany: State University of New York Press, 1994.

———. "The Quest of the Historical Muhammad." *International Journal of Middle East Studies* 23 (1991) 291–315.

Peters, John P. "A Jerusalem Processional." *Journal of Biblical Literature* 39 (1920) 52–59.

Peterson, Daniel C. *Muhammad: Prophet of God*. Grand Rapids: Eerdmans, 2007.

Pines, Shlomo. "Amr." In *Encyclopaedia of Islam*, edited by P. J. Bearman et al., 449–50. Leiden: Brill, 1960–2005.

Piovanelli, Pierluigi. "Qu'est-ce qu'un 'écrit apocryphe chrétien', et comment ça marche? Quelques suggestions pour une herméneutique apocryphe." In *Pierre Geoltrain, ou comment «faire l'histoire» des religions. Le chantier des «origines», les méthodes du doute, et la conversation contemporaine entre disciplines*, edited by Simon C. Mimouni and I. Ullern-Weité, 171–84. Turnhout: Brepols, 2006.

———. "What Is a Christian Apocryphal Text and How Does It Work? Some Observations on Apocryphal Hermeneutics." *Nederlands Theologisch Tijdschrift* 59 (2005) 31–40.

Porter, Stanley E. *The Criteria for Authenticity in Historical-Jesus Research: Previous Discussions and New Proposals*. Sheffield: Sheffield Academic, 2000.

Powers, David S. *Muḥammad is Not the Father of Any of Your Men: The Making of the Last Prophet*. Philadelphia: University of Pennsylvania, 2009.

———. "Sinless, Sonless and Seal of Prophets: Muḥammad and Kor 33, 36–40, Revisited." *Arabica* 67 (2020) 333–408.

———. *Zayd: The Little Known Story of Muḥammad's Adopted Son*. Philadelphia: University of Pennsylvania Press, 2014.
Pregill, Michael E. "Review of *Creating the Qurʾan: A Historical-Critical Study*, By Stephen J. Shoemaker." *Journal of the American Academy of Religion* (2024). https://doi.org/10.1093/jaarel/lfae008.
Proudfoot, Wayne. *Religious Experience*. Berkeley: University of California Press, 1985.
Rada, W. S., and F. R. Stephenson. "A Catalogue of Meteor Showers in Medieval Arab Chronicles." *Quarterly journal of the Royal Astronomical Society* 33 (1992) 5–16.
Ramadan, Tariq. *In the Footsteps of the Prophet: Lessons from the Life of Muhammad*. New York: Oxford University Press, 2007.
Raven, Wim. "Sīra." In *The Encyclopaedia of Islam*, edited by P. J. Bearman et al., 660–63. Leiden: Brill, 1960–2005.
Reeves, John C. *Trajectories in Near Eastern Apocalyptic: A Postrabbinic Jewish Apocalypse Reader*. Leiden: Brill, 2006.
Regnier, A. "Quelques énigmes littéraires de l'inspiration coranique." *Le Muséon* 52 (1939) 145–62.
———. "Some Literary Enigmas of Koranic Inspiration." In *Koranic Allusions: The Biblical, Qumranian, and Pre-Islamic Background to the Koran*, edited by Ibn Warraq, 248–62. Amherst, NY: Prometheus, 2013.
Renan, Ernest. "Mahomet et les origines de l'Islamisme." *Revue des deux mondes* 12 (1851) 1023–60.
———. "Muhammad and the Origins of Islam." In *The Quest for the Historical Muhammad*, edited by Ibn Warraq, 127–66. Amherst, NY: Prometheus, 2000.
———. *Vie de Jésus*. Paris: Lévy, 1863.
Reynolds, Gabriel Said. *The Qurʾān and its Biblical Subtext*, Routledge Studies in the Qurʾan. New York: Routledge, 2010.
———. *The Qurʾān and Its Biblical Subtext*. Routledge Studies in the Qurʾan. New York: Routledge, 2010.
Reynolds, Gabriel Said, and ʿAlī Qūlī Qarāʾī. *The Qurʾān and the Bible: Text and Commentary*. New Haven: Yale University Press, 2018.
Rippin, Andrew. "Muḥammad in the Qurʾān: Reading Scripture in the 21st Century." In *The Biography of Muhammad: The Issue of the Sources*, edited by Harald Motzki, 298–309. Leiden: Brill, 2000.
Robin, Christian Julien. "Introduction—The Development of Arabic as a Written Language." In *The Development of Arabic as a Written Language*, edited by M. C. A. Macdonald, 1–3. Oxford: Archaeopress, 2010.
Robinson, A. "Three Suggested Interpretations in Ps 84." *Vetus Testamentum* 24 (1974) 378–81.
Robinson, Chase F. *ʿAbd al-Malik*, Makers of the Muslim World. Oxford: Oneworld, 2005.
Robinson, Majied. "The Population Size of Muhammad's Mecca and the Creation of the Quraysh." *Der Islam* 99 (2022) 10–37.
Rodinson, Maxime. *Mahomet*. Paris: Seuil, 1961.
———. *Mohammed*. Translated by Anne Carter. New York: Pantheon, 1971.
Roggema, Barbara. *The Legend of Sergius Baḥīrā: Eastern Christian Apologetics and Apocalyptic in Response to Islam*. History of Christian-Muslim Relations 9. Leiden: Brill, 2009.

Rubin, Uri. *The Eye of the Beholder: The Life of Muhammad as Viewed by the Early Muslims: A Textual Analysis*. Studies in Late Antiquity and Early Islam 5. Princeton: Darwin, 1995.

———. "Muḥammad's Message in Mecca: Warnings, Signs, and Miracles." In *The Cambridge Companion to Muḥammad*, edited by Jonathan E. Brockopp, 39–60. Cambridge: Cambridge University Press, 2010.

———. "Prophets and Prophethood." In *Encyclopaedia of the Qurʾān*, edited by Jane Dammen McAuliffe, 4:289–306. 6 vols. Leiden: Brill, 2001–2006.

Rüling, Josef Bernhard. *Beiträge zur Eschatologie des Islam*. Leipzig: Kreysing, 1895.

Safi, Omid. *Memories of Muhammad: Why the Prophet Matters*. New York: HarperCollins, 2009.

Samji, Karim. *The Qurʾān: A Form-Critical History*. Berlin: de Gruyter, 2018.

Sanders, E. P. *The Historical Figure of Jesus*. London: Allen Lane, 1993.

———. *Jesus and Judaism*. Philadelphia: Fortress, 1985.

Sardar, Ziauddin. *Mecca: The Sacred City*. New York: Bloomsbury USA, 2014.

Schacht, Joseph. *The Origins of Muhammadan Jurisprudence*. Oxford: Clarendon, 1950.

———. "A Revaluation of Islamic Traditions." *Journal of the Royal Asiatic Society* 49 (1949) 143–54.

Schimmel, Annemarie. *And Muhammad Is His Messenger: The Veneration of the Prophet in Islamic Piety*. Studies in Religion. Chapel Hill: University of North Carolina, 1985.

Schmidt, Hans. *Die Psalmen*. Handbuch zum Alten Testament 1/15. Tübingen: Mohr Siebeck, 1934.

Schneemelcher, Wilhelm. *Neutestamentliche Apokryphen in deutscher Übersetzung*. 3rd ed. 2 vols. Tübingen: Mohr Siebeck, 1959–1964.

Schneemelcher, Wilhelm, ed. *New Testament Apocrypha*. Translated by R. McL Wilson. 2 vols. Philadelphia: Westminster, 1963–1965.

Schoeler, Gregor. "Character and Authenticity of the Muslim Tradition on the Life of Muhammad." *Arabica* 48 (2002) 360–66.

———. *Charakter und Authentie der muslimischen Überlieferung über das Leben Mohammeds*. Studien zur Sprache, Geschichte und Kultur des islamischen Orients 14. Berlin: de Gruyter, 1996.

———. "Foundations for A New Biography of Muḥammad: The Production and Evaluation of the Corpus of Traditions from ʿUrwa b. al-Zubayr." In *Method and Theory in the Study of Islamic Origins*, edited by Herbert Berg, 19–28. Islamic History and Civilization 49. Leiden: Brill, 2003.

Schürer, Emil, et al. *The History of the Jewish People in the Age of Jesus Christ (175 B.C.–A.D. 135)*. Vol. 2. Rev. ed. Edinburgh: T. & T. Clark, 1979.

Schwarb, Gregor M. "Amr (theology)." In *Encyclopaedia of Islam*, edited by Kate Fleet, et al. 3rd ed. Leiden: Brill, 2007–.

Schweitzer, Albert. *The Quest of the Historical Jesus: A Critical Study of Its Progress from Reimarus to Wrede*. Translated by W. Montgomery. London: Adam & Charles Black, 1910.

———. *Von Reimarus zu Wrede: Eine Geschichte der Leben-Jesu-Forschung*. Tübingen: Mohr Siebeck, 1906.

Shoemaker, Stephen J. *The Apocalypse of Empire: Imperial Eschatology in Late Antiquity and Early Islam*. Divinations: Rereading Late Ancient Religion. Philadelphia: University of Pennsylvania Press, 2018.

Bibliography

———. "Christmas in the Qurʾān: The Qurʾānic Account of Jesus' Nativity and Palestinian Local Tradition." *Jerusalem Studies in Arabic and Islam* 28 (2003) 11–39.

———. *Creating the Qurʾan: A Historical-Critical Study*. Oakland: University of California Press, 2022.

———. *The Death of a Prophet: The End of Muhammad's Life and the Beginnings of Islam*. Divinations: Rereading Late Ancient Religion. Philadelphia: University of Pennsylvania Press, 2012.

———. "Early Christian Apocryphal Literature." In *Oxford Handbook of Early Christian Studies*, edited by Susan Ashbrook Harvey and David G. Hunter, 521–48. Oxford Handbooks in Religion and Theology. Oxford: Oxford University Press, 2008.

———. "The Eschatological Reign of God in the Qurʾan: The *Amr Allāh*." In *Die Entstehung einer Weltreligion VI: Vom umayyadischen Christentum zum abbasidischen Islam*, edited by Marcus Groß and Robert M. Kerr, 720–33. Berlin: Schiler-Mücke, 2020.

———. "The Imperial Qurʾan: Scripture in the Service of Empire." In *Mélanges d'études shiʾites et islamologiques offertes au Professeur Mohammad Ali Amir-Moezzi*, edited by Orkhan Mir-Kasimov and Mathieu Terrier, forthcoming. Turnhout: Brepols, 2024.

———. "In Search of ʿUrwa's Sīra: Some Methodological Issues in the Quest for 'Authenticity' in the Life of Muḥammad." *Der Islam* 85 (2009–11) 257–344.

———. "The Jerusalem Temple and the Qurʾan's Holy House." In *Abschied von der Heilsgeschichte*, edited by Robert M. Kerr and Marcus Groß, 179–200. Berlin: Schiler-Mücke, 2023.

———. "Jewish Christianity, Non-Trinitarianism, and the Beginnings of Islam." In *Jewish Christianity and Early Islam*, edited by Francisco del Río Sánchez, 101–14. Turnhout: Brepols, 2017.

———. "Mahomet dans l'histoire." In *Le Mahomet des historiens*, edited by Mohammad Ali Amir-Moezzi and John Tolan, forthcoming. Paris: Cerf, 2025.

———. "Mary between Bible and Qurʾan: Apocrypha, Archaeology, and the Memory of Mary in Late Ancient Palestine." In *Extracanonical Traditions and the Holy Land*, edited by Harald Buchinger et al., forthcoming. Tübingen: Mohr Siebeck, 2024.

———. "Muḥammad and the Qurʾān." In *The Oxford Handbook of Late Antiquity*, edited by Scott F. Johnson, 1078–108. New York: Oxford University Press, 2012.

———. "A New Arabic Apocryphon from Late Antiquity: The Qurʾan." In *The Study of Islamic Origins: New Perspectives and Contexts*, edited by Mette Bjerregaard Mortensen et al., 29–42. Berlin: de Gruyter, 2021.

———. "The Portents of the Hour: Eschatology and Empire in the Early Islamic Tradition." In *Cultures of Eschatology: Authority and Empire in Christian, Muslim, and Buddhist Communities*, edited by Veronika Wieser et al., 298–320. Berlin: de Gruyter, 2020.

———. *A Prophet Has Appeared: The Rise of Islam through Christian and Jewish Eyes: A Sourcebook*. Oakland: University of California Press, 2021.

———. "Qurʾanic Eschatology in its Biblical and Late Ancient Matrix." In *Dreams, Visions, Imaginations: Jewish, Christian and Gnostic Views of the World to Come*, edited by Jens Schröter et al., 461–86. Berlin: de Gruyter, 2021.

———. "The Reign of God Has Come: Eschatology and Empire in Late Antiquity and Early Islam." *Arabica: Journal of Arabic and Islamic Studies* 61 (2014) 514–58.

———. "Theological Literacy in the Late Ancient Near East: Liturgical Catechesis and Not-So-Simple Christian Believers of Roman Arabia." *Journal of Orthodox Christian Studies*, forthcoming.

Bibliography

———. "Les vies de Muhammad." In *Le Coran des historiens*, edited by Mohammad Ali Amir-Moezzi and Guillaume Dye, 1:183–245. Paris: Cerf, 2019.

———. "'You Pass by Them in the Morning and in the Night': Lot, Laykah, and the Levantine Qur'an." *Studies in Late Antiquity*, forthcoming.

Sinai, Nicolai. "The Eschatological Kerygma of the Early Qur'ān." In *Apocalypticism and Eschatology in Late Antiquity*, edited by Hagit Amirav et al., 219–66. Beyond the Fathers 2. Leuven: Peeters, 2018.

———. "The Qur'ān." In *The Routledge Handbook on Early Islam*, edited by Herbert Berg, 9–24. Routledge Handbooks. London: Routledge, 2018.

———. *The Qur'an: A Historical-Critical Introduction*. Edinburgh: Edinburgh University Press, 2017.

Singer, Isidore, ed. *The Jewish Encyclopedia*. 12 vols. New York: Funk & Wagnalls, 1901–190.

Sivertsev, Alexei. *Judaism and Imperial Ideology in Late Antiquity*. Cambridge: Cambridge University Press, 2011.

Smith, Jane I. "Eschatology." In *Encyclopaedia of the Qur'ān*, edited by Jane Dammen McAuliffe, 2:44–54. 6 vols. Leiden: Brill, 2001–2006.

Smith, Joseph, Jr. *The Book of Mormon*. Penguin Classics. London: Penguin, 2009.

Sprenger, Aloys. *Das Leben und die Lehre des Mohammed: Nach bisher größtenteils unbenutzten Quellen*. Berlin: Nicolai, 1861–65.

———. *The Life of Mohammad from Original Sources*. Allahabad: Presbyterian Mission Press, 1851.

Stark, Rodney. "A Theory of Revelations." *Journal for the Scientific Study of Religion* 38 (1999) 287–308.

Starr, James. "Paraenesis." *Oxford Bibliographies: Biblical Studies* (2013). https://www.oxfordbibliographies.com/page/134#4.

Starr, James M., and Troels Engberg-Pedersen. *Early Christian Paraenesis in Context*, Beihefte zur Zeitschrift für die Alttestamentliche Wissenschaft 125. Berlin: de Gruyter, 2005.

Steingass, Francis Joseph. *The Student's Arabic-English Dictionary*. London: Allen, 1884.

Stubbe, Henry, and N. I. Matar. *Henry Stubbe and The Beginnings of Islam: The Originall & Progress of Mahometanism*. New York: Columbia University Press, 2014.

Stubbe, Henry, and Maḥmūd Shīrānī. *An Account of the Rise and Progress of Mahometanism: With the Life of Mahomet and a Vindication of Him and His Religion from the Calumnies of the Christians*. London: Luzac, 1911.

Tannous, Jack. *The Making of the Medieval Middle East: Simple Believers and Everyday Religion*. Princeton: Princeton University Press, 2018.

Tesei, Tommaso. "The Prophecy of Ḏū-l-Qarnayn (Q 18:83–102) and the Origins of the Qur'ānic Corpus." *Miscellanea Arabica* (2013–2014) 273–90.

———. "'The Romans Will Win!' Q 30:2–7 in Light of 7th c. Political Eschatology." *Der Islam* 95 (2018) 1–29.

Thackeray, H. St J., et al., trans. *Josephus*. Loeb Classical Library. 10 vols. New York: Putnam, 1926–1981.

Theissen, Gerd, and Annette Merz. *The Historical Jesus: A Comprehensive Guide*. Translated by John Bowden. Minneapolis: Fortress, 1998.

Thomson, Robert W., and James Howard-Johnston. *The Armenian History attributed to Sebeos*. 2 vols. Translated Texts for Historians 31. Liverpool: Liverpool University Press, 1999.

al-Tirmidhī, Muḥammad ibn ʿĪsā. *Al-Jāmiʿ al-Ṣaḥīḥ*. 5 vols. Edited by Ibrāhīm ʿAwaḍ. Cairo: Muṣṭafā al-Bābī al-Ḥalabī, 1965.
Tolan, John. *Faces of Muhammad: Western Perceptions of the Prophet of Islam from the Middle Ages to Today*. Princeton: Princeton University Press, 2019.
———. *Saracens: Islam in the Medieval European Imagination*. New York: Columbia University Press, 2002.
Trimingham, J. Spencer. *Christianity Among the Arabs in Pre-Islamic Times*. London: Longman, 1979.
Underwood, Grant. "The Prophetic Legacy in Islam and Mormonism: Some Comparative Observations." In *New Perspectives in Mormon Studies: Creating and Crossing Boundaries*, edited by Quincy D. Newell and Eric Farrel Mason, 101–18. Norman: University of Oklahoma Press, 2013.
van Bladel, Kevin. "The Alexander Legend in the Qurʾān 18.83–102." In *The Qurʾān in its Historical Context*, edited by Gabriel Said Reynolds, 175–203. New York: Routledge, 2008.
van Putten, Marijn. "The Development of the Hijazi Orthography." *Millennium* 20 (2023) 107–28.
van Sivers, Peter. "The Islamic Origins Debate Goes Public." *History Compass* 1 (2003) ME 058, 1–14.
Villeneuve, François. "La résistance des cultes bétyliques d'Arabie face au monothéisme: de Paul à Barsauma et à Muhammad." In *Le problème de la christianisation du monde antique*, edited by Hervé Inglebert et al., 219–31. Paris: Picard, 2010.
Vogel, Dan, and Brent Lee Metcalfe. *American Apocrypha: Essays on the Book of Mormon*, Essays on Mormonism Series. Salt Lake City: Signature, 2002.
Waines, David. "Agriculture." In *Encyclopaedia of the Qurʾān*, edited by Jane Dammen McAuliffe, 1:40–50. 6 vols. Leiden: Brill, 2001.
Wanke, Gunther. *Die Zionstheologie der Korachiten in ihrem traditionsgeschichtlichen Zusammenhang*. Beihefte zur Zeitschrift für die alttestamentliche Wissenschaft, 97. Berlin: Töpelmann, 1966.
Wansbrough, John E. *Quranic Studies: Sources and Methods of Scriptural Interpretation*, London Oriental Series 31. Oxford: Oxford University Press, 1977.
Wansbrough, John E., and Andrew Rippin. *Quranic Studies: Sources and Methods of Scriptural Interpretation*. Amherst, NY: Prometheus, 2004.
al-Wāqidī, Muḥammad ibn ʿUmar. *Kitāb al-maghāzī lil-Wāqidī*. Edited by Marsden Jones. 3 vols. London: Oxford University Press, 1966.
Watt, W. Montgomery. *Islam and the Integration of Society*. International Library of Sociology and Social Reconstruction. London: Routledge & Paul, 1961.
———. "The Materials Used by Ibn Isḥāq." In *Historians of the Middle East*, edited by Bernard Lewis and P. M. Holt, 23–34. London: Oxford University Press, 1958.
———. *Muhammad at Mecca*. Oxford: Clarendon, 1953.
———. *Muhammad at Medina*. Oxford: Clarendon, 1956.
———. *Muhammad: Prophet and Statesman*. London: Oxford University Press, 1961.
———. "The Reliability of Ibn Isḥāq's Sources." In *La vie du Prophète Mahomet: Colloque de Strasbourg, Octobre 1980*, edited by Toufic Fahd, 31–43. Paris: Presses universitaires de France, 1983.
Webb, Peter. "The Hajj before Muhammad: The Early Evidence in Poetry and Hadith." *Millennium* 20 (2023) 33–63.

Bibliography

———. "The History and Significance of the Meccan Hajj—From Pre-Islam to the Rise of the Abbasids." In *Hajj and the Arts of Pilgrimage: Essays in Honour of Nasser David Khalili*, edited by Qaisra Khan, 28–46. London: Ginko, 2023.

Weil, Gustav. *Geschichte der Chalifen*. 5 vols. Mannheim: Bassermann, 1846–51.

———. *Historisch-kritische Einleitung in den Koran*. Bielefeld: Velhagen & Klasing, 1844.

———. *Leben Mohammed's nach Muhammed ibn Isḥak, Bearbeitet von Abd el-Malik ibn Hischâm*. 2 vols. Stuttgart: Metzler, 1864.

———. *Mohammed der Prophet, sein Leben und seine Lehre: Aus handschriftlichen Quellen und dem Koran geschöpft und dargestellt*. Stuttgart: Metzler, 1843.

———. "Sur un fait relatif à Mahomet." *Journal Asiatique* 14 (1842) 108–12.

Weiss, Johannes. *Die Predigt Jesu vom Reiche Gottes*. Göttingen: Vandenhoeck & Ruprecht, 1892.

Wellhausen, Julius. *Reste arabischen Heidentums, gesammelt und erläutert*. Berlin: Reimer, 1887.

Wilken, Robert Louis. *The Christians as the Romans Saw Them*. New Haven: Yale University Press, 1984.

Witztum, Joseph. "The Foundations of the House (Q 2:127)." *Bulletin of the School of Oriental and African Studies* 72 (2009) 25–40.

———. "The Syriac Milieu of the Quran: The Recasting of Biblical Narratives." PhD diss., Princeton University, 2011.

Wüstenfeld, Ferdinand, ed. *Die Chroniken der Stadt Mekka*. 4 vols. Leipzig: Brockhaus, 1857.

———. *Das Leben Muhammed's nach Muhammed ibn Ishâk bearbeitet von Abd el-Malik ibn Hischâm*. 2 vols. Göttingen: Dieterich, 1858–1860.

Zeitlin, Irving M. *The Historical Muhammad*. Cambridge: Polity, 2007.

Index

A

'Abd al-Malik, 38, 95, 107, 109, 131
'Abd al-Razzāq al-Sanʿānī, 14
Abraham, 10, 88, 103–4
    sacrifice of son, 82, 89–91, 94
Abu Bakr, 26
Abū Ṭālib, 59
Africa, North, 63
agriculture
    in Mecca, 43–44, 49, 61
    in the Yathrib oasis, 45
    practiced by Qurʾan's opponents, 44
Aisha, 36, 57
Alexander the Great, 105, 118, 129
Ali ibn Abū Ṭālib, 57
Allah, 10, 90, 96–97, 99–100, 106, 112–13, 130
Ambros, Arne, 98–99
America, Book of Mormon and, 78–79
amir al-muʾminin, 107, 131
Amir-Moezzi, Ali, 119, 127
amr (Allāh), 96–107
    as "reign" of God, 96, 100–104, 112–14, 116–17, 121–23, 125, 131
Andrae, Tor, 25, 28–29
angels, 63, 99, 101, 103–4, 114, 123
anointing / anointed, 121
Anthony, Sean, 59, 119
apocalypticism, 21, 24, 26–28, 64, 68, 73–74, 77, 80, 95, 97, 100, 102, 106, 111–14, 119, 120–23, 125–26, 128–31
apocrypha, 17, 22–24, 29, 68, 71–74, 76–80

apostles, 72
Aqaba, 54–55
al-aqṣa, al-masjid, 93
Arabia/Arabian, 6, 16–18, 31, 37, 42–43, 45–48, 50–54, 59, 61–63, 79, 83
Arabic, 6, 13, 22, 36, 50–51, 55–56, 68–69, 77, 79, 84, 86, 90–91, 98–100
Arabs, 6, 17–18, 63, 66, 106, 109, 130
Aramaic, 51, 56, 84
Armenian, 40, 60, 62, 66, 126
Asia, western, 28, 40, 43, 50, 60, 63, 65, 68, 110
Association pour l'étude de la littérature apocryphe (AELAC), 72
al-Azmeh, Aziz, 41
al-Azraqi, Muhammad ibn ʿAbd Allah, 90

B

Baḥīrā, Sergius, 5
Bahrām Čōbīn, 106, 130
baka, 84–87, 94
bakka, 43, 83–84, 86–88, 94
Baljon, Johannes M. S., 96, 98–100, 103
Bashear, Suliman, 92, 94
basileia, 100, 113, 121
Baur, F. C., 8, 12
Bayt al-Maqdis, 86
Beck, Daniel, 92
Becker, Carl, 18–19
Beit HaMikdash, 86

Index

Believers (name of Mumammad's new religious community), 31, 43, 65–66, 82, 87, 92, 101–2, 104, 107, 113, 117, 131
   interconfessional nature, 31, 66
Bell, Richard, 28, 97, 113, 117–18
Benedict XVI, Pope, 24
Bible / biblical traditions, 71, 73–79, 84–85, 87–89, 100, 109, 112–13, 120–23, 125–27, 131
   in Arabic, 53, 56
biblical criticism, 1–3, 7–8, 11, 37, 70
Blachère, Régis, 31
Bostra, 59
Brock, Sebastian, 40
Brown, Jonathan A. C., 24
Buhl, Frants, 16, 25
Byzantine Empire, 92, 102, 104–6, 113, 126, 129–30

C

Caetani, Leoni, 3, 18–19, 30
caliph, 11, 38, 109
canon, biblical, 71–72, 80
capitalism, in Mecca, 20–21
Casanova, Paul, 25, 26, 30, 98
Christ, eschatological role of, 120, 122, 126–28, 131
Christianity / Christians, 2, 5, 19, 24, 28–30, 38, 40, 42, 54, 65–66, 69, 79–80, 82, 94, 99, 101–7, 110, 113, 121–22, 125–27, 129–31
   among the Believers, 31, 66
   in Mecca and Medina, 29, 52–56
   study of early, 7–10, 12, 26–27, 41, 64, 80, 111
circumambulation, 91
clouds, 104, 114
Cole, Juan, 21
Constitution of Medina, 52, 65, 94
Cook, David, 27, 97, 112–13, 119, 120, 127
Cook, Michael, 27, 40, 42, 44, 62
criterion of dissimilarity / embarrassment, 36, 94
Crone, Patricia, 19, 22, 27, 31, 40–43, 46, 48–49, 59, 61–62, 83

Cross, restoration of, 105, 129

D

Davies, W. D., 79
de Prémare, Alfred-Louis, 70, 109
Decharneux, Julien, 29
Dome of the Rock, 82, 95
Donner, Fred, 27, 31, 65, 104, 113
Dubai, 45
Dye, Guillaume, 70

E

earthquakes, at the eschaton, 114–15, 122, 125
eclipse, 114
Ehrman, Bart, 24
El-Badawi, Emran, 29
Ephrem, 28, 125
epilepsy, 5, 15–17
Eschaton / eschatology
   delay of, 78, 101, 105, 116, 118, 123–24, 129
   imminent 25–27, 37, 64, 82, 98, 100–2, 105, 108, 111, 114–18, 122–24, 127–29
   imperial, 27–28, 64, 93, 102, 104–7, 129–31
   in Qur'an 64–65, 71, 74, 79, 93, 95–106, 111–31
   Muhammad as prophet of, 225–28, 64–65, 105–6, 108–9, 111, 117, 123
Essene Gospel of Peace, 73
Ethiopia, 28, 46, 53
Eucharist, 75, 126
Ewald, Heinrich, 6–9, 12

F

Fatima, 4, 57
Form criticism, 37, 70–72

G

Gehenna, 85
Geiger, Abraham, 9–12, 28–29

Index

Gog, 118–19, 122, 125
Goldziher, Ignác, 3, 17, 30, 34, 36
gospels, 9, 10, 24, 66, 70, 72–74, 98, 111, 122–24
Greek / Greeks, 40, 55, 63, 76, 90–91, 99, 102 121, 126
Griffith, Sidney, 77
Grimme, Hubert, 18–19, 98

H

ḥadīth, 26, 59, 64, 120, 127
Hagar, 89
Hagarism, 40–42
hajj, 48, 84, 89
Har HaṢofim, 90
al-ḥarām, al-masjid, 92, 94
ḥarām, Meccan, 93
Hawting, Gerald, 31, 48, 83
Haykal, Husayn, 22
Hebrew, 84, 86, 90
Hegra, 55
Hellenism, 76, 99, 126, 128
Heraclius, 105–6, 129–30
Hijaz, 18, 42, 46–54, 56–57, 63, 82, 87, 91
hijra, 36, 57
Hirschfeld, Hartwig, 16
Hodgson, Marshall, 4
Holy Land, 28, 81, 102, 105, 129
    Islamic, 43, 94
homilies, 28–29, 69, 73–77, 125–26
Horovitz, Josef, 25, 32
Hour (eschatological event), 96, 102, 112, 114–19, 121, 123, 125, 127–28
House, Qur'an's Holy, 47, 81–95
Hoyland, Robert, 19
Hubāshah, 59
Hurgronje, Snouck, 16, 25–26

I

Iblis, 104
Ibn Hishām, 3, 6–8, 13, 90
Idolatry, 31, 63, 84
Indian Ocean, 45

Inscriptions, ancient Arabian, 50–51, 55
intertextuality, 87–88, 95
Iran, 102, 106, 128, 130
Ibn Isḥāq, 6, 13–14, 22, 35
Ishmael, 89, 91, 94
isnāds, 33–36
Israel, 66, 79, 85, 93, 104, 106, 121, 123, 130

J

Jacob of Edessa, 61
Jacob of Serug, 125
Jeffery, Arthur, 15, 24, 28, 30, 37
Jerusalem, 28, 43, 63, 81–82, 84–85, 87–95, 105, 129
Jesus, 1–3, 7–12, 14, 15, 20, 21, 24, 26–27, 36, 56–58, 64, 66, 89, 98, 108, 111–12, 119–25, 127
    as eschatological prophet, 26, 111
    see also Christ, eschatological role of
Judaism / Jews, 2, 7–9 11, 29, 38, 42, 56, 65–66, 69, 71, 76–77, 79–81, 82, 85–86, 90–91, 99, 101–7, 109–10, 120–21, 123–31
    in Yathrib/Medina, 52–54
    among the Believers, 31, 66, 94
jihād, 27, 63–65
John the Baptist, 122
Josephus, 90
Judaism, 2, 7, 9, 11, 52, 56, 76, 79–80, 91, 94, 103–6, 110, 113, 121, 123–31
Judgment, Final, 25, 27, 37, 64–65, 96–98, 100–101, 104, 112–15, 117–19, 121, 128, 131
Junod, Éric, 72–73
Jurash, 59
Juynboll, G. H. A., 34

K

Kathisma Church, 89
Ka'ba, 91
Kerr, Robert, 90–91
Khadija, 57–59
Khosrow, 106, 130

Kingdom of God, 98, 104, 113–14, 119, 121, 123–25

L

Lammens, Henri, 3, 18, 30, 46
leather, and the Meccan economy, 49–50, 58–59, 61–62
Lebanon, 61
linguistics, historical, 13, 51
literacy, 50–53, 55–56, 110
liturgical traditions, 69, 71–73, 75, 85
lives of Jesus, 1–2, 8, 21, 24
lives of Muhammad, apologetic, 15, 20, 22–24
lives of Muhammad, eschatological, 15, 24–28
lives of Muhammad, pathological, 15–17
lives of Muhammad, political and economic, 15–22, 45, 64
lives of Muhammad, traditional Islamic, 3–7, 9, 12–15, 17, 19, 21–22, 30–33, 35–37, 40, 53, 57–58, 61–63, 66, 67, 90, 117
Logos, 99, 103
Lot, 62

M

Macdonald, Michael, 51
Madā'in Ṣāliḥ, 55
Maffly-Kipp, Laurie, 79
Maghāzī (of al-Wāqidī), 13
Magog, 118–19, 122, 125
malkūt, 100, 113
Margoliouth, David, 16–18, 22, 30, 46
al-Marwa, 89–90
Marxism, 20
matn, 36
Mayer, Wendy, 75
Mecca, 10, 18, 20–22, 29, 33, 42–56, 58–63, 65, 67, 81–84, 87–94, 109, 110
  arid climate 18, 43–44, 58, 61
  Christianity, absence of, 29, 52–56
  economy, 18, 20, 21, 44, 47, 49–50, 58, 60–62, 83
  flooding, 43, 104
  food, scarcity of, 43, 49–50
  Judaism, absence of, 53
  myth of long-distance trade in luxury goods, 18, 22, 45–49, 58–61
  nonliterate culture, 51–53, 56
  pastoralism, 21, 44, 48–49, 51, 58, 60–62, 82–83
  pilgrimage, 47–49, 82–84, 89–90
  population, 43–44
  as sanctuary (ḥarām), 47, 49
  shrine, 48–49, 82–84, 87–88, 93–94
  as wealthy, 18, 22, 45–47, 49, 59
Medina
  See Yathrib
memory
  collective, 32
  limitations, 11, 33, 38–39, 109–10
memre, 69, 75
Mesopotamia, 53, 56
Messiah / messianism, 105–6, 114, 119–21, 123, 125–27, 129–31
midrash, 85
migration, 18, 36, 42, 57
Mingana, Alphonse, 28, 30
mining, 47, 60
Mishnah, 90–91
monotheism, 5, 19, 25, 31, 55, 62–63, 65, 69, 96, 102, 127
moon, 101, 103, 114, 122
Moriah, Mount, 89–90
Mormon, Book of, 17, 73, 78–79
Moses, 10, 27, 104
Muhammad, 1–48, 50, 52–54, 56–67, 73–75, 78, 81, 87–88, 90, 92, 94–95, 104–13, 117, 119, 123, 129–31
  death, 57–58, as epileptic, 5, 15–17
  as eschatological prophet, 25–28, 64–65, 105–6, 108–9, 111, 117, 123
  historical, compared with historical Jesus, 1–3, 8–9, 111–12
  marriage, 57–58
  from Mecca, 42–43
  as merchant, 54, 58–62
  migration to Yathrib, 57
  political leadership, 63

as political organizer, 18–20
as prophet, 6, 11, 16–27, 35, 53,
  56–58, 60, 62–65, 108, 111, 123
and Qur'an, 10–13, 15, 30–31,
  38–40, 78, 87, 110–11
as shepherd, 58–60, 62
as social reformer, 5, 20–22, 26
as tanner, 60, 62
Muir, William, 13–15, 17, 46

N

Nabataean, 42, 51, 55
Nagel, Tilman, 16, 20, 97
Nagel's, 16, 97
Nativity, in the Qur'an, 89
Nehmé, Laïla, 55
Neuenkirchen, Paul, 29
Neuwirth, Angelika, 87–89, 94–95
Noah, 103–4
Nöldeke, Theodor, 12, 15

O

oral transmission, 11, 14, 33, 35, 38–39,
  48, 50–52, 65, 75, 109–10, 125

P

paganism / polytheism, 31, 47, 62–63,
  102
Palestine, 57–59, 61, 105, 126, 129
Paraclete, 28, 119, 120, 127
paraenesis, 70, 73, 76
Paret, Rudi, 20, 99, 117
Passover, 84, 90
Persia, 105, 129
Peters, 20, 39, 54, 85
philology, 12–13, 98
Phoenicia, 61
Pietism, 85
pilgrimage, 47–49, 81–92, 95
Pregill, Michael, 39
Promised Land, 63, 65–66, 89, 93, 95,
  116
psalms, 69, 74, 84–88, 91, 95, 123

Q

Qumran, 121
Quraysh, 45, 59, 92
Qur'an, *passim*
  as apocryphon, 68–80
  as Arabian/Arabic scripture, 37, 79
  and Book of Mormon, 17, 73, 78–79
  canonization, 37–38, 109
  and eschatology, 64–65, 71, 74, 79,
    93, 95–106, 111–31
  Holy House of, 47, 81–95
  and Jerusalem Temple, 84–95
  Muhammad and, 10–13, 15, 30–31,
    38–40, 78, 87, 110–11
  opponents, 44, 62–63, 115
  As scripture, 11, 71, 76–80, 101, 109
  Shi'i memories of formation, 109
  Sunni tradition of formation, 109.

R

Regnier, Adolphe, 87
Renan, Ernest, 1–3, 7, 9–10
Reynolds, Gabriel, 29, 73–74, 76, 103
Rippin, Andrew, 37
Rodinson, Maxime, 20
Rome / Roman Empire, 8, 34, 42, 47,
  49–50, 53–55, 59, 61, 78, 90, 92,
  102–3, 105–6, 128–30
al-Rūm, Sūrat, 102

S

sabbath, 101
al-Ṣafā, 84, 89–90
Safi, Omid, 24
Sanders, E. P., 24
Sasanian, 47, 104–6, 113, 129, 130
Schacht, Joseph, 33–34, 36
Schweitzer, Albert, 8–9, 15, 21, 26, 56,
  64, 111
Scopus, Mount, 90
Sebeos, 60–63, 66
Septuagint, 86, 90
Shavuot, 84
Sinai, Nicolai, 74, 76, 77, 79, 125–28
Sinai, Peninsula, 46

sīra
  See lives of Muhammad, traditional Islamic
Scopos, Mount, 90
Smith, Joseph, 17
socialism, 18–19
Sodom, 62
Ṣofeh / Ṣofim
  See Har HaṢofim
Sophronius, 63
soteriology, 126–27
Sprenger, Aloys, 13–15
stars, 101, 103, 114, 122
Strauss, David Friedrich, 8, 9, 12
Stubbe, Henry, 5
Sukkot, 84
Syria, 54, 59, 126
Syriac, 28–29, 40, 69, 73–77, 105, 125–26, 129

T

al-Ṭabarī, 6, 13
Tabuk, 55
Taif, 49, 55
Tanakh, 77
Tannous, Jack, 53
Taymā, 59
Temple, Jerusalem, 81–95
Tesei, Tommaso, 102
Tolan, John, 8
Torah, 74
Trinity, 31, 103
trumpet, 104, 113, 119, 122, 125
Tübingen, 8–9, 12, 24
Tyre, 61

U

Uthman, 11, 26, 38, 109

V

Virgin Mary, 72
Vulgate, 86

W

Wansbrough, John, 37, 42, 111
al-Wāqidī, 13, 90
Waraqa, 53
Watt, Montgomery, 19, 20, 22, 32, 44, 46–47, 117
Weil, Gustav, 2, 5–9, 11–13, 15, 30
Welch, Alford, 20
Wellhausen, Julius, 48, 82
Witztum, Joseph, 29
Wüstenfeld, Ferdinand, 13

Y

Yarmuk, 78
Yathrib (Medina), 10, 19, 29, 33, 42–45, 47, 50–55, 57–58, 62, 65, 67, 94, 109–10
Yemen, 46, 54

Z

Zayd, 57
Zeitlin, Irving, 20
Zerubbabel, 123
Zoroastrianism, 102–3, 105–7, 129–31
al-Zuhrī, 35